Yachtsman
in Red China

Yachtsman in Red China

DAVID J. STEELE

JOHN DE GRAFF, INC.
Tuckahoe, New York
1970

© *1970 by David J. Steele*
ISBN 0-8286-0042-2
Library of Congress Catalogue Card Number: 71-112702
Manufactured in the United States of America

No part of this book may be reproduced in any form, by print, photoprint, microfilm or any other means without written permission from the publisher.

John de Graff Inc.
34 Oak Ave., Tuckahoe, N.Y. 10707

TO ARTHUR PIVER

Contents

1. The South China Sea 1
2. The Linda Niña I 6
3. Manilo Ho! 28
4. In Quest of Dragons 37
5. The Temple 56
6. The Linda Niña II 79
7. Saigon, Adieu 98
8. The Vietnam Coast 109
9. Mayday, Mayday 120
10. Trawler 203 135
11. Red China 143
12. Twenty Questions 153
13. The Thoughts of Mao 172
14. Canton and Release 182
15. Hong Kong 202

1 / The South China Sea

Although the wind had held fairly steady at twenty knots from the northwest, the seas between Vietnam and Hainan became increasingly rough throughout the afternoon, and by nightfall the *Linda Niña II* was bucking and pitching into six-foot swells.

I sat in the aft cockpit, ducking occasional spray thrown up by the swells pounding against the weather float, and thinking dark thoughts about the weather. In spite of the cheery and unvarying forecasts emanating from VPS-60 in Hong Kong, the breezes had not been overly cooperative on the run up from Saigon. Force 3/4 winds had been predicted daily along the Vietnam coast. In fact, they had been light to negligible all the way, and after the first good day's run out of Saigon, I had spent the rest of the week limping up the coast with slack sails. On this day too, in spite of the usual optimistic outlook, the wind had shifted to the northwest toward midmorning and had built in strength throughout the afternoon. Now, approaching early evening, the swells were up to six feet, topped by curls of white foam. They crashed and banged against the floats of the *Linda Niña*, and from time to time gusts of salty spray came flying back into the cockpit. The sky was overcast, and gray clouds scudded along out of the northwest.

It was a jouncing ride and my shoulder was becoming sore from banging against the mainsheet traveler each time the boat lurched over a swell. I finally worked myself into a position where the life jacket absorbed most of the jolt, and found a three-point seating arrangement of reasonable comfort: one foot braced against the port cockpit seat, my back against the mizzenmast, my left hand on the helm. My safety belt was snapped onto the diamond stay fitting at the base of the mizzenmast.

From time to time I considered putting the self-steering on, saying to hell with it all, and going below to relax in my bunk. Each time I vetoed the idea, for awhile at least. It was not all that uncomfortable and the occasional lashing of salt spray added a certain savor to the situation, leaving me feeling like a small edition of Chichester. Although I was growing tired, it was nonetheless exhilarating to sit at the helm, braced against the jolting of the boat, guiding her northward into the wind and swells, and feeling the breeze and spray in my face. I had a lively sense of participation in the whole affair; a feeling of being an active element in the combination of boat, wind, and sea.

We were now two days out of Danang, the *Linda Niña* and I, en route to Hong Kong. With any luck, and no typhoons, we would reach Hong Kong within another week. From there, I planned to sail down the northwest coast of Luzon to Manila, and thence to Singapore, where in another few months I was due to start work on a new assignment with Esso. After four years as supply manager at our Saigon office, I had seen enough of Vietnam and had not been too sorry to see the shoreline of Quang Tri Province fade astern.

The *Linda Niña II* was a thirty-two-foot trimaran, one of Arthur Piver's *Herald* designs, with a lot of reverse sheer longitudinally and athwartships as well. She was a rakish-looking craft, a bit heavy in the bow, but she sailed well enough. On the first day's run out of Saigon we had averaged over seven knots for the twenty-four-hour period, with a fifteen-knot wind on the quarter. Between the outer edges of the twin twenty-seven-foot floats that flanked the main hull, she had a nineteen-foot beam. Like all trimarans, she was extremely stable.

Her skipper, at age thirty-nine, was also becoming somewhat heavy in the bow, and a bit astern to boot, but was bearing up cheerfully enough under these encroachments of incipient middle age. In this corner, weighing 175 pounds, 5 feet 11 inches, in ragged khaki shorts, no shoes, crew cut, old sport shirt, yellow life jacket, and attached to the mizzenmast by a safety belt and six feet of $\frac{1}{2}$-inch nylon rope: D. J. Steele.

At various moments of your life you look about, and back, and take stock; and sometimes you wonder at the long chain of circumstances that led up to your being here, at this particular hour and locale. The results of these introspective musings are at times discouraging, but at other times, if you are lucky, they can be gratifying.

At the moment, jouncing over swells, banging against the mizzenmast, and wiping salt spray off my glasses, I felt they were as satisfying as they could ever be. I think no man can ask more than to be able to fulfill a long range ambition, a dream of years. Should it somehow come out to less than expected in my case, at least I had had my chance at it.

From boyhood I had harbored romantic and adventurous thoughts about the South China Sea and had imagined what it might be like to be involved in a quest for some nameless and exciting goal in the Far East. The lure of Oriental culture, teeming marketplaces, babble of exotic tongues, sloe-eyed women, strange cultures and religions, and a host of other images had engaged my imagination over the years. I was particularly attracted to the South China Sea with its monsoon winds, waves pounding on unknown shores, long traditions of piracy, and the fierce typhoons that sweep its upper latitudes.

I thought again about all of these things, and marveled at the good luck and circumstances that had led up to this particular day. I was here, in good health, on a boat that I had built with my own hands, sailing alone on the South China Sea. The wind and the waves were high enough to be exhilarating, yet not quite to that point which quells adventurous idealism and makes one wish he were somewhere else, back in a more conventional clime.

From my vantage point beside the mizzenmast, I appreciatively eyed the lines of the *Linda Niña II* as she sliced and surged her way northward towards Hong Kong. My admiration was tinged with the pride, sentiment, and other emotions that come when sailing on the open seas a boat built with one's own hands. I thought of the long year I had spent in building her; a year of complete sacrifice of time and energy—every weekend, every holiday, during lunch hours, and after work—to the complete exclusion of other activities. One might have called it an obsession, but it was no such thing. I was driven by the simple realization and practical conclusion that if I wished to have a boat in the water by the time my long vacation came due in mid-1967, there were only two possible ways: to have someone build it for me, or to spend practically every waking minute doing it myself. I had chosen the latter course, and had never regretted it. It had been a complete commitment of time and effort; yet, to me, this was all part of the package that made it so satisfying.

This boat was *mine*. I had put into her a considerable investment of resources—financial, physical, emotional. I knew every frame and piece of marine plywood in her. I had driven every nail, screwed down every bolt. She was mine, and I in turn was a part of her. Perhaps there is a tendency to anthropomorphize any material thing into which one has put such an intensely personal investment, but to me the *Linda Niña II* was much more than just a boat.

In the context of all the foregoing, I sat in my cockpit enjoying waves and spray, and mulling over the circumstances that had led to all this. I thought over the long series of turning points in my life and wondered: Had one of them been substantially different, would I be here now? What if I had joined another company, and not gone into an overseas career? Or had been assigned to other places, isolated from the allure of the sea? Or had not spoken Spanish and been transferred to Colombia, where I built my first small boat and thus became irrevocably embarked in a spiral of ever-escalating interests—bigger boats, bigger ideas? What if I had not been transferred to Esso Standard Eastern; would I be back there now, in Colombia, or perhaps in Coral Gables, behind a desk? Certainly I would not be in the Far East, and certainly not by myself in the middle of the South China Sea.

Yes, time and circumstances had indeed been good to me. I had been damned lucky.

But now night was falling, and the gray light was fading with the usual rapidity of tropical sunsets. I abandoned my musings and turned to the more practical considerations of getting the self-steering gear set up for the night.

The nylon line on the safety belt was long enough to permit me to clamber into the aft cockpit and reach over the mizzen traveler to the rudder, on which the vane was mounted. After a few moments adjusting the thumbscrews on the adjustable sleeve, I got the vane oriented to hold a northerly course, and returned to the main cockpit. The helm was now attending to itself, so I ducked into the cabin to get a can of warm beer and a cigar. I sat for a few minutes on the port-side seat, back against the cabin, sipping beer, smoking, and watching the last of the light fade from the sky.

The ocean was now dark, except for the lashing of whitecaps out over the water and the luminous rush of breaking foam in the wake of the boat as she broke through the approaching swells. Gray clouds pushed across the sky from the northwest, but soon they too had dissolved into a uniform blackness, unbroken by any hint of stars or moon. The *Linda Niña II* surged northward into the night.

I flipped the switches for the mainmast toplight and the compass, and returned to my vantage point in the cockpit to finish the cigar before going below to fix supper.

I had been caught under the spell of awareness of time and circumstance, and was loath to leave it for the moment. These times in life are few and magical—the realization of Self in some introspective moment, where the elements of nature and circumstance are focused into an intensified awareness of passing time, of perspective, and of the great inner satisfaction of standing for one brief moment at one of those peaks in your life. The spell is brief, an elusive moment of mental and emotional witchery, perhaps the essence of which lies in the casting off, for a trice, of the chains that tie you to the rest of the world and to conventional experience. You are here, now, alone, unique.

The spell does not last, and soon your thoughts return to the present-day realities of the weather, what you will cook for supper, the outlook for the morrow; and thus you return to your old world. But for a few moments you have achieved a sort of personal Nirvana and perhaps, with luck, it will come again on some future day.

And these are the days to be lived for, and worked for, and planned for. One day like this is worth a year of ordinary living.

The cigar had burned low, and regretfully I threw it out to sea and went below. It had been a long day, and a tiring one, yet I was not ready for sleep. Earlier thoughts kept crowding back, of the past and of the circumstances that had put me here on this day. I thought particularly of the last four years in Vietnam. They had been full years, indeed! There had been problems, but life had never been dull. I remembered the search for the dragons, the building of the first *Linda Niña*, the day my mast had come down en route to Manila, and the war in Vietnam. A host of associated memories came flooding back as I mused over these recent years.

No, it had not been dull at all.

2 / *The Linda Niña I*

These days, when I get to talking to close friends about Life, I find myself using the term "escalation," as I apply the word to adventuresome tendencies and to personal accomplishment in some field or other. Perhaps a simpler way to state it is: If you want to do something big that appears beyond what you consider to be your natural abilities, then start small and work your way up. It's a very simple concept, and it *works*.

Until I was well into my thirties, I had never sailed a boat, much less built one. From time to time I wistfully viewed some graceful craft slicing through the waters offshore, sails taut in the wind, and distinctly envied both the lucky dogs who were doing the sailing and the talented fellow who had built the thing. However I had never had any exposure to boat-building, and maximum accomplishments in the field of carpentry had been limited to simple cabinets or shelves. Their quality from a woodworking standpoint can best be demonstrated by the fact that they usually stayed behind whenever I moved.

From inclination and from mechanical engineering, I was fairly conversant with machine tools and felt reasonably confident fashioning things out of metal. But wood was another matter; the world of saws, planes, routers, and joiners was complex and forbidding.

After graduation from college, I joined Standard Oil of New Jersey and promptly was posted overseas to Aruba, in the Netherlands West Indies, where the company has one of its largest export refineries. In the "Lago Colony," as our housing compound was called, many people had their own home workshops, and many of

The Linda Niña I

them had built Sailfish, which are twelve to fourteen-foot long surfboard-like affairs with a centerboard and a lateen-rigged triangular sail. People had a great time sailing these craft about the reef-enclosed harbor, where there was almost always a ten to fifteen-knot breeze. A friend would take me out on his boat occasionally and I started taking an interest in sailing, but I could never work up the confidence to try building a Sailfish.

After four years in Aruba, I was transferred to our new refinery in Cartagena, Colombia. My home there was also near the sea, and had a fair-sized garage that had great potential as a workshop. After having gotten settled, I decided to try my hand at building a small boat. Nothing ventured, nothing gained. I bought a small power saw with tilting table, a saber saw, an electric drill, and a few hand tools, and had a go at boat-building.

For the first project I decided to make a small eight-foot pram-type sailboat with a simple catboat rig, that is, a single self-supported mast with no jib or stays. I obtained the plans from one of those *23 Boats You Can Build* type of publications.

This particular boat was about as simple as you can get. The whole hull was essentially no more than five pieces of plywood: the bottom, the transom, the two sides, and the sloping pram-type bow piece. It had a simple coaming, a centerboard well in the middle with a seat on each side, and a seat across the back. The mast was simply stuck through a hole in the small forward deck, and stepped in a block of wood on the floor. Next to building an orange crate, it was as simple a carpentry project as you could find. Anyone who could use a hammer, a plane, and a jig saw could build it readily.

As it turned out, I spent a few months on it, although looking back, I probably didn't put in much more time than the equivalent of four or five weekends. I had golf and other interests, and the half-finished hull would lie for weeks at a time gathering dust in the workshop before I could get back to it. As it neared completion, however, my enthusiasm suddenly increased and I finished it up in a few consecutive weekends. Surprisingly, it did not look at all bad. (It's marvelous how many mistakes you can hide with plastic wood.) After I had carefully sanded it all down and applied a few coats of white paint, with red trim about the waterline and on the rub rails along the side, it looked downright attractive.

I made a small wagon out of a discarded golf cart, and one sunny Saturday morning, accompanied by my yard boy, who had the improbable name of Calisto, I trundled it a block to the bay and put it into the water. I well remember my thrill of pleasure to see this small boat floating gently on the water, and the feeling of accomplishment when I climbed in and pushed off from the shore. There was a light offshore breeze, and the boat responded well. For a happy hour or so I tacked back and forth offshore in the calm bay. I let Calisto have a shot at it too, and he had a great time. Calisto was a small brownish man, a *mestizo* from the coast, of indeterminate age and philosophical disposition. I asked him how he liked it.

"*Homb'e, que bueno!*" he exclaimed with simple pleasure. "*Sí que naviga bien!*" He was getting as much of a kick out of the whole thing as I was.

We would take the boat out frequently on weekends thereafter. She sailed well, and aside from a bit of seepage about the centerboard joint, didn't leak. After awhile I started thinking about building something a bit larger, and sent away to a friend in Aruba to send me plans for a Sailfish.

This is where the escalation element comes in: my simple eight-footer had turned out fine, and I now had the confidence to tackle a project that I had not previously dared attempt.

The Sailfish plans eventually arrived, and I started making the frames. Partway through the project, I was transferred to Bogotá, eight thousand feet up in the central highlands of Colombia, and far from the sea. The frames gathered dust on my garage shelves for a year. Thereafter, I returned to Cartagena, and promptly resumed work on the Sailfish.

It took me about five months, again working in spare time. Similarly to the previous boat, I probably could have made it in about a month and a half if I had worked through every weekend.

The Sailfish was a little more complicated than the pram, having an internal framework, but work progressed steadily with no particular problems. I had already had some experience with the basic woodworking elements of planing, driving screws, and making glue on the earlier boat, so in these respects the Sailfish was just more of the same. It was nearly twice as big, but I have found that this is not necessarily a criterion in building boats. The bigger ones take more time, obviously, and in some aspects present different problems, but by and large it is just "more of the same." So, if you can build a small boat successfully, you *know* that you can build a larger one. Put another way, let's say you knock together a six-foot pram. Having accomplished this successfully, you build a ten-foot sailboat. You will encounter a few additional problems in building the ten-footer, but the problems will be far *less* than the ones you had to overcome to build the six-footer. And, having built the ten-footer, you will find yourself quite confident to tackle, say, a sixteen-footer, and so on, until stopped by finances, lack of building space, or time, but not by confidence or ability. This is what I mean by "escalation" of abilities or accomplishments.

The Sailfish was completed in due course, and turned out beautifully. I finished her off with a few coats of synthetic varnish over a mahogany-stained finish, and she looked fine. I put a coat of non-skid deck paint over the deck aft of the spray boards, to prevent slipping off when the deck was wet (as it usually was).

The great day finally arrived, and we trundled her down to the bay and placed her in the water. Again, it was a thrill to climb aboard for the first time and tack out into the bay. She sailed really well, much faster than the pram. However, she had a discouraging tendency to turn over if I didn't tack just right, and the first few weekends I spent much of my time spluttering out of the water and climbing on the centerboard to get her righted.

It was with the Sailfish that I had my first boating adventure, if one could call it that. As I look back, perhaps it is worth mentioning, for in a way it was the forerunner of things to come—a first step in this process of escalation, but this time as applied to adventure. Building boats is an accomplishment, of which I use the term escalation in the sense of gaining increasing confidence to tackle bigger and bigger boats. But what you *do* with these boats is another form of escalation.

If you have a twenty-footer, and venture to take it along the coast of Connecticut, this is one thing. But when you learn navigation, and take it on your two-week vacation for a sail across the sound to Plum Island and Montauk Point, this is something else again, and represents a considerable escalation over previous endeavors. Depending on your outlook, it might logically be expected that, having made the run to Montauk Point successfully, you would start itching to do it one better, and perhaps would consider a run to Cape

Cod. Having accomplished this successfully, you will find yourself casting about for something more challenging on the next go-around, and assuming that by now you have a suitable boat, you may start thinking about making a run to Bermuda. (Don't laugh; it's only about seven hundred miles from New York, and you could make it there and back in the month that many people now have for vacation.) The point is, of course, that after three or four outings of ever-increasing scope, you will find yourself considering challenges that you would never have dreamed of some time ago.

As regards my outing on the Sailfish, I decided to start early one Sunday morning to see if I could take it out to sea and circumnavigate the island of Tierra Bomba. This island lies adjacent to the city of Cartagena on the Caribbean, and is about ten miles long.

After a whole morning of tacking against a light wind, Calisto and I finally made the mouth of the bay and emerged onto the sea. Although it was a relatively calm day, the sea was moderately choppy, and it was a bouncy ride on the flat-bottomed fourteen-foot Sailfish. By noon we were proceeding southwestward along the outer coast of Tierra Bomba when a rain squall blew up without warning. Clouds suddenly filled the sky, and the rain came down in buckets, so thickly that we could no longer see the shore. The wind suddenly strengthened and changed direction sufficiently to backwind the sail. The boom swung around with a crash, and I knew we were going over.

"*Calisto, homb'e, agarre el almuerzo!*" I cried, as the boat capsized. Calisto was nearest the lunch, which consisted of sandwiches and a few bottles of Coca-Cola wrapped in a large plastic bag, and he managed to grab it as he slid gracefully into the Caribbean.

We floundered about, and after awhile managed to get the boat righted again. We turned towards the shore, where we beached her and waited for the squall to pass over. After a half-hour or so it did, and we set to sea again, soaked and a bit chilly. We ate the sandwiches en route to Boca Chica, a small fort at the other end of Tierra Bomba. Tourist boats run every day from Cartagena to Boca Chica, where guides show them about the old Fort. There is also a small refreshment stand there.

We finally arrived in the late afternoon, excruciatingly hungry. I had only a few pesos in my pockets, enough to buy soft drinks and a few sandwiches. About five o'clock we started back, this time on the inland side of the island. As luck would have it, the wind died down and shifted to practically dead ahead. We crawled along. I could see the refinery off to starboard, abeam, and as night fell its lights went on. Ahead, the lights of Cartagena could be seen, ten miles or so away. The clouds had blown over, and the night was full of stars. We ghosted along at a little over a knot against the nearly dead breeze.

It was nearly midnight, and we were both dead tired, when a searchlight sprang up a few hundred yards off our bow. We heard the rumbling of engines and presently a Colombian Navy patrol boat hove up alongside.

"*Señores, que están haciendo aquí, tan tarde?*" the officer of the deck inquired. Under the circumstances, I thought his tone was remarkably polite. I explained what had happened. The officer and crew chuckled, and offered assistance back to the base, which was only about a mile from my house. Since it looked like hours at least before we would have reached Castillo Grande, we accepted with alacrity. They hauled the Sailfish aboard the patrol boat and went roaring back to the base. We thanked them and obtained permission to leave the boat until the next day.

The guard on duty gave us a lift in a jeep, and we arrived home about one, to find the maids frantic and the dog barking. I wolfed down a few sandwiches and dropped into bed, exhausted, leaving Calisto to explain to the maids. A few days later one of them informed me with a grin that Calisto had confided to them: "*Homb'e, espero que el Señor Steele no me vuelva a invitar a navigar en ese bote!*" I hope Mr. Steele doesn't invite me to go sailing again on that boat!

But it had been undeniably interesting, and an accomplishment of sorts, considering the size of the boat. Already I was starting to think about larger boats and longer trips.

Then came my transfer to New York, and my boating ambitions languished for a year while the Sailfish rested mummy-like, wrapped in burlap, in the basement of the apartment building. However, I already had an idea what I wanted to do next. Oddly enough, the idea had suddenly crystallized at about 25,000 feet above the Caribbean, while flying back to Cartagena after my transfer job interview in New York.

I had gotten into a conversation with a fellow on the plane and found that we were both interested in boats. Furthermore, he just happened to have in his pocket the spec sheets and study plans for a boat he was considering building. He was full of enthusiasm for this new type of boat that was coming out, the trimaran.

It appeared that trimarans consisted of a main central hull, with an outrigger-type float on each side. Of course, there was nothing basically new about outriggers, but to date no one had really developed them along the lines of modern yacht design. The plans that the man showed me were those of the thirty-foot *Nimble*, designed by Arthur Piver in California.

The trimaran was supposed to be extremely fast, very stable, and nonsinkable. It looked to be just what I wanted.

During the year I was in New York, I looked further into trimarans. At that time, Arthur Piver was the only one pioneering them, although soon many other designers were to get into the business. Art Piver was one of those unusual men who have the unsurpassed combined ability for creative thinking, initiative, persistence, and that special ingredient x, which drives a man into following up his dreams and making something of them. I promptly dug up his book *Trans-Atlantic Trimaran*, in which he describes his earlier experiments with trimaran design, culminating in a voyage across the Atlantic in the *Nimble*.

By the time I was transferred and reached Vietnam a year later, I had exchanged several letters with Piver, and had decided to build the twenty-four-foot model, the *Nugget*. Once settled in my house, I started getting a workshop together and ordered the plans. I was extremely lucky to have a monstrous garage, which was nearly thirty feet long, by fifteen high, by twelve feet wide. There was plenty of space to build the hull and semi-wings of the *Nugget* and I could later move it out into the front yard to attach the rest of the wings and floats.

I had ordered a new power saw from Singapore, and while waiting for it to arrive, I made a partial balsa wood model of the *Nugget*, along with a model of *me*, to scale, so I could see how everything would fit. The model helped give me a feel for the inside accommodations. I never did finish it, since once the power saw arrived and I got the workshop set up, I wasn't about to spend time with balsa models when I could be working on the real thing!

I spent a week or so of spare time setting up the strongback on the garage floor just the way I wanted it. The strongback base consisted of two two-by-fours about three feet apart, running the length of the boat, with one-by-four-inch planks laid crosswise at each frame location. I nailed them down loosely and later installed shims as necessary to bring the top of all the crosspieces dead level. Shims were also necessary under the base pieces, to compensate for the drainage slope of the garage floor.

Prior to commencing actual construction, I used the strongback itself as a convenient base for laying out all of the lines of the boat to check for smooth continuity. I laid out a centerline, with taut string, down the center of the strongback, and from this laid out transverse lines at right angles at each frame location. Using the offsets from the plans, I marked out on the crosspieces the lines of the horizontal plan view at the sheer and at the chines, and the line of the keel. I then connected all these points with a flexible batten to check for a smooth curve in each case. I was glad that I did this, for there was an obvious discontinuity at one of the aft bulkhead locations, where the offset table read 1/16" when it should have been 11/16". It would have been annoying to find this out after making and installing the frame, even though it could still have been corrected by adding make-up strips along the side of the frame.

After making a few minor adjustments to the designer's offsets, based on my layout with the batten, I started making the frames. These are very easy on Piver's trimarans, since they have straight sides and a V-angled bottom. It was simple to lay out the 3/4-by-3-inch frame lumber over the pattern sketched on a sheet of plywood, tack it down, nail the keel and chine gussets in place, and tack on a crosspiece. The gussets were 3/8-inch marine plywood, with both mating surfaces coated with resorcinol glue and nailed down with stainless steel grip-fast nails. I tacked a temporary batten across to connect the tops of the frames and at the same time serve as a base for mounting the frames (upside down) on the crosspieces of the strongback. As soon as the gussets had been tacked in place, I would remove the frame and rest it nearly vertically against the wall while the glue dried. Next day I would add gussets on the other side, trim the gussets flush with the frames with the saber saw and presto, Instant Frame! Once I got started I found that I could turn out a frame in less than an hour. Even on the larger boats, say thirty-five feet, all of the frames can be made in a few weekends of spare time. While I was making frames for the main hull, I made all the ones for the floats as well. There were about a dozen for the main hull, spaced about two feet apart, and fewer for the floats.

Once the frames were complete, I set them up on the crossarms, upside down, and connected them with temporary battens until I had them all lined up vertically and checked with a level. Next came the sheer stringers and chines, which were one-by-two-inch and one-by-three-inch lumber, respectively, spliced to about twenty-eight-foot sections from two lengths of lumber. The frames were notched as required, much like building model airplane fuselages, and the stringers attached in a bed of resorcinol glue, with two countersunk 1-1/2-inch bronze wood screws at each joint.

Next came the keel which was about 1-1/2 inches thick by 3 inches wide. I had a bit of trouble bending it, and no facilities for steaming, so I finally sort of cheated and helped it out a bit by making some transverse saw cuts on the inner surface of the keel. I have since found that a much easier way to make keels is to laminate them, that is, install a 3/4-by-3-inch inner piece, which would bend readily, and then follow up with an outer piece fastened with wood clamps and resorcinol glue. I have seen this done on a number of boats, and it is a painless way to make keels.

The intermediate stringers and the stem piece went on rapidly. Within a month I had the framework complete. Probably the toughest job was beveling the keel and the chines to fair smoothly with the surface of the bottom of the boat. As you plane, you lay a straight batten along the bottom to check for smooth fairing. I found this to be one of the more tiring jobs on the boat, next only to sanding down fiberglass, but both of these can be made easy with the power planes and sanders available today.

It was a very pleasant day when I started planking. One starts to feel a sense of completion, somehow, as the hull becomes planked and solid-looking. Planking is a simple job with 3/8-inch plywood. I would lay a sheet over the part of the hull to be covered and trace on the back side the stringer and frame locations. Then I would remove the plank and cut the outer edges to shape in a jiffy with the saber saw. I would drill a few small (nail-sized) pilot holes here and there from the back to indicate the centerlines of the frames and stringers. Then, when the sheet was tacked back in place, it was a simple matter to connect the pilot holes with penciled lines to indicate the locations of the framing for nailing.

Prior to installing the planks, I would cut the butt blocks to size and tack them in place. These are eight-inch-wide pieces of plywood that fit between the stringers and serve as backup splices where the ends of the planks butt together. Although some people advocate putting them in later, I have always felt that it is easier to put them in as each plank is installed. I would cut them to fit snugly and tack them with temporary nails to hold them in place while I drilled pilot holes for the screws. When the plank was tacked on for the second time, I would drill holes for one-inch bronze screws, remove the plank, coat everything with resorcinol, replace the plank, fasten it to the butt blocks at both ends with screws, and fasten all the rest to frames and stringers with one-inch grip-fast stainless steel nails on about two-inch centers. I fastened the planks to the stem with 1-1/2-inch bronze screws. I planked the bottom first, planed down the edges smooth at the chines, and then planked the sides to overlap the bottom at the chine. The chine was then rounded off slightly with a plane, for fiberglassing. Where the keel is a right angle section, one half of the bottom overlaps the other, but toward the stern, where it flattens out, this is a difficult joint to match closely and I was left with a bit of a chink between the two bottom planks. I filled it in with wood slivers and a sort of mastic made of sawdust and resorcinol glue. It sets up hard as a rock, and can later be planed and sanded to a smooth surface.

Fiberglassing came next and was much simpler than I had expected. You merely fit the cloth over the hull, which has been sanded smooth and cleaned thoroughly, stretch it taut with Scotch tape or something else suitable about the edges, mix the resin, and apply it with a brush. After letting it set overnight, you put on another coat to fill in the mesh of the cloth, perhaps with still another coat for good measure, and finally sand it down. I had had no experience with fiberglass and thought that the 1% of hardener to be mixed with the resin was sort of small, so it might be a good idea to put in a little more for the pot, say about 2% of the total. I had been brushing for about five minutes when the pot felt funny when I put the brush in it. I looked down and found that the resin has turned into a species of green jello! I dumped it out on the ground and within another minute it had set up hard. It was hot to the touch from the heat of the reaction. That was the last time I ever added a "bit for the pot" when mixing fiberglass resin hardener. Thereafter I added 1% scrupulously and things went well. I would normally mix about a quart at a time, enough for ten or fifteen minutes of brushing, then come back and mix another quart in the same can. The brush will remain flexible as long as you keep using it with fresh batches of resin. After I was through for the day, I'd leave the brush suspended in a can of synthetic lacquer thinner, which is about the only thing that will cut fiberglass resin.

Sanding down fiberglass is a chore! As it sets, it tends to thin and run through an internal heat reaction that lessens the viscosity. Unless you keep going over it for ten or fifteen minutes to smooth out runs as they appear, you are left with a lot of sanding work the next day. (I hear there are improved resins on the market these days which don't run.)

Perhaps the most annoying thing about sanding fiberglass, next to the work, is all the prickles you get in your skin from the tiny particles of glass. They go away after a day or two, fortunately.

Finally the day came to turn over the hull. As a matter of interest, I weighed it by propping up each end on a bathroom scale and taking the sum. It turned out to be about four hundred pounds. With the aid of a few friends, I managed to turn it over without trouble and built a cradle to hold it upright for the rest of the construction period. I put several two-inch pipes under the cradle so we could roll it out of the garage when the time came.

I had started the boat in the spring of 1964, and continued to work on it in spare time throughout the year. By the time it was ready to be launched, I had worked on it about fourteen months. However, this is in no way indicative of the usual building time for I was later to complete a much more complicated thirty-two-foot boat in exactly one year. I spent many of my weekends playing golf, so it is not surprising that it took so long.

The remainder of the year was spent making the cabin, internals, wings, and cockpit on the main hull. Early in 1965 I trundled her

The Linda Niña I

Partway through construction of the Linda Niña I.

out into the front yard and started construction of the floats. These went rapidly, being much simpler than the main hull. The *Nugget* floats were simply V-frames, although larger models now have chines.

The remaining carpentry on the main hull was relatively simple. Roof framing was something of a chore but everything else was straightforward, requiring only the simplest of cabinetwork-type skills. Working on the inside is rather fun as the internals begin to take shape. In the midst of my labors I would relax on the settee with a cold beer and it began to feel as though I was inside a real live boat. As it approached completion, I started imagining that magic day when I would put her into the water and what I would do with her then. It's great material for daydreaming and there were afternoons when I would get little done except drink beer and imagine the trips I would make in her. By this time she already had a name, *Linda Niña*, which means "pretty girl" in Spanish.

In the spring of 1965 I started studying navigation in preparation for the great trip, whenever that might be, and bought a second-hand sextant for fifty dollars from one of our retired tanker cap-

Wings have been partially finished, and port float completed.

tains in Singapore. About this time, too, I bought a three-inch Japanese refractor telescope and started taking an interest in the stars. Carried along by enthusiasm for this new interest, I spent several months early in the year out in the yard in the evening with telescope and star charts, studying like mad. I had picked the right time of year since the skies become clear over Saigon toward the end of November and by January they are clear most evenings. Also, at this time of year the constellation Orion is right overhead along with a host of other constellations and first magnitude stars.

Learning about stars is quite simple. You just buy a set of inexpensive star charts and then go out and *look*. A few nights of mild eyestrain are generally sufficient to locate all of the constellations in your part of the sky and identify the principal navigational stars. It is nice to have some sort of telescope but not vital. A telescope will bring distant galaxies and nebuli closer and you can see a lot of things that are beyond the range of the naked eye.

Peering through a high-power telescope at the moon is fascinating. It suddenly takes on a depth and reality beyond anything you ever imagined. Viewing the planets is equally fascinating. I'll never forget the day I focused on Jupiter for the first time. Instead of a twinkle of light, it suddenly took on substance, a small ball hanging in the vast reaches of space with little white dots of moons about it. It was with a similar feeling of wonderment that I first viewed Saturn and actually *saw* it, surrounded by its luminous rings. You read about these things in books and see pictures and know they exist but it is a special sensation to see them with your own eyes for the first time. One of the surest things that can be said in favor of studying astronomy, aside from the benefits in connection with navigation, is that you will never again step outside of your house on a clear night with indifference to the heavens. I suppose it is like any study; one becomes aware of things that were previously seen but not noticed. I recall the time I read a few books on heraldry. For the next few months I was bemused at the way shields, flags, and other heraldic devices seemed to be popping up all over the landscape and intruding themselves on my consciousness. Of course they had been there all the time but through lack of knowledge or interest I had been completely unaware of them. So it is with the stars.

I think one of the best all-around books I have ever read on astronomy is *Astronomy*, by Fred Hoyle. It is full of fascinating little sketches to explain all manner of things astronomical, bits and pieces of history, old navigational instruments, beautiful illustrations, and everything else required to make a first-rate and most interesting book. At the same time it is a good introduction to the study of navigation.

There is an excellent book on navigation that everyone seems to endorse, George Mixter's *Primer of Navigation*. Mixter has a straightforward, friendly, pipe-smoking knack for making things simple and interesting. His book will undoubtedly long remain a favorite in this field. There are many others, of course, but I wholeheartedly recommend Mixter.

Assuming that by now I have talked you into having a shot at navigation, you will need a *Nautical Almanac* (published every year), and the H.O. 249 Tables, which are three loose-leaved books, good indefinitely. The *Almanac* lists the exact angular position, relative to the Greenwich Meridian, for each hour of each day in the year, for the sun, the moon, Venus, and a mysterious and astrological-sounding point called the First Point of Aries from which the stars are in turn located. The fifty-seven navigational stars are listed on each page with their sidereal hour angle relative to Aries. Tables are provided at the back for interpolating between the hourly positions given on the pages of the *Almanac*. The H.O. 249 Tables are a set of tabled figures from which solutions to the navigational triangle may be readily looked up. Although this is hardly the place for a treatise on navigation, the reader may be interested in a very brief description of the process.

Navigation consists of getting a so-called "line of position" (LOP), calculated by taking a sight on the sun or on some other heavenly body. A "fix" requires generally two sights at about the same time on two different bodies; where the respective lines of position cross is your position. Line of position may be described with a simple analogy.

Suppose you are somewhere in New York. There are no street signs, but you think you are somewhere in the vicinity of Fifth Avenue and 42nd Street. You can see the top of the Acme Building, which let's say lies due south, and you can also see the top of the Smith Building, which lies to the west. You have a sextant, and you get the top of the Acme Building sighted in it, and then gradually swivel the mirror on your sextant and "bring it down" to the street. You check the reading on your sextant, and it says fifty-five degrees. Making a further analogy to degrees versus nautical miles, let's assume the streets of New York are set apart from each other a distance such that for each street you get closer to the Acme Building, the angle increases by one degree. In other words, as you walked south toward it, by one block from where you are now, the angle would increase by one degree and you would read fifty-six degrees on your sextant.

Now, suppose you have the equivalent of the H.O. 249 Table for New York City, and this table is set up by the different buildings in New York. You look up the Acme Building and run your finger down to the line that says 42nd Street, which is where you *think* you are, and you come up with the number from the table "fifty-seven degrees." You mull over this for a moment and think there must be something wrong somewhere, since when you measured the angle on your sextant you got fifty-five degrees. The only thing that's wrong is that you are obviously *not* on 42nd Street. Where are you, then? Well, you know that for each Street toward or away from the Acme Building, the angular measurement changes by exactly one degree. You wound up with an angle two degrees less than what you should have gotten if you really were on 42nd Street. That means that you are actually two blocks further north, since the further away you get the less is the angle; hence, you are somewhere on 44th Street. As yet, you don't know exactly *where* on 44th Street, but 44th Street becomes your line of position, which runs at right angles to the line of direction between yourself and the Acme Building to the south.

You may say that this is all very logical (or maybe very confusing?), but why can't you fix your position on 44th Street at the same time? If you know that the Acme Building lies, say, between Fifth and Sixth Avenues, and if it is truly south, isn't it logical to assume that you are on 44th Street between Fifth and Sixth Avenues as well?

It is logical, but not too applicable in practice, since the celesital bodies being observed—or rather the "shadows" that they cast on the earth's surface—are usually thousands of miles away. You could indeed take a compass reading on them (as a matter of fact this information, called the azimuth, also pops out of the tabled figures when you look up the solution in the H.O. 249 Tables). However, assuming a possible error of only a tenth of a degree in the compass reading, by the time you had mapped this on a large-scale chart and brought the line back to your line of position, the error would have been magnified into many miles.

Therefore you have to run through the same procedure again, this time using the Smith Building. By an identical procedure, you find that the actual reading you got on your sextant is, say, one and a half degrees more than you should have gotten had you been on Fifth Avenue. Assuming the avenues were laid out in the same manner as the streets, this would bring you a block and a half closer to the Smith Building, that is, to the west. Therefore your line of position becomes a north-south line running parallel to and halfway between Sixth and Seventh Avenues. Now you have two lines of position; where they cross, on 44th Street halfway between Sixth and Seventh Avenues, is your true position.

What have you done, in essence? You have assumed yourself to be in a certain position and you have taken sights on a known landmark. Checking back into the tables to get the proper number corresponding to your assumed position, you have found that it differs from the one you actually got. By simple inspection, you have concluded that you are nearer to or further away from the landmark than you had assumed, and have located your line of position accordingly.

Obviously, there is a limited analogy between the top of a building a few blocks away and a star moving through the heavens at approximately 1,000 miles per hour, considering the speed of the spot directly under it traveling along the earth's surface. The procedure is roughly the same, however, in principle. Although it appears complicated at first, once you develop a feel for it, it becomes logical and straightforward, and not at all difficult to carry out.

Once I got the hang of it, I used to spend frequent evenings in the front yard with my sextant, sighting different stars and "bringing them down" to the level of an arbitrary line that I had marked on the fence at about eye level. Later I would drop down to the Club Nautique in the evenings and practice off the dock. Eventually I improved to where I could get lines of position within ten miles of Saigon, which I felt to be quite satisfactory considering deviations in my watch since the last time I had checked it against a time-tick, plus the fact that I had only an approximate horizon to work with.

As spring wore on, and completion of the boat approached, I started collecting the odds and ends required to finish her off. These final trimmings are what cost the money! The wood and glue for a boat are relatively inexpensive, but when you start getting into compasses, chronometers, sails, stainless steel rigging, etc., it begins to pile up. I was fortunate in two of the items: A friend in the Marine Department of Esso in Singapore gave me a salvaged lifeboat compass, which was ideal for the *Linda Niña*, and another friend in the AID Mission in Saigon gave me a brand new chronometer. On local vacation for a week, I flew up to Hong Kong and ordered the sails of bright red terylene. I stressed the need for speed, and was able to pick them up on the day I left, a week later.

I also bought fittings, cleats, and assorted hardware to finish up the boat, including miscellaneous items such as bilge pump, stain-

The Linda Niña I

...and the Linda Niña I is ready for sea.

Stepping the mast...

Getting her ready to launch.

less steel sink, rope, and blocks for the running rigging. Somehow I brought it all back on the plane without any excess baggage. I reflected, looking at the pile, that I was bringing back everything but the kitchen sink; and upon further reflection, grinned at the thought that I was bringing *that* back too!

All ready to go, complete with American ensign and 5 hp Evinrude.

The Linda Niña I

It was a tight squeeze out the Nhabe gate.

Spring passed into summer, and my biannual two-month vacation was fast approaching. I gave up golf on weekends, and really started putting myself to it to finish the boat by June. The last few weeks were a strain, but I completed it about the time my vacation started. This meant spending another week or two of vacation getting her launched and fitted out.

In the water at last, just as it started to pour buckets.

The great day finally arrived and we arranged for a flat-bed trailer to haul her out to the Esso oil terminal at Nhabe, where I would finish the final assembly of wings and floats, slap the final coat of antifouling on her bottom, and we'd put her in the water. I had a fair number of friends who had been watching developments over the past year with interest. They all pitched in and helped with the launching.

We tied her temporarily alongside the Nhabe pier, and retired to drink beer.

It was quite an occasion. We had a big launching party at Nhabe, and quite a few people showed up. Unfortunately it started to rain just as we were getting her into the water and everybody got soaked! The launching proceeded successfully otherwise, and she floated nicely in the water. The thrill appears to increase in proportion to the size of the boat and to the amount of effort. What a great moment! We broke a bottle of champagne over her bow (on a steel plate thoughtfully provided for the purpose), and slid her in the water. It was still drizzling, so we moored her alongside one of the tanker piers until the next day, and retired to drink beer and relax for the rest of the afternoon.

The next day I went down to Nhabe again, and with a few friends we putt-putted back up the Saigon River, with a little five-horse Evinrude that I'd recently brought back from Singapore. It was a sunny day, and a glorious sensation to be proceeding up the Saigon River.

I was afloat at last, in a real *boat* that I could call my own!

3 / *Manila Ho!*

The *Linda Niña* had barely been put into the water when vacation was upon me. I had about two months coming, and had planned the vacation essentially around the boat. First I was going to sail her across the South China Sea to Manila; thereafter, my plans were flexible.

Looking back on it, I shudder at my optimism. I had never sailed a boat, aside from the Sailfish, and here I was all set to take a twenty-four-footer across the nine hundred miles between Saigon and Manila. I think this realization began to dawn upon me during the final weeks prior to the launching. I had been planning the trip for so long that of course I had to go through with it now, although I would not have a chance to take the boat on any sea trials. Hence, as the day of departure drew near, I was in something of a mental sweat, growing ever more aware of the fact that I was setting out in an untested boat, and with nil experience in deep-sea sailing. However, it was too late to back out, so I set forth with determination, if not with the romantic enthusiasm that had carried me along during the long months of building the boat.

I had given a lot of thought to getting down the Saigon River to the sea. The river winds and twists from Saigon down to Ganh Rai Bay, by Cap St. Jacques, where it opens onto the South China Sea. As the Vietnamese crow flies, it's about thirty-five miles from Saigon to Cap; but the twists and bends in the river add ten miles at least to this. At any rate, security was generally doubtful along this section of the river. Although theoretically the Government forces controlled this portion of the delta, the area was undoubtedly infested with Viet Cong. To date there had been no incidents on the commercial shipping coming up the river, but a small boat proceeding downstream alone could conceivably offer an irresistibly tempting target for casual snipers.

After some thought, I finally decided to get a tow down the river with an Esso tanker. It was no problem to tie in my trip with a tanker, since we had one coming into Nhabe about once a week. Fortunately, the next tanker in after the start of my vacation was the *World Success*, captained by an old friend with the unlikely name of Sydney Beer.

Captain Beer was an English gentleman of the old school, with a hearty ho-ho-ho approach to life, and a Santa Claus figure to match. I first met him through normal company channels in the course of my dealings with tankers, and we became good friends. Whenever he came into town we would usually arrange a dinner or a night out together. He followed with interest the various stages of construction of the boat, and was interested in my ambitious plans for vacation.

Hence, when I apprised him of my plan to take off for Manila, Captain Beer was only too pleased to offer a tow down the river, after completion of his discharge operations at Nhabe. He expressed some concern about the speed of towing, since outgoing vessels usually go full speed down the Saigon River, but I assured him that the *Linda Niña* could easily take towing at the twelve to fourteen knots of the *World Success*.

The *World Success* arrived about on schedule, and the Captain and I had dinner together on a Wednesday evening. The vessel was due to depart again Friday morning.

On Thursday, accompanied by little fanfare, I completed the loading of the final stores at the Club Nautique, and took off in the afternoon for Nhabe. The two-hour run down the river was uneventful, and I tied up alongside the Nhabe barge pier to spend the night. It was hard to get to sleep that night. Next morning was to be the big day.

On Friday morning I had breakfast on the boat, and about nine o'clock it looked as though they were starting to cast off the mooring lines on the *World Success*, so I fired up the little five-horse Evinrude, and made a long circle out into the river and back to come alongside the outboard side of the *World Success*. As I approached the gangway, the portly figure of Captain Beer loomed regretfully over the gunwales to announce that the Pilot had refused to let him tow me downriver. Some regulation or other....

Well, *shikata ga nai*, as the Japanese say. This took it out of my hands, so after exchanging a few farewells with the Captain and the Chief Officer, I revved up the outboard without further ado and headed down the river towards Cap.

The river was full of traffic that morning, and one of the first basic lessons I learned about boat-handling is that you must keep your eyes open every moment to all sides. As I was going downriver I decided to duck into the cabin for a minute to get a chart. I was only there for a few seconds, it seemed, when I heard an angry hooting aft. I looked out, horrified, through the hatch to see a large passenger liner, the Messageries Maritime's *Viet-Nam* of about ten thousand tons bearing down on me a hundred yards astern! For a moment it took the breath out of me, and then I reacted leaping out into the cockpit and grabbing the tiller. I bore off hard to starboard, and a minute or so later a white avalanche went scudding by a hundred feet to my port, still hooting angrily and throwing up a monstrous bow wave. Tourists crowded the rails to take pictures of the nice little sailboat, as I rocked and wallowed in the wash. *Choi oi*! From then on I kept a close watch on what was going on in the river!

The rest of the trip down the river was uneventful, although fraught with a certain amount of tension. There was plenty of company, though. I kept passing liners and freighters going up and down the river, and LCU's, and a variety of patrol boats. It took about six hours to get down to Ganh Rai bay, and I arrived at four thirty in the afternoon.

Ganh Rai Bay is about ten miles long. Looking at it on the map, at the upper left corner the Saigon River empties into it, coming down from Saigon; on the lower right corner is Cap St. Jacques, which faces on the strait connecting Ganh Rai Bay with the South China Sea.

As I entered the bay, I decided to haul up the sails and make it across to Cap St. Jacques under sail to get a feel for it, and then perhaps lie off Cap for an early morning start. After some effort, I finally wrestled them up. However, by this time, what little breeze there was had died down, and the sails luffed and flapped listlessly. I kept the outboard on and continued out into the bay. As I passed the last point of land to starboard, and got out into the open bay, I found there was a nasty chop running, which chop seems (based on subsequent experience) to blow up just about every evening. Although the chop was not much to look at, being only a few feet, it was of just the right amplitude to rock the *Linda Niña* back and forth like a pendulum.

Suddenly I realized with a shock that there was something wrong with the rigging. The mast was swaying back and forth in the step! Something was horribly wrong, since the shrouds had been tight the last time I had checked them.

For a few moments I watched the shrouds on each side grow taut and then slacken noticeably, as the mast rocked back and forth. Before I had a chance even to assess the situation, much less do anything about it, *thunk!* went the starboard shroud, whipping up into the air, and with a splintering of plywood as the lower lamination of the mast step ripped apart, the mast leaned over tiredly to port and then went down like a majestic cypress, with a rocking crash and a billow of tangled sails and rigging!

Choi oi! I sat and watched it go over, thinking to myself resignedly: *Well, there goes the old trip to Manila!* I felt an overwhelming sensation of frustration and despair, and yet I would not be completely honest if I didn't acknowledge a hint of relief among the other emotions. It wasn't exactly that my heart wasn't in the trip, but I was very much aware that I was setting off under inauspicious circumstances as regards the condition of my boat and my familiarity with it. Add to this the great strain of the past weeks wondering whether the boat would be ready on time, the launching, the frenzied last-minute carpentry, which lasted up to the day of sailing, and one can see where the sudden taking of all of this out of my hands in a somewhat providential way would engender a certain amount of relief.

So there I was, about five in the afternoon in the middle of Ganh Rai Bay, with the mast overboard, and Cap St. Jacques still about five miles off. I spent the next ten minutes or so in wrestling the mast aboard, which was a real chore, with a tangle of sails and rigging, slippery deck, 100 pounds or so of combined mast, boom, and sails, and the *Linda Niña* bouncing about on the chop. I finally got it hauled on deck and lashed down, and then fired up the outboard and headed toward Cap. St. Jacques.

The chop had not yet finished with us, however. Waves kept washing up about the outboard and finally swamped it. After sweating over it for ten minutes I finally started it; however, after another fifteen minutes it got swamped again, and this time it was out for good. I worked on it for another half-hour, but with no luck. It was getting past six by now, and I had only an hour and a half before nightfall, with Cap St. Jacques still nearly five miles away. About this time, however, the fishing boats started coming in from the Vietnam coast, and were passing only a quarter of a mile or so from where I was, en route back to their villages for the night.

They couldn't hear me hailing, so I got my ensign, which was mounted on a short flagpole mounted atop the rudder, and waved it back and forth. Finally one of the boats veered off and came over to see what the trouble was. The trouble was pretty evident, when you got up close, and I didn't have to say much. They came in after making a turn or two about the boat, and attached a towline. I asked whether they could tow me to Cap, but they said no, they had no time, but that they would take me on in to their village. All of this was conducted in shouted Vietnamese accompanied by a lot of gestures.

After a half-hour or so we got to shore, and continued up a river leading inland from Ganh Rai Bay, somewhat to the north of Cap St. Jacques. We passed one or two fishing villages along the river, and finally stopped at a village that I later found out was named Binh Dinh. As we pulled up to the fishing boat piers, there was a large crowd of people along the shore to greet the returning fishermen. They were asking the fishermen what was going on, and I heard a fisherman yell "*con ca lon*" to the crowd, which amused them highly. *Con ca lon:* a big fish! When we moored, some of the crowd gestured to ask me what kind of odd boat mine was. I told them "*con ca lon*," which evoked much laughter. It was quite a catch at that, since the fisherman wanted a thousand piastres, or about eight dollars, for bringing me in, which I paid without demur. This was probably a few weeks worth of fishing revenue.

Thank heavens for my Vietnamese! I don't know how I would have gotten by without it. Apparently there was no one in the village who spoke French, let alone English, and had I not known a moderate degree of Vietnamese, communication would have been a real headache. As it was, we dickered back and forth at length, accompanied by a good deal of gesturing, and I told the fisherman that I wanted him to tow my boat back up the river to Nhabe the following day. We finally settled on a price of 2,000 piastres, or about fifteen dollars, which seemed pretty reasonable. The fisherman advised that we would leave next morning about four o'clock.

I spent the evening on the boat, surrounded by a crowd of curious urchins who scampered about the boat, peering in the windows. They waited with considerable interest to see how I was going to eat, drink, urinate, or whatever else the roundeyes might do. In the Orient, life is surprisingly open to public view, and they were all disappointed when I finally had someone chase them off the boat. Even then they remained perched on neighboring boats, and never did disperse until nightfall had made further observations impractical, at which time I thankfully went below, drank a can of fruit juice, and crawled into my bunk.

I managed to get a fair amount of sleep, although I would wake up from time to time as boats were moored nearby and people walked across the boat. At about four in the morning I woke up again, this time as they were untethering the *Linda Niña* from the nest of vessels tied up along the pier. By half past four we were putt-putting off into the darkness. The skies were beautiful, full of stars, and there was a bright moon. I assumed the fishermen knew where they were going, and after a bit I yawned and went below again to grab some more sleep.

If I had been worrying about the Viet Cong before, I would have worried more now, for when I woke up about seven and emerged into the cockpit, we were in a completely unfamiliar channel somewhere deep in the delta! The fishing boat was moored placidly about twenty yards in front of me, tethered with the mooring rope, and the two fishermen were busy in the cockpit stuffing themselves with their morning rice. They grinned and waved when they saw me. I went below again to fish up something for breakfast.

Presently we started off again. They fired up their little pop-pop diesel, and we took off at about four knots. Back and forth we went, along a variety of inland channels. From time to time we saw other small boats of the sampan type. I had my .38 loaded and ready in my pocket by this time, although the extent to which it would have been of any use if I had run into any real problems is questionable.

As we were running along a small channel, just before reaching a junction where it emptied into a considerably larger river, we suddenly came upon an abandoned temple on the left side of the bank. It was fascinating: an old, abandoned temple out in the middle of nowhere. There was not a soul to be seen, and it appeared that the brush and weeds had grown up about the grounds. The temple had pagoda-like roofs. To the left was a separate little building with an altar of some type, and atop this building was a cupola-like roof on the second story, with ceramic dragons mounted on the roof.

I stared in fascination as the boats nosed slowly by this old temple. *Those dragons!* They appeared to be about five feet long and a few feet high, and there were four of them, one on each corner of the roof. They were coated with some sort of glaze, and the sunlight reflected richly off the green coloring of their serpentine bodies and the brown of their rooster-like tails. Most unusual animals! I sat spellbound, and finally gathered up enough presence of mind to grab the camera and get a quick shot of the temple, although by now it was nearly out of view behind the trees.

Some day, I thought, I must come here again and look for those dragons!

Shortly after noon we came out onto the main river, into the commercial channel, at a point that I recognized as being just below the Coral Bank lights. I was back in familiar territory. A few hours later we pulled up at Nhabe, and I tied up the boat to the wharf and paid off the fishermen.

It was Saturday afternoon, and Dave Baillie, the terminal superintendent, was understandably amazed to see me back so soon! I rustled a cold beer out of him and told the story; then I hitched a ride into Saigon on an Esso tank truck. The maids were equally surprised to see me, since I was supposed by now to have been on my way to Manila. It had been only a little over a day since I'd left home, but it seemed much longer.

Over the next few days, I went back and unloaded the boat, and made arrangements with Dave Baillie to have her hauled up onto the bank until I returned from vacation. I started making alternate plans for tickets and reservations, which the travel people took with good grace. They fixed me up on short notice, and I was soon ready to take off on a more conventional vacation. Well, it had been a good try.

Manila Ho! indeed. I didn't get very far! Yet I could look back on it with a certain degree of wistful philosophy. Things sometimes just don't work out the way you think they will, and there is no use moaning and groaning about it. All you can do is have a better shot at it next time.

I had closely examined the shrouds after we got back and found that both turnbuckles had worked loose in spite of the lock nuts; the starboard one had given way first. Lesson number one, learned the hard way was: Wire down your turnbuckles!

Well, I would have another try at it, one of these days.

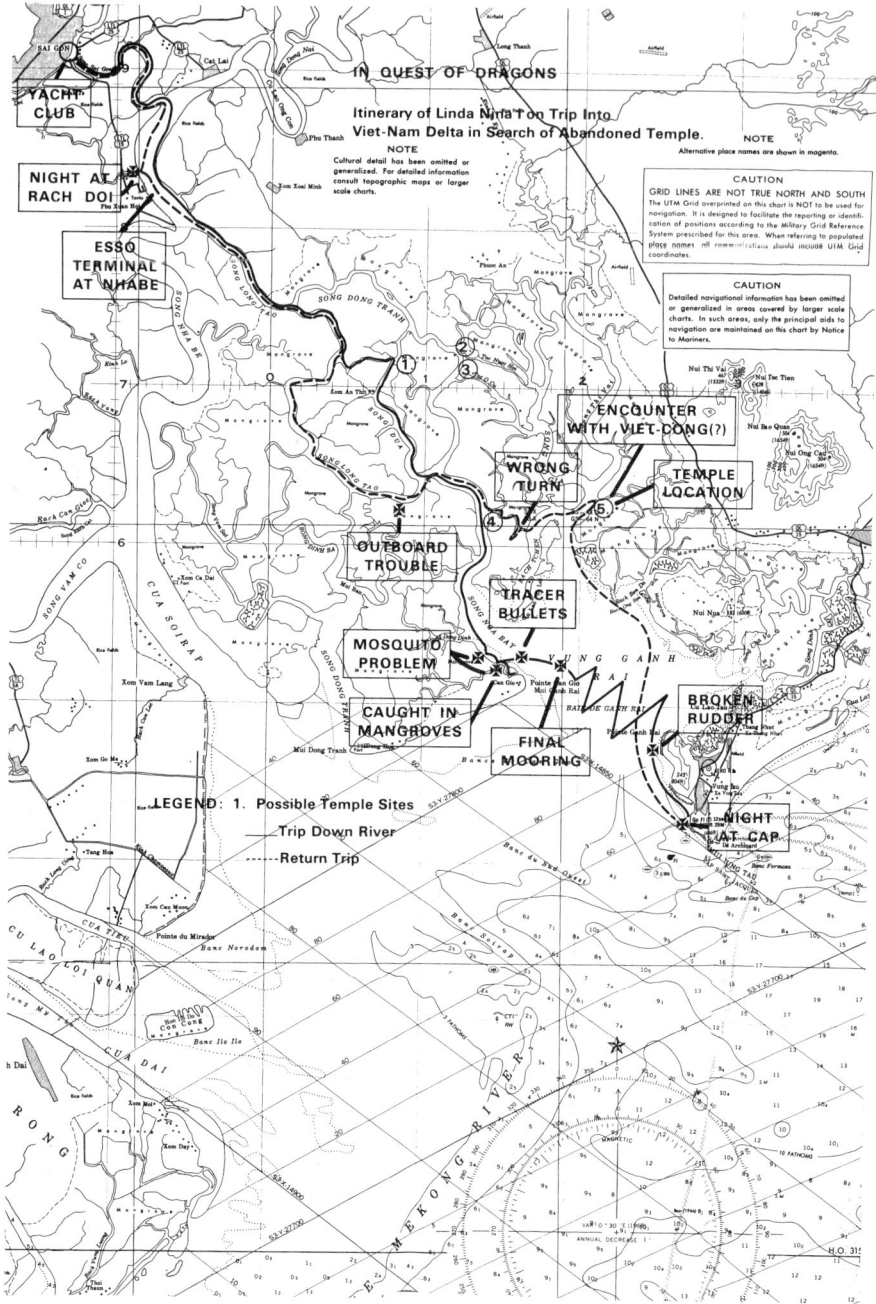

4 / In Quest of Dragons

On the first weekend after my vacation, having settled again in Saigon, I made a trip to Nhabe to check the status of the *Linda Niña*. Although she had been covered with a tarp, the rains had come in and the hull was nearly half full of murky water. It had apparently become the favorite mosquito hatchery of the Nhabe area, and I retreated in haste. After a few hours with buckets and rags I had her cleaned out, however, and although the varnish had suffered considerably, at any rate the marine plywood seemed unaffected. I made arrangements with a local boatyard to put her up on blocks for fiberglassing of the bottom and repainting.

A few weeks later we got her into the water again, with the assistance of the Nhabe fork lift truck and a team of coolies, and the Nhabe launch towed me down the river to the Sovicotra boatyard. They had her up on blocks within a few days, and started scraping the bottom of the hull and floats preparatory to installing additional fiberglass, since there were several leaks along the keels.

Work on the *Linda Niña* under way, I started thinking about the next project: the dragons.

I racked my memory for what I could remember of the temple, and where it had been located. We had passed it on the left side of a small channel, just upstream of where the small channel had emptied into a considerably larger river, and we had turned right upon entering the larger river. Thereafter, the boats had meandered through a variety of small and large channels before finally emerging onto the commercial river by the navigation lights at Coral Bank. The photo that I had taken of the temple had come out well but gave no particular information of use in locating it again.

I obtained a number of large-scale military maps of the delta area between Saigon and Cap St. Jacques from some friends in MAC-V, and also referred to a chart I already had, number 3268 "Eastern Approaches to Rivière de Saigon," which showed most of the channels. I was looking for a point somewhere between Cap and Coral Bank, on a route that the fishermen might conceivably have taken, and where a small river emptied into a large one. I finally came up with five possible locations (see map), numbered in order of probability.

The end of 1965 came and went, and then we were approaching Tet, the Vietnamese equivalent of Chinese New Year. It fell on a Thursday, January 20th, and we would have the rest of the week off—four whole days in which to hunt dragons. The Viet Cong had apparently agreed to a cease-fire during this interval, so hopefully the risks associated with traveling about the back channels of the delta would be minimized.

By the end of December, the *Linda Niña* had been repaired and was back in the water, resplendent in a new coat of white paint. The mast step had been repaired, and the stays on the mast were carefully wired at all points to preclude any further slippage of turnbuckles! The interior had been refinished and varnished.

On weekends thereafter I would take her up the river, on the five-horse Evinrude, to the annex of the Club Nautique to have lunch aboard and watch the water-skiing and the bikinis by the pool. Water-skiing was a popular sport upriver from Saigon, and not without a certain spice, for from time to time casual shots had been reported from shore. Whether these were from Viet Cong or perhaps just some of the ARVN troops having a bit of Sunday sport, no one ever found out.

The Wednesday afternoon prior to departure I put the finishing touches on the boat and got everything loaded aboard. I had a fair amount of food, mostly of the canned Chef Boy-ar-dee variety. I was up to my ears in stuff left over from the abortive Manila trip, including meatball stew, beefarone, ravioli, spaghetti with meatballs, and spaghetti without meatballs. To round out the pasta diet I had a lot of smaller cans of spinach, beets, etc., plus a goodly

The Linda Niña I after repairs.

store of Camp's pork and beans. The cook came up with a couple of loaves of French bread, which were wrapped in aluminum foil. Eight eggs were tenderly enclosed in paper towels and carefully packed in a plastic box. I also had such staples as tea bags, sugar, pepper, salt, and cooking oil. To wash down the above motley assortment, I had two bottles of red wine (*toujours le gourmet*), about ten half-gallon plastic bottles of water, and a few dozen assorted cans of beer and soft drinks.

Other supplies included cooking utensils, a small kerosene stove (courtesy of Esso), camera, binoculars, and a small tape recorder for recording impressions along the way. I also had a few books, the radio, a couple of changes of clothes, first aid kit, fishing equipment, and a fair variety of tools and rope. All in all, I could probably have made it to Manila, with all the junk I had aboard.

On Thursday I got to the Club Nautique dock just before nine, got the *Linda Niña* unmoored from her posts near the club, and hauled her alongside the dock to load on the last few bits and pieces prior to departure.

The river was practically motionless, due to the Tet holiday, and after leaving the Nautique I drifted down a traffic-less river. I had the outboard purring lazily at half-throttle (it was not completely run in yet), and proceeded downriver at about four knots. The sun was well up in the sky now, and it looked as though it was going to be a beautiful day. I was comfortably slouched on the cushion on the port side of the cockpit, chewing on a toothpick, leaning against the back end of the cabin, and steering the tiller with one foot. I wore socks and tennis sneakers, an old pair of khaki pants and old knit shirt, sunglasses, and what I referred to as my "French planter's hat," a wide-brimmed old straw hat that I had picked up in the Saigon market for boating and other activities not requiring a great deal of fashion.

By about nine thirty I had passed the Arroyo Chinois, the channel that runs between Saigon and Cholon. From time to time I had to steer to avoid the small sampan ferries that cross the river, driven by energetic old ladies wielding paddles, each with a few local denizens seated in the bottom. I was starting to get a bit thirsty but was loath to duck into the cabin, remembering the last trip when I had nearly been run down by an ocean liner.

I finally did duck into the cabin for a pair of dividers to check the distance on my chart to estimate how long it would take me at this rate to reach Pointe de Feu Rouge. Sure enough, I was in there for just a second, and by the time I came out the boat was slewing around at a forty-five-degree angle and heading towards the bank. You can't leave the things for a second. I resolved to rig up some sort of friction device for holding the tiller steady.

Checking the distance from the Nautique to the Arroyo Chinois, I calculated that I was making about 4-1/2 knots, and that it would take another two hours or so to get down to Nhabe, and another seven hours to get to Ganh Rai bay. The ebb current was starting to slacken off, though, and I wondered how well I would do with the motor still at half-throttle against the oncoming flood tide. As it turned out, it was several more hours before the tide really changed, by which time I had passed the running-in time and had the outboard up to full blast, all 7-1/2 horsepower of it.

A small coastal freighter, the *Tien Phong*, went by at a good rate and threw up a considerable bow wave. It was a good test, and I rode into it with interest, watching to see how the mast would hold out. The *Linda Niña* rocked like a pendulum, but there was little noticeable slackening of the shrouds and the mast didn't budge an inch. This left me feeling optimistic about everything in general. Several other boats went by, a Vietnamese gunboat and a small craft with the river police. The police peered over uncertainly as they went by but I grinned and waved and shouted a few greetings in Vietnamese and they grinned back and waved. The gunboat went by more sedately, in keeping with increased size and dignity, but they all waved too, in response to my salute. A few minutes later the Esso tug *Dong Tien* went by, pushing a fuel oil barge toward some bunkering rendezvous upriver. Mother Esso was always before me: Halfway down to Cap St. Jacques, I passed our LPG tanker plowing upriver, and down at Cap one of our fuel oil tankers was waiting for a pilot to come upriver, plus an Army Y-boat that we had just loaded at Nhabe the day before.

By about half past ten, things had settled down considerably, and I had passed beyond the limits of the Saigon harbor and out into the curving river that leads down to the main river. Suddenly it became extremely quiet, with not another boat in sight. I relaxed a little and settled back for what was obviously going to be a long day. I set up the tiller with a friction cord that held it very well, requiring only an occasional adjustment to hold the boat on course. I ducked into the cabin to get a cold beer, and for the first time since I'd left the Club Nautique I really had a chance to relax and watch the river banks go by.

Actually, watching the river banks go by in the delta of Vietnam is dull sport, after the first mile or two. The shores are uniformly unexciting, consisting of mud flats and a variety of small scrub trees that grow to a height of ten feet or so. The land is amazingly flat; it is a true alluvial delta, silted up over the ages, and with no hills (except down in back of Cap St. Jacques) to break the monotony. Along the shore there is frequently a scrubby type of small palm tree that grows in clumps, and which is apparently planted by the Vietnamese as a kind of erosion control. They plant rice paddy up to about thirty feet from the river bank, and plant these scrub palms along the river edge to serve to break the bow waves of the ships that go by. Further down the river, where there is no paddy, it's even scrubbier—an unalluring miscellany of sparse grass, small brush, and only an occasional bird call to break the stillness. One eerie aspect of this low-lying land is that you can see vessels a long way off that are coming up the river, and due to the flatness of the land and the bends in the river it looks for all the world as though these ships are sailing over the delta land.

The sun was higher in the sky now, and I sailed placidly down the middle of the river. There was little haze and hardly a cloud to be seen; the sun hung in the sky, a glowing ball, bright and hot. Way up there was a long contrail made by some unseen jet.

At about eleven o'clock I reached Pointe de Feu Rouge and started to turn out into the main river. Suddenly there was quite a bit of boating action. A large sampan had been coming up behind me for the past ten minutes and was just drawing abreast as I came out by Feu Rouge light. At the same time, two Vietnamese patrol boats, moving along at a good clip, came up the main river and turned into the channel. What a bunch of cowboys those patrol boat jockeys are! One came at me on a collision course until he was no more than a hundred yards away. I kept steering to starboard and he kept steering to port, and finally I decided to chicken out and steered to port. He maintained his course and passed no more than a dozen yards away. He threw up a hefty bow wave, and the *Linda Niña* heeled and wallowed drunkenly for a few moments until the water subsided. I wrenched at the tiller, cursing.

Meanwhile, the sampan had come up from behind and passed to my starboard. About this time the second cowboy came roaring up in his patrol boat. We all passed within a few yards of each other; the sampan crossed my bow to avoid the patrol boat, who in turn slashed across his bow going off to starboard, and for a few seconds, there never seemed to be so many boats and so many waves in one place at the same time.

I finally escaped into the tranquil sanctuary of the main river, and for the next few hours worked my way down toward Nhabe and Pointe du Lazaret. By noon I had passed Nhabe, and the oil tankers discharging at the Esso and Shell piers, and was approaching Pointe du Lazaret and the branch-off where the Soirap River meets the Long Tao coming up from Cap St. Jacques. In the open bay in this area additional mooring buoys have been installed

In Quest of Dragons

and are being used as a lightering port to supplement the Saigon wharves. There were perhaps a half-dozen old Victory ships moored there, discharging into junks and barges alongside. Most of them were beat-up looking hulks, left over from World War II and only recently hauled out of mothballs to meet the burgeoning demands of the war in Vietnam. I wended my way among them, and was about halfway to the Long Tao River when the outboard kicked off with a gasping cough.

There is an awful quiet finality about outboards when they kick off. You have lived with their reassuring splutter for hours and it sort of grows on you. When they suddenly conk out it seems so *quiet* around! I was fairly sure the gas tank had just run dry, which indeed it had, but nonetheless had a moment of incipient heart failure until I had verified this. I took out the auxiliary gas tanks and filled the small service tank, managing to slop a fair amount of gas about the cockpit in the process.

Outboard motor gasoline, with its oil content, is extremely messy when spilled. The gasoline obligingly evaporates promptly, leaving an oil residue, which leaves the deck properly slippery until it can be mopped up with a kerosene-soaked rag.

I drifted among the Victory ships for a few minutes and had the gassing up completed, when it occurred to me that I was getting hungry. I got the motor started again, set the tiller for a relatively clear course, and ducked below to see what was handy. I will never gain weight living on boats, perhaps a good thing, but on the other hand I become a little undernourished since I never seem to have time to prepare anything halfway decent to eat while under way. In this case I came up with a dry roll from the galley, and cracked a can of Coca-Cola. It wasn't too bad; anything tastes good when you're hungry. So, I wended my way toward the entrance of the Long Tao, chewing on the roll and sipping the cola.

Once into the Long Tao, things quieted down again, and I coasted along alone. It started to cloud up a bit, but the sun was still very hot. I rigged up a tarpaulin over the boom to shade the cockpit. I had the sail wrapped around the boom, with the roller-reefing, and had hauled the boom up with the topping lift to a fair level above the top of the cabin. Over the last six feet or so I rigged up the canvas cover I used to protect the cockpit with a pair of whisker poles on either side to keep the side up, and lashed it with a variety of lines to the wing nuts on the float hatches and inspection ports on either side.

On the trip downriver to Pointe Velero and the Coral Bank lights, I had some time to think further about this matter of the dragons, pursuit thereof. Up to this time I had not absolutely decided whether I was going to take off into the back channels of the delta looking for the dragons or not. On one hand my better judgement kept telling me not to be an idiot; that I had a pleasant life here in Saigon and in general, and all sorts of interesting things to look forward to in the future, and wouldn't it be silly to jeopardize it all and end up hung by the heels from some tree just because of an idealistic and supposedly romantic quest for a couple of pieces of ceramic atop an old temple.

Of course this was the chicken in me coming out. On the other hand, I rationalized that there might very likely be little chance of an encounter in the delta. The Viet Cong, I reasoned, would never expect anyone to be such a bloody ass as to come nosing about in the back channels in a small boat; hence they might equally not be expected to be prepared to accost such an interloper with any degree of efficiency. Well, I argued it back and forth for awhile, but by the time I had reached the Coral Bank lights I'd decided that I was definitely going after the dragons.

As mentioned previously, the only part of the route that I remembered was returning to the main river via the little channel that connects with it just south of the Coral Bank lights. I planned to go east on this channel until I reached the Song Dua river, at which juncture I could check whether location No. 1 was the jackpot or not. If not, I could go down the Song Dua and check out another location shown on an Army map I had dug up, indicating a sort of temple at the junction of a small stream with the Song Dua just north of the village of Xom An Thit.

It took about three hours to work my way down to the channel in question. Progress down the main river was slow. The current was starting to change to flood tide, and the outboard made little progress, although by now I had passed the running-in time and had the outboard revved up full. A bit more traffic had appeared on the river by now—some sampans, Vietnamese patrol boats, and a variety of large vessels that commenced to appear heading upriver from Cap. Their bow waves were most troublesome, mostly due to the problems with the outboard. The outboard was of standard length, and reached just far enough down into the water to cover the anti-cavitation plate when mounted on my outboard mounting. Every time I went over the bow waves from passing vessels, the stern of the *Linda Niña* would lift out of the water and the outboard would race furiously, forcing me to shut it back to half-throttle, which was barely enough to hold my own in the ever-increasing flood current. Since a fair number of ships went by for the next hour or so, the going was slow. Relax, I told myself, and cracked a can of beer.

By three in the afternoon I had reached the channel branching off from the main river and turned into it. From now on I would be off the main channel and would be wending my way through the back delta. I was understandably nervous from here until I got back down to the main river at Quatre Bras.

I plugged along up the quiet channel. Not a soul could be seen. Prudently, I kept to the middle of the channel. From time to time I looked around with forced casualness to see whether there was anyone on the river bank aiming anything at me. *Choi oi!* By now the clouds were clearing up and the sun was comfortably hot on my shoulders, being low enough to shine in below the end of the tarp. The boat cut a quiet wake up the center of the channel, and the outboard purred on steadily.

It took about half an hour (it seemed longer!) to reach the Song Dua, and as I rounded the curve out into the river I looked forward to seeing whether the junction was where the temple had been. I had thought it the most likely spot, all things considered. However, a few minutes of inspection verified that such was not the case; this junction was completely different from the one on which I had seen the temple.

I stopped for a few minutes by the river bank to gas up again, and then restarted the motor and went chugging down the river toward the town of Xom An Thit. It took about fifteen minutes to reach the village; on the way I verified that the other small channel just above the town did not hold any temples of interest. As a matter of fact, I couldn't even find the channel, and concluded that it must have been very small and become grown over since the maps were made.

The town of Xom An Thit was a small fishing village sitting on one side of the river, about a half-mile long along the shore, with mostly thatched-roof accommodations, although I did see a concrete structure or two. One item of particular interest that I noted was the predominance of Vietnamese flags about. There was one on every boat moored along the river bank, and at least one or two prominently exposed in front of every house on the shore. Most were bright new flags, brilliant yellow with three bright red stripes running lengthwise down the middle. Apparently aircraft come by every so often and shoot up sampans and other moving craft that do not fly the Vietnamese flag. I didn't suppose anyone would shoot up the village of Xom An Thit, but apparently the residents were taking no chances.

I putt-putted along the shoreline to have a good look at the village, and all the local urchins came running out on the river bank to wave and shout as I went by. They cried "hello" and "okay" and "numbah one." I wondered where they picked up these expressions, so far down in the delta. From American patrol boats, presumably. I waved back, and cried hello and okay back at them, and passed the village, heading down toward Quatre Bras and the bay.

It was something of a relief to be on the main channel again. There were no ships; it was still a lonely river, but at least it was the main commercial channel to Saigon. There would be traffic passing by eventually, and presumably the Viet Cong restricted their nefarious activities to less patrolled waterways. In another half-hour I had worked my way down to the entrance of Ganh Rai Bay and was facing out into open water. The weather had quieted down, with just a slight breeze blowing, and the water was quiet. The sun was going down over to the west, low on the horizon and colorful behind the clouds. To the east the skies had cleared up considerably, and it looked as though it would be a clear evening.

Facing out into Ganh Rai bay, however, the wind freshened up a bit again, and the bay was getting a bit choppy. As I ventured out into the open water the chop was rough enough to make the outboard troublesome, so I decided to put up the sail and see what could be done. I shut the outboard off and went forward to haul

In Quest of Dragons

up the mainsail. It was quite a job to get it up. By now there was enough of a chop running so that the *Linda Niña* bounced about quite a bit, and it was slippery work to balance myself on the forward deck and try to handle sail, lines, and D. J. Steele at the same time, with only two hands. The wind had the sail all billowed out, and it kept getting tangled in the stays and spreaders. The running rigging kept flapping about and fouling, and had to be shaken out or slacked off. Finally I got the sail up at about six o'clock.

The boat lay in stays for awhile and I couldn't seem to get her started off. I thought I might need the motor to get her headed into the wind, and was just starting to gas up the service tank again when presto! the wind shifted a wee bit and I looked up to find the *Linda Niña* sailing along sedately at three or four knots. I tacked out toward the bay, hoping to make it to Fort Can Gio and anchor there for the night. Of course I had long since given up any thoughts of making Cap St. Jacques by that evening.

The tacks went slowly. It was difficult coming about; in the choppy bay the boat wouldn't get up enough headway to carry her about when tacking, and she would keep getting caught in stays. I finally had to light off the motor to get about, feeling most unseamanlike about the whole thing.

By six thirty it was beginning to get dark, and it was becoming obvious that I wouldn't make it to Fort Can Gio either, so I started casting about to find some likely spot to anchor. There appeared to be a little channel on the south shore of the bay, about two miles northwest of Fort Can Gio, where it looked as though I could sneak the boat in and settle down for the night. I tacked about once more and headed toward the inlet.

I just about made it on one tack, and glided into the channel, which was about forty feet wide. By the time I reached it the wind was increasing noticeably, and the chop had also increased. It was getting up to a mean three feet, which doesn't sound like much, but the frequency was just right to start the *Linda Niña* rocking like a pendulum. As we yawed and pitched I would have liked to have had an inclinometer in the cockpit; we were really tilted over on some of those last rolls! The mast and rigging had a good test. On some of the more extreme pitches, the forestay slackened a bit, and I thought fleetingly of what would happen if it should ever give way and the mast came down, straight back; I would have been crushed. If one of the side shrouds gives way, as had happened on the trip to Manila, the mast falls forward and off to one side. If the forestay gives way, though, it comes smack down on the cockpit.

I entered the channel just after seven o'clock, and coasted to a stop against some mangrove trees along one side of the channel. The water was quiet here, and it looked like a peaceful spot to tie up and spend the night. I went forward to tie up and haul down the sail, and suddenly discovered that we had a problem.

Mosquitoes! They were voracious, and they came in clouds! I cannot recall ever having seen so many in one place at one time. They were eating me alive, settling hungrily on every exposed patch of skin and digging in! I was literally covered with dozens of black spots, biting away, while dozens more came homing in. It was unbelievable!

I ripped down the sail in a frenzy, tying it clumsily, and ran back to the cockpit, slapping madly at my arms and neck and legs. I made it into the cabin and closed the doors and hatch, and sat for a few more minutes slapping away at the last survivors, rubbing my exposed surfaces, and breathing heavily. I had never in my life seen so many mosquitoes!

I sat for a moment in temporary relief, but wondering what I was going to do for the rest of the night. It would be too hot in the cabin to sleep without the windows open. Also, apart from the mosquitoes, the boat was washing back and forth against the dry branches and leaves of the mangroves, and I knew that any thought of sleep was out of the question with all that grinding and rasping going on all night. I finally decided the only solution was to take the boat out of the channel again and anchor in the bay.

The decision made, I gritted my teeth and plunged out onto the deck again to push off the bow, get the outboard started, turn the boat around, and head into the bay. The whole process probably took no more than a few minutes, but it seemed like years. I would have liked to have had lights fastened to various extensions of my anatomy and had it all photographed as a time and motion study, because there was one hell of a lot of motion in a very, very short time.

In Quest of Dragons 49

Once out into the bay a bit, the mosquitoes magically dissipated, and I dropped the hook a few hundred yards off shore, with relief. The boat rocked placidly, headed into the chop and the breeze, and I sat in the cockpit for a few minutes, rubbing my arms reflectively and thinking about the mosquitoes. They had been truly incredible.

It was quite dark by now, so I went below to dig up something to eat and to light the lantern. I had been in the cabin only a few minutes, it seemed, when I glanced out through the window and, with a shock, saw what appeared to be a tree drifting past the window. I blinked once or twice, and suddenly realized that the anchor had slipped and the boat was drifting ashore!

I dashed out on deck, but it was too late; the boat was already washing up against the outermost of the mangroves along the shoreline. Fortunately there no mosquitoes in this particular location; thank God for small favors, and maybe not so small at that. I had drifted into an area that appeared to be shallow mud flats, with occasional mangroves protruding from the water here and there. The actual shoreline appeared to be a few hundred feet away.

I grasped desperately against the mangrove, trying to hold the boat there until I could think what to do, but the inexorable tide and the swells and wind all combined to push the *Linda Niña* around the mangrove and up onto the mud flats. She lodged alongside another mangrove, bumping against some underwater obstruction, and wedged herself between the tree and the obstructions on the bottom.

I walked about the deck attempting to assess the situation, and things looked black indeed. I tried to get a grip on the mangrove to shove the boat backwards and get her floating again, but with no success. Finally, I stripped down to everything but my shirt and a pair of rubber beach shoes and got out to shove.

The water was not too cold, but for some reason I hated to wade around in the mud. Away from the security of the boat, I suppose. It made me a little uncomfortable at first, until I had gotten used to it.

The water was warm and about waist-deep, and I waded about the hulls to assess the situation and to see just how she was lodged. The bottom was a slimy mud into which my feet would sink about four inches. There were a number of underwater hummocks, which appeared to consist of mud held together by old mangrove roots. Some of these hummocks actually stuck out of the water; others were submerged a few feet. I tramped around trying to chart them roughly in my mind, and came up with a rough mental picture as indicated in the sketch. From this it was immediately evident that the only way the boat was going to leave was the same way it had come in, namely, via the channel between mangroves numbered one and two.

There appeared to be only one thing to do, and that was to shove like hell, so I went to the front of the boat and tried to push her out. No luck whatsoever; the wind and the waves were too much. I would barely get her started, and they would heave her back in my face. I stayed there grunting and shoving for fifteen minutes or so until I was completely fagged out, and it was evident that I was getting nowhere.

It is difficult to describe how fatigued I was. I had been driven on by desperation, putting everything I had into it, plagued by thoughts of the *Linda Niña* winding up high and dry at low tide on the mud flats the next morning, and me sitting there like an idiot, hoping that no Viet Cong patrols were in the vicinity. After fifteen minutes of this wrenching activity I was completely bushed, and had a splitting headache to boot.

I don't recall what possessed me at the time to put up the mainsail. I think the wind had shifted and was blowing more or less in the direction I wanted to push the boat, and I thought perhaps the sail would help. At any rate, I got it up. *That* was a job. The wind billowed it out and it tangled in the mangrove, and then got stuck on a spreader. It was dark by now, of course, although I had lighted the latern in the cabin to give me some light to work by, and when I started to haul up the main halyard I hauled on the wrong end and the free end went spiraling up beyond reach! So I had to climb halfway up the mast to get it down again. That was fun, too, what with the boat pitching in the waves and bumping against the mud hummocks and the mangroves, coupled with my fatigue. Thank God for having installed the mast steps, I thought. I climbed slowly, hugging the mast, which was slippery with spray, and trying not to think about slipping and bouncing off the deck some fifteen or twenty feet below. I got the halyard down and the sail halfway

In Quest of Dragons

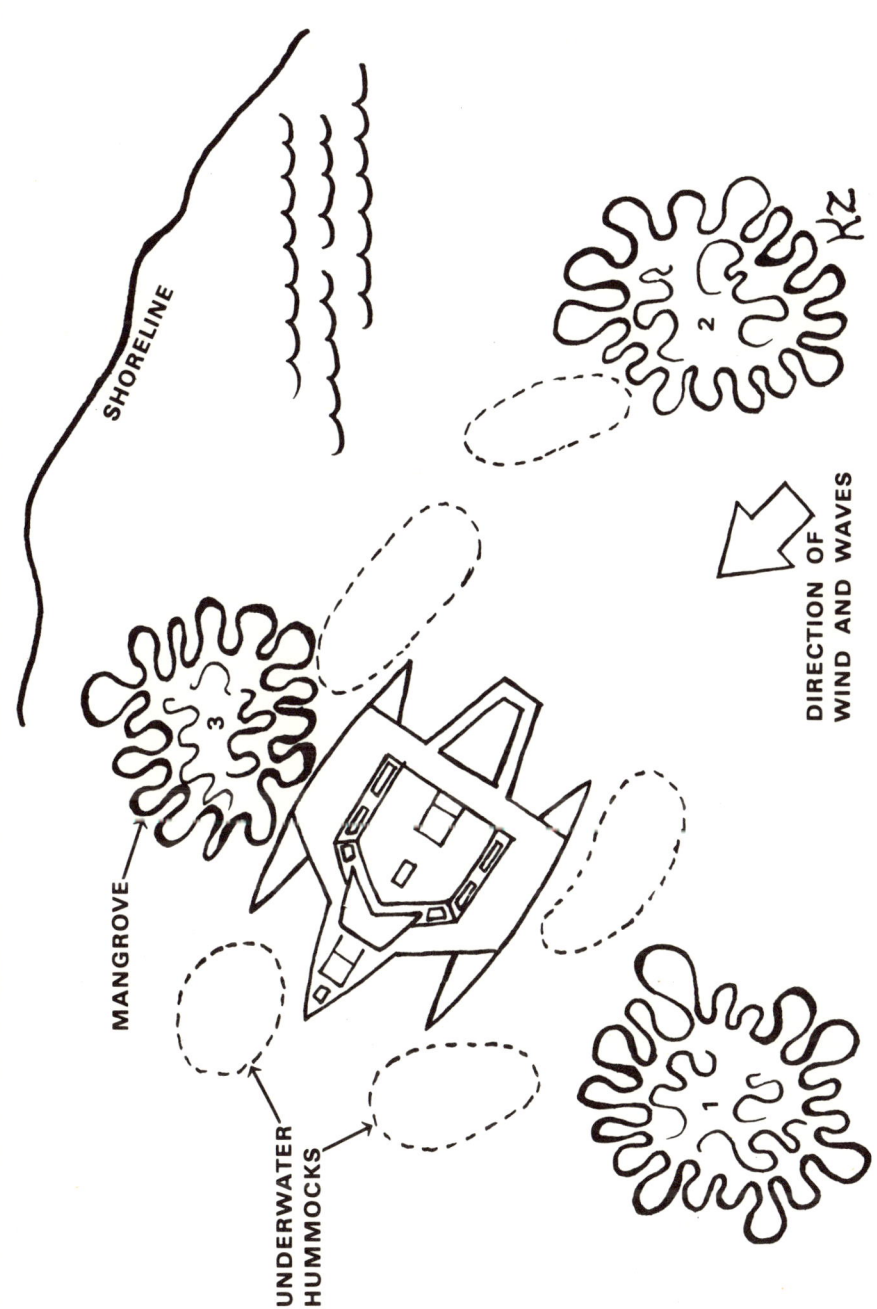

up, and then *it* jammed on one of the spreaders, so I had to go up the mast again. *Choi oi.* I finally got the sail up, but I didn't do much with it and finally lowered it again later that night.

I splashed about a bit more trying to get the boat loose, but without any real enthusiasm, and finally got back aboard, dried off, and lay back on the bunk, completely shot, and with my headache. I was very discouraged, and lay there sighing to myself and wondering what had ever possessed me to get into the boat-building business in the first place. As to getting the *Linda Niña* off the mud flats, it occurred to me that high tide was not until about two in the morning; perhaps I could sleep some and get up later for another shot at it when the water was higher. The flood tide was coming in strong; of course this was one of the reasons, combined with the wind, that I couldn't get her out. Later in the evening the waves washing against the shore should die down, with the impending change in tides, and perhaps the wind would die down too.

This thought encouraged me a bit, and I tried to sleep a little, but it was impossible. The waves kept bumping the *Linda Niña* up and down and grinding her against the mud banks, and I could hear things scratching against the mangrove tree. Sleep was out of the question.

I lay there brooding, and finally had an idea. Considering the orientation of the mangrove trees, it appeared possible that a line hooked up from the boat over to mangrove number two could be used to haul her in the desired direction, so she could be turned to go out the channel. I thought I had enough rope and could tie it about the base of the mast and rig up a kind of Spanish windlass to apply pressure. The more I thought about it the more promising it seemed, so finally I gave a martyred sigh, dragged my weary frame out of the bunk, and started looking for rope.

Fortunately I had one long warp of $\frac{1}{2}$-inch manila, about two hundred feet, which I thought would be adequate. The tree was fifty or sixty feet away. I got out and wrapped the rope around the base of the mast, and stepped into the water to take it over to the tree.

I hated to get back into that water. There was a cool breeze blowing, and I was dog-tired, and the water seemed a lot colder than before. I got out to put on my wet shirt and the rubber shoes, and then went in again. I lost one shoe on the way over to the tree and thereafter didn't bother. My feet would sink several inches into the ooze, which kept sucking the shoes off my feet. I finally got over to the tree and made the double loop of line fast about the trunk. It was an unpleasant experience: As I grabbed the trunk my hand came down on something small and slimy, which dropped off into the water. A leech? A snail of some type? Also, there were numerous old mangrove shoots that came curving up from the base of the mother tree, terminating in sharp splintery stubs just below the surface of the water, and just below waist level. I had visions of stepping on a soft patch and suddenly sinking down, and taking one of these things in the crotch. So I walked very gingerly about the base of the tree, affixing the rope with one hand, and with the other hand firmly protecting my crotch. I must have presented a ludicrous figure.

One item worthy of mention was the phosphorescence, which I had read about but had never seen before. As I walked through the water, little patches kept lighting up in the water beside me, like blue fire. One of them was on my arm when I pulled it up out of the water, and it was an eerie sensation to watch it glowing briefly on my skin before I brushed it away. Some sort of plankton, I presumed.

I returned to the boat with the rope and, rather than tying it around the base of the mast, decided to snub it around the outboard mount on the back of the stern. This enabled me to stay in the water and pull and guide the boat, and at the same time keep snubbing the rope about the motor mount.

It worked out fairly well. On the first heave I moved the boat back a bit, snubbed the line, and on the next wash of the waves she remained in place. A few more tries met with equal success, and I was very encouraged. I got the boat out about ten feet, and was beginning to think I had the world by the tail, when she got stuck, and try as I could, I could make no further progress. I panted and tugged and wrenched until I was bone-weary again, but could pull the boat out no further. Finally I tied down the rope and trudged, gasping, about the floats and main hull to see what was wrong.

I found a taut line dropping down from the front of the hull, and on the other end of it: the anchor! The damned thing had fallen into the water somewhere along the line, and had caught nicely in a mangrove root. I had spent the last half hour tugging against wind and tide and about ⅝ inch of good braided nylon rope. *Mi madre!*

I lugged the anchor aboard, wryly, and got back to the stern, and from then on everything went better. I backed the boat up a sufficient amount, and then rigged another line from the bow over to the same tree to keep her headed into the sea.

By now the wind had begun to slacken a bit and the swells were not quite so high; and the work became progressively easier. I got the miscreant anchor and walked out into the bay up to about neck level, sixty feet or so out, planting it solidly in the bottom and tamping it down with my feet. Then I walked back and cast off the other lines and hauled in on the anchor line until the boat was out in the bay beyond the mangroves. For the first time I could draw a deep breath.

It was nearly eleven o'clock by the time I got out of the mangroves. I had been battling wind and waves steadily since eight o'clock, with the exception of the half-hour I had spent in the bunk, and I was as fatigued through and through as I can ever remember.

I fired up the outboard, and headed out into the bay, picking up the anchor on the way. I took her out a fair distance, half a mile or so, and dropped the anchor in about ten feet of water. This time I sat around for quite a while to make sure it was holding!

Finally it appeared to be fast, and I sat for awhile breathing deeply and thinking over the events of the last four hours. It had been a personal struggle, and I was highly satisfied at having been able to get the boat off the flats. In retrospect, I could not honestly say I regretted having been in the situation, although I certainly would not care to have to go through it again. But I had learned a few things about winds and tides and dragging anchors and lee shores, and perhaps the lesson was worthwhile. It would not easily be forgotten, just as I would never forget the lesson learned with turnbuckles on the first abortive try to Manila. Maybe it's the only real way to learn.

It was nearing midnight, and the sky was incredible; an absolute maze of bright stars. I sat looking at them, gratefully, for awhile. It was the most beautiful part of the heavens to begin with, that fantastic band of constellations and first magnitude stars—Orion, Taurus, Perseus, Auriga, Gemini—but most impressive were the thousands of minor stars that provided a backdrop to the panorama, so many that it seemed almost hazy. I marveled at the difference in the sky between Ganh Rai Bay and Saigon. In Saigon on a clear night I could pick out the constellations and brighter stars with ease, but I had never realized to what extent the haze in the city concealed the thousands of stars. It was absolutely beautiful, and a soothing balm to the soul after the last few hectic hours.

I had something to drink, made a sandwich, and prepared to stretch out on the bunk, dead tired. The evening was not over yet, however. The sail started flogging in the breeze, and after lying there awhile I decided I couldn't let that go on all night, so I got up and took it down.

I lay down again, and at twelve o'clock all hell broke loose at Fort Can Gio, about half a mile off my starboard beam! Suddenly there were flares in the sky and the insistent rattle of machine gun fire. I leaped out of the bunk and ran out into the cockpit. Then the tracers started: red glowing dots arcing up into the sky and petering out at the top of their trajectory. Two guns were firing, and the tracers were arcing all over the place. Some of them headed out in the general direction of the boat, and after eyeballing their trajectories I thought it likely that the unseen pieces would be coming down uncomfortably in my general vicinity. After my initial shaken-up reaction, I decided they were just celebrating Tet, since tonight was the first night of the Chinese New Year. Looking off into other directions I could see flares elsewhere, far away over the delta, and hear distant gunfire.

Well, back to the old outboard. I wearily started it up again, and motored further out into the bay.

In half an hour or so I was a few miles further out, and by one o'clock in the morning the firing had died down to an occasional rattle and the flares had stopped. Things had more or less returned to normal.

After checking the anchor for a goodly time, I finally went below and climbed, for what seemed the umpteenth time, into the bunk. After thrashing about for a long time, I finally dropped off to sleep.

It had been a long day.

5 / The Temple

I woke up at about six thirty and lay in the bunk until seven, savoring the peaceful morning. The bay was placid as a lake, mirror smooth, and the deceptive quiet of Fort Can Gio and the early morning sun shining on the quiet mangroves near the shore, were hard to reconcile with last night's mood of desperate activity.

After a can of fruit juice to start off the morning, I proceeded to clean up the mess from the night before. The decks were covered with the slimy mud that I had dragged aboard on numerous occasions. I suddenly recalled my impression of the previous evening as to what constitutes the most slippery thing in the world; a wet backside sliding over a boat deck painted with white Epikote. I didn't have any arrangement of steps to climb from the water onto the boat; I just had to grab hold of something and kind of swing my rump up and onto the deck, frequently sliding right off again. On one occasion I had just hitched myself aboard when the boat gave a sudden heave and I slid about five feet straight down the deck on my fanny. In spite of my despondent mood, I couldn't help but chuckle to myself at the time.

After two hours of cleaning, the boat looked better than she had when I'd left the Club Nautique the previous day. As I finished, a couple of fishermen with a small boy came by in a sampan to tend their nearby nets, and they stopped by the boat to peer curiously into it. I eyed them warily as they approached, and had the .38 to hand, but they were quite friendly and my suspicions were soon allayed. We exchanged some conversation, although I have found that the lower level the native, the harder it is to communicate.

The Temple

They mumble and use slang Vietnamese, and we had a difficult time understanding each other. They were from Fort Can Gio, where there is apparently a small town, and I told them I was from Saigon and heading for Cap. I brought out some cans of Mott's A&M 5-Way Fruit Juice, had one myself, and opened a can for each of them. They sipped it cautiously, after I explained that it was "*nuoc tat ca qua dua*," or juice made of many fruits.

About nine I was ready to take off for Cap St. Jacques, and went forward to pull in the anchor. It got caught on the way in on the underside of one float, and I realized that the water was shallow indeed. The trouble with trimarans, if you can call it a trouble, is that they are so stable that in calm water it is difficult to tell whether you're grounded or not, unless you go out to the edge of a float and deliberately bounce around to make the boat rock. At any rate, it was not grounded very much, and one of the fishermen helped me push it off towards deeper water. The rudder kept dragging so I took out the brass shear bolt and folded it up. It's a kick-up design, which pivots on a stainless steel bolt; further down, near the bottom of the outer cheeks that encase the rudder, there is another small diameter brass bolt that goes through. The idea is that if the rudder is hit going across a reef or something, the brass pin will shear off and the rudder will kick up, rather than tearing out the lower gudgeons and pintles.

We shoved the boat off into deeper water with no trouble, and I gave the fisherman a hundred piastres, for which he was quite pleased. This was probably the equivalent of a couple of days' fishing. We all waved goodbye, I fired up the outboard, and was off toward Cap St. Jacques.

The day was beautiful, and the water was very calm. The sun was well up over the horizon by now, and there were no clouds in the sky. A gentle breeze was blowing. By the time I got abreast of Fort Can Gio, however, the wind had freshened considerably, and a low swell was starting to come in from the South China Sea.

There was no other traffic of any sort about except for a lone chopper, which came clattering over lazily from the north and settled down into a field near the Fort. After that everything was quiet again. I was well out into Ganh Rai Bay now, north of the Fort, and shortly after nine I stopped for awhile and put up the jib and the mainsail. As usual it was a battle, and what with one thing and another it was nearly ten by the time I was all finished. This was partially complicated by the wind and current which wafted me over among some fishing stakes, and there were a few delicate moments of maneuvering with the outboard to get clear. I thought I had given myself plenty of sea room, but putting up the sail took longer than I had expected, and I drifted nearly into the nets before I was through.

There are quite a few such stakes and nets all around the fringes of Ganh Rai Bay. They are marked to some extent on the charts, and vessels are warned to keep clear of them. These nets are quite elaborate affairs, stretching perhaps two hundred feet, and projecting twenty feet above the surface. They are guyed up by a complicated system of vines and ropes to rocks sunk on either side on the bottom, and nets are slung from them to catch fish that come up and down the channel with the tides. Small houses are perched on a few piles, and presumably people live there to watch and tend the nets, although I never saw any sign of them.

By ten I had the sails up and was headed off on a north-northeast tack. For the rest of the morning and early afternoon it was a matter of tacking up to Cap St. Jacques dead into the face of an east wind and an ever-increasing chop. The sails worked well, and I made from three to five knots, depending on the wind. One problem that I encountered, similar to the day before, was that I kept getting caught in stays when I tried to come about, due to not being able to get up enough speed with the modest wind and the chop to get the boat fully about for the next tack. After awhile I tired of lighting off the motor to achieve this and finally started jibing my way around. This is a little tricky, and I did it very cautiously, going downwind and getting the main really close-hauled before coming about. Even so, it whips across with a startling bang, and I wouldn't dare do it with a strong breeze.

I made a long tack to north northeast and then headed back more or less south southeast. The water was becoming choppier by now, nearing ten thirty; the swells were up to between two and three feet, and the boat was taking some water over the deck. I was wearing a pair of swimming trunks this morning, along with sunglasses, French planter's hat, and little else. The water started com-

The Temple

ing in the front windows, and two lanterns that I had hung in the front were swinging about and knocking against the cabin side, so I tied down the tiller and went inside to mop up the water and move the lanterns. I set the tiller at the place where I had been holding it and went inside with minimum delay, expecting that the boat would gradually come about and head up into the wind. But no—surprisingly, she was apparently balanced on this particular combination, and was self-steering. I was pleased. For the next half-hour the wind held steady; I didn't lay a hand on the tiller, and the boat sailed herself at about five knots going south southeast with never a variation of more than two or three degrees off course.

About ten thirty I tacked back toward north northeast, since I was heading for the fish nets east of Fort Can Gio and I obviously wouldn't make it anywhere near Cap on this tack. I was having a bit of trouble gauging the wind, so I made a couple of telltales from cellophane bags that I had aboard—about 18 inches long and a half-inch wide—and they worked well, being light enough to flutter straight out with the breeze. I kept the main boom trimmed about in line with the telltale, just on the taut side of luffing, and the boat seemed to sail fairly efficiently. I was making about forty-five degrees off the wind, which I didn't think too bad, with the modest breeze and the chop being encountered. The wake was quite straight with little leeway, which was gratifying. I had worried whether the lack of a centerboard would result in problems in that respect. Actually the *Linda Niña* was somewhat deeper in the water than Piver's design, with her heavier construction and her floats being about four inches deeper in the water, both of which helped compensate for the lack of a centerboard.

I tacked back toward south southeast after awhile, but it was evident that I wouldn't make it to Cap on this tack either. The weather was very pleasant for awhile; the sun was hot on my shoulders, and the chop had died down a bit. The boat scudded along at about five knots. I had the radio out and was listening to pleasant music from AFRS, the military radio station in Saigon. I reflected that there are some truly nice moments in boating—when the weather is right, the sun is hot, you're making good time with a clean boat, and the world all seems right—but they seem to be few and far between. If any lesson is to be learned from boating, it's that you have to take the bad—sometimes very bad—with the good, but it is all worthwhile in the long run if you persevere. Perhaps this lesson applies to life, too, except that you seem to have more control over boats.

I was comfortably ensconced on the now-dry cushion in the cockpit, and for awhile lolled back, letting the boat sail itself, watching the fluttering of the telltales from the shrouds and the billow of the bright orange sail, hearing the water flow by, and momentarily feeling at peace with the world. I almost felt guilty, with my lovely boat and my leisure, while other people were toiling, but then I thought about the sacrifices in building it, the fiasco on the trip to Manila, and the problems of the previous night, and concluded that I shouldn't feel too guilty after all; I had worked considerably for the few pleasant moments I now had, and at that, they probably wouldn't last long anyway.

I was right, they didn't, as it turned out. I finally turned back and decided to make one last long tack far over to north northeast to get in a position where I could definitely get back into Cap on the final tack. I jibed about carefully and spent the next hour or so heading toward the north shore. About one o'clock I made the final turnabout and commenced the long tack (about six miles) back toward Cap. By now the weather had freshened considerably and the chop had increased. The boat started to plow and buck her way through the chop, and a lot of spray was coming aboard. On this last tack, when I came about the jib boom got caught under the spray board that I had nailed above the window on the forward cupola. It hung up there for a moment, and before I had a chance to tie the tiller down again and get up forward, the wind blew up strongly, the jib billowed out, and the boom ripped loose with a crash, tearing off the spray board and ripping off the forward hatch cover as well as it whipped across to the other side!

I sat in the cockpit, ruefully watching the few pieces of white board flying out into the spray and disappearing rapidly astern.

The picnic was over for the moment; the wind was really picking up, and the chop had angry whitecaps along the top. I was being inundated by clouds of spray, as the weather float kept burying itself in the chop, which was now coming from the port side on the south southeast tack. The boat bucked and plunged steadily along. By about two I was approaching the land at Pointe Ganh Rai north

The Temple

of Cap, and estimated that at this rate I'd be into the harbor in another hour at the most. We were boiling along pretty well now, despite the chop, and the wind continued to strengthen. It must have been up to twenty knots by now.

Suddenly, the wind strengthened even further, and it must have been blowing somewhere between thirty and forty knots! It was exhilarating! The books on multi-hulls all claim that the trimarans can top twenty knots, and I believed it now. The wind held, and the *Linda Niña* hesitated for a moment, and then...perhaps the most apt description would be that she picked herself up out of the water and started *skittering* across the top of the chop. We were doing at least twenty knots! I held on for dear life! The sail was billowed out taut as a bowstring, the boat was heeled over only slightly, and she was really tearing along! As the hulls lifted out of the water and she began surfing, the balance changed considerably, and she developed a strong weather helm, presumably due to the loss of the stabilizing underwater profile of the hulls. As a result, I had to really pull on the tiller to keep her on course. For a few glorious moments we skittered across the bay, definitely over twenty knots, gaining speed, practically flying, it felt, and then *crash!*—the rudder gave way with a fractured rasp of splintered wood, and the boat suddenly came about into the wind and stopped dead, with a rock and slosh of waves!

Chol oi! I sat there holding a dead tiller in my hand, a little glassy-eyed, wondering what had happened. Apparently the strain on the rudder, which must have been considerable, was just too much. I cursed the Sovicotra boatyard, who had made this replacement rudder after mine had been stolen. Mine had been solid $3/4$-inch plywood; when I looked at the shattered remnants of theirs I saw that they had sandwiched two $3/8$-inch pieces together with a few copper rivets; no wonder it hadn't held!

I wrestled the sail down, lashed it about the boom, and turned on the outboard again to head for Cap. The next few hours were miserable, and I didn't make more than two knots. In the high chop, the outboard kept lifting out of the water with every bounce of the transom, and overspeeding. I thought: What am I doing to the poor motor? I didn't know too much about outboards, but it seemed as though that type of service must be rather tough on their innards. Anyway, I beat my way painfully up the coast toward Cap. It took about two hours, and by the time I made the harbor I was tired and covered with salt.

I putted peacefully into the quiet harbor at about four, happy to be out of the open part of the bay and the chop. There were a number of boats anchored in the cove, and I approached slowly, gauging the layout to see where I could anchor. One fairly large cabin cruiser sat in the middle of the bay, and it looked vaguely familiar. Of course! it had been alongside the Club Nautique pier the day before, when I was preparing to leave. There were a few Frenchmen sitting about in the aft cockpit, and they waved as I came in.

"*Bonjour!*" I cried over the outboard's splutter, "*Ou peut-on mouiller l'ancre?*" They waved and indicated an open spot a few hundred yards from the beach, not too far from their boat. I drifted in, shut off the outboard, and dropped anchor. After checking it for a reasonable interval, I went below to wash up, keeping a weather eye out.

Well, the damned anchor slipped again, and I suddenly realized that I was drifting toward the Frenchmen's boat! I ran out on the deck to start the outboard, mashing one toe on one of the wing nuts on the starboard float hatch cover in the process, and nearly ripping off a toenail. This did not help my temper any. I fired up the motor, got the boat back to the desired position, and dropped the anchor again. This time I sat in the bow to watch it for a good ten minutes, grimly, toe throbbing, but it appeared to be caught well this time. Watched kettles never boil; watched anchors never drag, I guess.

One of the Frenchmen came across in his dinghy with the boat-boy and was most helpful. He offered me the use of the dingy to get back and forth between my boat and the shore. I explained the problem with the rudder, and that I needed more gas. They paddled off, returning soon with an old man, who apparently watches the boats in the cove and is of general assistance to boatsmen in the vicinity. I explained in Vietnamese that tomorrow I wanted to go into town to get gasoline and that I wanted to have a spare rudder made, and this had to be ready by tomorrow morning too. This last was a bit more trouble, since everyone was on holiday for Tet, but eventually three hundred piastres solved the problem, and he agreed to have the rudder by tomorrow. We took out the bolts and I gave him the remaining piece sandwiched between the kick-up cheeks to use as a pattern for the rest of the rudder.

The old man left, the Frenchman returned to his cruiser, and I went below to wash up, using a bottle of fresh water and a pair of underpants as a washcloth. I put on some dry clothes and felt like a new man. I hailed the Frenchman's boat, and his boat-boy came over to give me a lift to shore. At the one allegedly halfway decent restaurant in Cap St. Jacques I had a steak, then sat and had a beer, pondering the happenings of the last few days. The room seemed to rock gently; I guess it was the two days on the boat. It was an odd sensation.

When I got up to leave, I found that a sort of delayed *rigor mortis* had set in. My God, but my bones had stiffened! I supposed it was the reaction from the activities of the previous evening. At any rate, I limped out of the restaurant and returned painfully to the beach, where I got one of the local fishermen to run me out to the *Linda Niña* in his sampan, for forty piastres.

It was shortly after seven, and I was indeed ready for the old sack. I decided to go whole hog tonight and use a *sheet*, by George, so I made up the bunk carefully, opened a few windows to let the breeze in, turned on the radio, and lay in the bunk for awhile listening to the music before going to sleep.

The stars came out, and the other boats were lit up to varying degrees. The large vessels way out in Coconut Bay anchorage were lit up like a lot of floating cities. It certainly felt like a more secure anchorage than that of the previous evening!

From Cap St. Jacques could be heard an occasional cry and the popping of scattered firecrackers. The soft lap of ripples from the incoming tide washed against the hulls. I turned off AFRS, and relaxed gratefully into my pillow.

In the morning I woke up about seven, and after mulling it over for awhile I got up and went out into the cockpit to brush my teeth. I sat for awhile to watch the sun come up over Cap St. Jacques. It had been a good night's sleep, but my muscles were still sore and stiff.

I cleaned up the boat a bit and started making breakfast. It was the first time I had tried out the kerosene stove, but it worked well.

I put the stove out in the cockpit and cooked from inside. I heated up a kettle of water for tea and then cooked a couple of eggs. The tea was pretty weak for the longest time, and then it occurred to me that you have to take the tea bags out of the little paper envelopes they come in, which just goes to show you what kind of a cook I am. I finally sipped my tea and ate the eggs with a bit of roll, and it all tasted good.

Meanwhile, the old man had come by to help me with the gas, and he sat crouched on the transom, watching me eat. He asked if I had a cigarette but I told him I didn't smoke and offered him a warm beer instead. He accepted with alacrity, and sat sipping it with gusto. These early morning drinkers. I gave him another can to have in his boat, to cement relations.

We went into town and picked up two full tanks of gasoline at an Esso station, and then drove over to the carpenter's house to pick up the rudder. It was an unpleasant surprise, since he'd made it about a foot too short. Apparently there had been a foul-up in communications somewhere along the line. Well, it would be enough to steer by, perhaps, so I accepted it and we went back and put it on the boat. There was only about a foot projecting below the bottom of the transom, but I thought it might be enough for steering downwind. We loaded the gas tanks aboard, and I paid off the old man, took a last look at Cap, and fired up the outboard. I headed out on a 290-degree course toward the mouth of the Song Go Gia, about ten miles across the bay to the northwest.

My plan was to go up the Song Go Gia past the number 5 choice of possible temple locations, and then on up and via the Tac O Cu channel over to the Song Dong Tranh river. If that wasn't it, I'd go up past the Tac Nuoc Hoi, around and down to the first location I'd checked, and out through that channel back to the main river south of Coral Bank. I felt it increasingly likely that the fishermen had originally gone up the Song Go Gia and across via the Tac O Cu or the parallel Tac Nuoc Hoi, and was sure that by following the above route I would cover all the possibilities.

Shortly after nine I was wending my way across Coconut Bay and through the numerous ships that were moored out there, including an Esso tanker. There was a long gentle swell coming from the sea with the incoming tide. I was well out into the bay, when the out-

The Temple 65

board quit on me again. This time it wasn't gas, and I was in a sweat!

I got it started once or twice but had to keep squeezing the rubber bulb on the suction line to keep it going; apparently the trouble was with either carburetion or the basic gas supply. Finally even the additional pressure generated by squeezing was insufficient, and the motor coughed out for good. I took off the cover and peered at it but there was nothing obviously wrong, such as the carburetor having fallen off, and little that I could do. I dreaded the thought of trying to take the carburetor apart for cleaning out in the middle of Ganh Rai Bay. I removed the filter from the gas tank and it seemed clean enough; in desperation I even took the filter off and tried to start the motor, but it gave up after a few asthmatic coughs. I dabbled and tinkered around with it for awhile and adjusted the high and idle speed needle valves and tried again, and by George, it started. It was still a bit rough, but I found that a few more adjustments on the high speed needle valve helped a lot, and finally we were under way again. Evidently the high speed jet had been clogged with something that I dislodged when I tinkered with it.

It took a few hours to reach the north shore of Ganh Rai Bay. The sun was getting high and the bay was calm, and for awhile I had another of those short periods when the weather is nice and the boat is purring along and for a change everything seems to be working. By eleven the wind had freshened and there was a bit of a chop, and I had to cut the outboard back to three-quarters throttle. I reached the north coast and turned to run northwest along it to the entrance to Song Go Gia. The lee along the coast cut down the chop and I was able to put the outboard full on again, and by quarter to twelve I was rounding the corner and turning up into the river.

The location I had marked as number 5 was only a short distance up the river, and by twelve I was approaching it and could see what looked like something projecting above the trees. My heart beat with excitement—could this be *it*? The trees were higher in this area than the scrubby brush I'd seen coming down the other rivers, and it looked about the size and type that I'd remembered from the picture of the temple. Slowly I made my way up the river. The object barely visible above the trees kept appearing and disappearing as I changed course and/or as the trees came up to block the view. It was all very elusive and exquisite mental torture. I grew increasingly hopeful that this was indeed the temple, although I had never thought it was this far south.

By all precedents, this was just the time the outboard motor should kick out, but it kept purring impassively along.

By a bit after twelve I was less than a quarter of a mile away. The trees finally cleared, and I could see it. *It was the temple after all!* My heart jumped, and I thought *I've found it!* Probably full of Viet Cong monks running around fixing lunch, I thought wryly. Nevertheless, it would be a considerable satisfaction to have found the temple again, even if I had to return dragon-less to Saigon. The 64,000 piastre question now was, whether the temple was abandoned or not.

I rounded the corner into the small channel. The temple was in clear view off to my starboard. I passed the remains of the brick pier, or whatever it had been, at the junction of the two channels, and then motored quietly up the smaller channel, and the temple came into full sight. It was indeed abandoned. The roof was in a bad state of repair, and weeds had grown up to choke the whole area. There was no sign of life.

From the roof the sun caught the green reflections from the glaze on the *dragons*! They were still there, as I had remembered them, crouched and glaring.

I nosed the boat over gently to the bank downstream of the temple, where there was some solid-looking ground and some stakes to tie the painter to. I cut the outboard, jumped ashore, and tied up, then stood for a breathless moment looking at the temple. The boat floated gently in the flood current. The sun was high and hot in the sky, and everything was quiet. There were no birds; only the slight rustle of wind through the trees.

There was a small stream running along the tidal flat between where I stood and the temple, crossed by some old piles at one point where there had obviously once been a bridge. It must have been pretty then, I reflected. I tried to cross the stream at a shallower point, but it was very oozy and I started to sink in ominously, so I more prudently went upstream to where the old piles were, but where it was deeper, and crossed there. It was about up to my

The Temple

I moor the Linda Niña along the mud flats.

waist; I stumbled and splashed my way over to the other side, clutching at piles with one hand and holding my camera and the .38 over my head with the other.

At length, dripping wet, I stood before the temple. All was quiet. Apparently it was or had been unfriendly territory; on one wall of the temple was painted crudely in black paint "*My-Diem*," or American-Diem, what the Viet Cong called Ngo Dien Diem for what they called collaborating with the West.

Weeds were all over, and dry brush that had grown up over the years. Branches kept straightening out behind me as I walked, and I couldn't resist the urge to turn around once or twice and make sure nobody was behind. I was pretty jumpy.

The building to my right contained an empty space about fifteen by twenty feet, with nothing in it. I suppose it was originally some sort of semi-open patio. It was completely open now, because the roof had fallen in a long time ago. There were red tiles all over the ground below.

The central structure was thirty feet long by fifteen wide and consisted of an open patio in front, with an approachway leading up to the altar, which was about six feet long by four deep, and was sheltered under a roof. Within the altar there were a number of plaster figures, once apparently painted but now shabby and weathered. They appeared to be a group of Vietnamese Buddhas in contemplation. Before the altar were a number of blue glazed dishes, with the remnants of long-ago offerings and long-extinguished joss sticks.

There was a strong dragon motif about the whole place. Two large plaster dragons coiled their way down the two pillars at either side of the altar, and two similar dragons were coiled on two other pillars in front. From where I stood in front of the altar I could

There was apparently once an old bridge. . .

The Temple

Temple cupola with dragons (my specimen is at upper left).

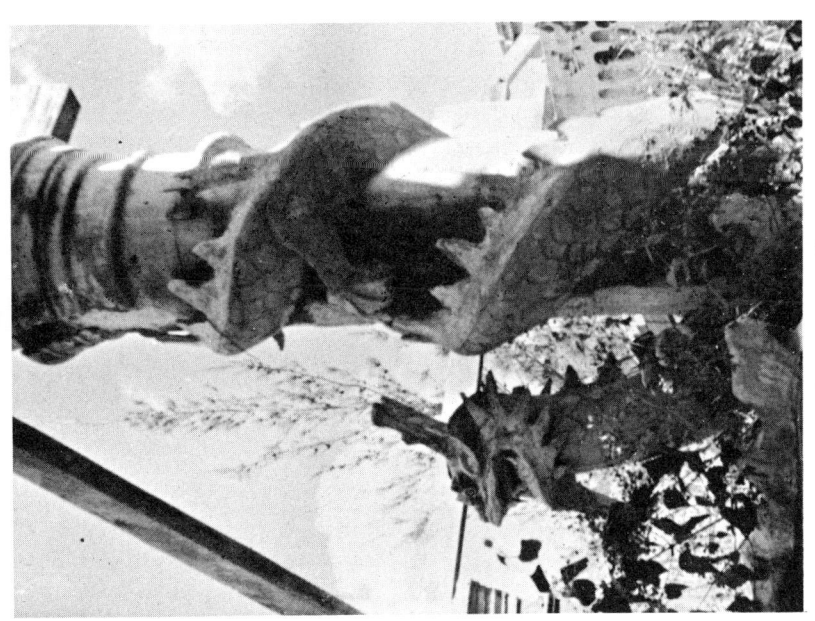

Dragon motif.

look up at the cupola to my left and see the ceramic dragons on the roof, undulating and glaring. On the walls to either side of the altar there were Chinese designs in a sort of frieze, which had weathered with the years but still appeared fairly legible. They were beyond the scope of my meager fund of characters, so I took a few pictures with a view toward deciphering it all when I got back. The front of the altar was overgrown with weeds, and there were quite a few big red ants about. I must have stepped in a patch, since a few minutes later I felt the first bite and it was quite awhile before I got rid of them all. They are very well organized; the first one bites, then the others wait and get you at one-minute intervals.

I finally worked my way over to the building at the left, where the dragons were. It was about two stories high, with a sort of veranda running about the second-floor level and a smaller altar up above topped with a cupola where the dragons were mounted. Up and down the entrance pillars to this particular section were a number of beautiful ceramic tiles with exotic designs, about six inches square. They were exquisite, and I wished that I had the time to pry a few of them off.

It was time to go after the dragons—the culmination of the hunt. I cast about for an easy way up to the first level of the temple, but finally had to settle for jumping up and catching myself by the fingers on a small cement cornice and hauling myself laboriously up and over the veranda. I remembered having been told about the mountain-climbing schools in Switzerland, and how the guides could pull themselves up by the very tips of their fingers. I had a lot more than that, up to the first knuckle at least, but it still was a job. I finally got up, huffing and puffing, to the veranda, and found that it was floored with rotten boards. The veranda was about five feet wide and appeared to run all around the second story. I stepped cautiously over to the altar in the center, which was floored with cement, crossing the rotten planks in a location where I could see a crossbeam under the chinks between the planks.

The dragons were just out of reach about six feet above me, mounted on the roof joints on all four sides. Apparently the two dragons in the front were males, since they had exotic and complicated heads, with horns and striped barbels, and gaudy colors; the two at the back appeared to be more sedately ornamented females.

The Temple

One of each appeared to be in good condition; the other two were beat-up by time and weather, and had several pieces broken off. Over on the roof of the main temple there were two more larger dragons, but also very deteriorated and headless. Between them was a ceramic decorative device of some sort, holding up a large crystal ball.

I stood for a few moments gazing at the dragons above me and recalling some of the things I had read about these serpents. According to descriptions, the Vietnamese dragon usually appears with "...the head of a camel, the horns of a buck, the eyes of a demon, the ears of a buffalo, the neck and body of a snake, the scales of a carp, the claws of an eagle, and the paws of a tiger. Hanging from both sides of its mouth is a long barbel, and under the dragon's tongue there is hidden a precious stone. The top of its head shows a decorative protuberance, which is the mark of intelligence, and along the backbone a crest of eighty-one extra large scales runs from the neck to the end of the tail."*

The specimen on the roof above me seemed to generally fit the description. He was about three and a half feet long, and about a foot and a half high. The sun reflected off the bright green glaze of the serpentine body that culminated in a rooster-like tail of brown glaze. Brown spines marched along the arching back. The snake-like body was about five inches thick and attached to the temple by two feet, which were grouted into the roof.

Close up, I could see that the body was put together in four pieces: the head; the first undulation of the body; the arching back; and the final undulation with the rooster tail. The back was connected into the two body pieces with something like a bell-and-spigot pipe connection, with the bell being on the body pieces. The back was connected into the bells on the body, and the joints stuffed with cement. The head was mounted on a sort of male joint projecting up out of the front of the body, which joint was also sealed with cement.

It was apparent that I was going to need a rope to get up to the roof, and I was also going to need something to get the dragons down. The pieces would have to be lowered gently from the roof to

---

*The Smaller Dragon, Joseph Buttinger (Frederick A. Praeger).

the ground, since they were extremely fragile, which fact I verified by knocking a few pieces off a part of another dragon that had fallen to the veranda at some time in the past. Apparently the dragons had been cast in some sort of local clay and fired in a kiln, and perhaps glazed and refired. The material was porous, however, and easily breakable.

I went back to the *Linda Niña* and by now the tide was coming up appreciably. I moved her into the small stream a bit upstream of the piles where the bridge had been, calculating that as the tide came up, the current would carry the boat over and rest her against the piles, all ready to go when I wanted to leave. For a change, it worked out that way. I took a coil of rope and a ball of twine, and returned to the temple, once more huffing and puffing my way up to the first-story veranda. I would have hated to have to do it again.

Well, old Tom Mix made up a lasso, and heaved it up toward the top of the cupola with the idea of settling it over the pinnacle and using it to climb up. Unfortunately my foot slipped as I heaved, and my leg went crashing down through the rotten planking of the veranda that I had clean forgotten about! Meanwhile, the rope had settled about the top of a ceramic figure perched atop the cupola and had pulled tight. I wasn't about to start putting my weight on a piece of porous ceramic, not with an eight-foot drop from the edge of the cupola roof to the veranda, with those rotten planks, and another ten feet or so to the ground beneath. After giving it a bit of thought, and unsuccessfully trying to shake the rope loose, I finally got the lower end of it wrapped around some beams on the underside of the eaves, and made a loop that I could step into. This would get me high enough to grab the lowermost support to which the dragon was grouted, and haul myself up on the roof.

At last I was there, at one o'clock or so of the afternoon, perched, panting, atop the cupola of a temple roof in the south delta of Vietnam. I took time to look about a bit.

The sun was high, and I could see for miles around the flat country of the delta—out over the main river, and well back along the small channel. It was not too comforting to consider that I might be *seen*, as well as see, for an equal distance, and I hoped the local population, wherever they might be, were not in the habit of facing the temple for prayers or something every hour.

The Temple

The problem of getting the dragons ungrouted was solved readily. As I shifted my weight, there was a slight *crunch*, and the back footing shifted loose from the roof. I had been sort of perched up and behind the dragon, balanced on the forty-five-degree tilt of the roof, with my feet resting against the back "foot" of the dragon. I shifted weight hastily, and got down to the business at hand.

I reached over for the head first, prying it loose from the body with little trouble. What a beautiful head! Such sculptured detail, and such bright colors! It was a real prize; I was elated. I wrapped some twine about the head and then, leaning over near the edge of the roof, I lowered it slowly until I could feel it gently come to rest against the wood flooring. Then I cut the string, and got another piece ready for the next joint of dragon. It was quite a good technique, but I nearly had heart failure when, shifting about, I dislodged several roof titles, which went clattering down below approximately where I had lowered the parts of the dragon! Fortunately they missed.

The back came loose easily from the parts of the body, and it followed the head. This part of the dragon was fairly heavy, and I wrapped a double layer of string to be on the safe side. It must have weighed nearly fifteen pounds, what with the big hunk of cement attached to the foot, which I never did get around to removing until I was back in Saigon. That left the front, which was still firmly grouted in. I tapped about the base cautiously with the hammer and presto! it had cracked loose, and I could dislodge it with no further trouble.

I had one dragon down, and one to go. I carefully worked my way around the roof to the other side, toward the back, where there was a (female?) dragon in good condition. I tried to get the rope dislodged from the ceramic at the top of the cupola, now that I was there, but I had forgotten to leave any slack when I tied it under the eaves, and now I couldn't pull enough of it up to be of any practical use.

I got down to the second dragon and removed the head, but suddenly discovered I was out of string! That about tore it. I had been up on that cupola for long enough, and didn't at all relish the thought of having to climb all the way down, return to the boat for more string, and then fight my way up to the top of the temple again. To clinch matters, while I was shifting about, a piece of the second dragon's tail broke off, so I thought to hell with it; I had had enough for today! I used my remaining small piece of string to tie the dragon head to my back, out of harm's way, while I once again circumnavigated the roof back to my rope. It was a difficult job, swinging down over that roof again backwards, trying to keep the dragon head from rolling off my back and swinging about and getting broken, while fishing about for the loop in the rope with my free foot, but I was finally down. I gathered all the pieces of the dragon together, and using the same pieces of string still attached, lowered them the final step down from the veranda to the ground. I threw the rope down after and climbed down myself, and took a deep breath. I was nearly done.

I carried the dragon and the camera in several armfuls to the shore by the piles, where by now the current had lifted and sure enough the *Linda Niña* was riding easily against the piles. I pulled her further in toward the shore, and started ferrying the pieces out and laying them on the deck.

About this time I heard the sound of a motor coming down the small channel! *Choi oi*! I looked up the channel, and coming slowly down around the bend a half-mile away was what looked like a medium-sized sampan. I dashed and splashed back to the shore and got another armload of dragon, ferried it back to the boat, and returned for the last armload of dragon, camera, and .38. I got them all aboard, freed up the rope, and pushed the *Linda Niña's* nose around to head out into the channel. I had been moving really fast for those last few minutes, and my throat was dry and I was exhausted. I had no idea what the sampan contained, but all I could think about were Viet Cong, and I wasn't about to start taking chances at this juncture.

I leaped aboard the boat, losing my French planter's hat in the act (which blew over and was last seen floating tranquilly in the inlet), started the outboard, and headed out into the channel, just as the sampan came abreast. It was being steered by a medium-sized Vietnamese, and there appeared to be a few other people under the deck shelter.

I'll never know whether he was Viet Cong, or a member of the local chapter of the Society for Prevention of Cruelty to Dragons, or what, but he looked pretty mean, and he deliberately steered the sampan to draw it up alongside the *Linda Niña*. As he approached, I shouted "*Chao ong!*" with a smile, but he remained impassive in the face of my greeting and continued to approach. He edged his boat over against my starboard float, and had his foot balanced on the tiller in such a manner that it appeared obvious that he was going to step aboard.

We locked glances for one long instant. I grinned at him like Burt Lancaster and shifted my right hand significantly to where the .38 was sticking out of my breast pocket, and put my hand over the butt. I guess I looked pretty mean too. I was half covered with mud, brown from the last few days on top of my normal tan, and had a four-day growth of beard to boot. The two boats proceeded side by side about five of the longest seconds of my life, while he stared at me and I grinned at him, throat dry. I supposed that I would have to shoot him if he had stepped aboard; in the circumstances there would have been little choice. I could feel my heart beating as I waited.

Apparently he decided the odds weren't very good, which they weren't, and finally his boat lost way and dropped behind as the *Linda Niña* proceeded out into the Song Go Gia River. He stood looking at me from across the widening distance, and then went down into the cabin of the sampan. For all I knew he was going to get a rifle so I too went below into the cabin to put a few more layers of plywood between me and anything unfriendly that might be coming my way, and took out the .38. However, he stayed under cover for awhile, and then came out and started down the river, on a somewhat different course from mine.

It looked as though I was getting out of the woods. There were still a few problems, as it turned out, but the end was coming into sight. I spent the next hour or so working my way around to the inlet of a small channel that the map showed to cut over and join with the Song Nga Bay a few miles downstream of Quatre Bras. I kept the sampan in sight for a long time, since he seemed to be taking a similar route, but on the other side of the river, and had he crossed to enter the small channel I wasn't about to follow him in. I would have had to take a longer way around to get to Song Nga Bay. Happily, he continued south until he was lost to sight; so much for my friend.

I came to the entrance of the small channel about two thirty, and started in. I reached what I thought was the junction on the chart and turned left, but after about twenty minutes found the boat was coming to a choked-up dead end in the channel! I still had headway on, and drifted to a stop among some more damned mangrove trees. There was a small current running, and it was pushing the boat on into the tree-clogged channel! I had to get out into the water, and wrestle the boat about, half-swimming, half-clutching at mangrove branches, until I could get the front and turned around to go back out the channel. I remember feeling vaguely like that character in the *African Queen*, trudging about in the reeds and trying to get that boat through to Lake Victoria. At least there weren't any leeches.

I finally succeeded, and it took about twenty minutes to return to where I had made the wrong turn, and another twenty minutes to get up to the big fork that opened into the main river. The channel kept curving about and narrowing down and I worried whether it would choke up too, forcing me to go all the way back to where I'd come in and then take the long way around. Fortunately this didn't happen, and I emerged onto the main river about three thirty.

I set the tiller to steer up toward Quatre Bras, and then sat back to take stock. Things looked pretty good; I was on the commercial channel again, and I had my *dragon*! I took the pieces in from the deck and arranged them carefully on the bunk. It was not a trophy I cared to air all the way up to Nhabe. I cleaned up the boat a bit, and then sat back in the cockpit to relax and mull over the happenings of the last few days.

But I wasn't out of the woods yet. As I rounded the bend at Quatre Bras, the outboard kicked off again. This time it sounded quite definite. I tried to start it again, but it made rasping noises as I cranked it, and I was afraid it had developed some major internal ailment.

About this time two Vietnamese LCT's came up the river, and I hailed them down and asked for a tow to Saigon. However, they were going just a little way up the river, so they regretfully refused, waved, and took off.

I tried to start the outboard again. This time it caught and it seemed that the rasping noises were not so bad. At any rate it managed to keep limping along and didn't sound too bad at half-throttle, so I gratefully left it at that.

Thank heavens it was flood tide or I never would have made it. As it was, the boat crept along at only a few knots—painfully slow; I could have walked as fast. Up past Pointe du Kervella; around Pointe de l'Est; by now it was well past six, and the sun was getting low on the horizon. It was apparent that I was going to have to run upriver, along the insecure portion of the Long Tao, at night! *Choi oi*!

By about seven I was passing the Coral Bank lights, and I passed the channel I had taken in pursuit of the dragons two days before. It grew pitch dark. The outboard kept running, and I continued upriver with fingers crossed.

By nine I had reached Pointe Phami, across the way from Pointe du Lazaret, and the end was finally in view. There is a small fort across the river on the east side, and they gave me a bit of a start as I went by, firing a couple of flares into the air above the boat to see what sort of animal I was. I felt bare and defenseless, sitting in the cockpit with the white flares bathing me in their naked glare. There was not a soul to be seen on the river bank and no sound—only the white glare of those flares, floating silently down. It was a bit eerie.

By nine I was getting out into the harbor area where all the Victory ships were anchored, and I could finally say to myself, more or less, that I had made it back! The lights of the ships were comforting and friendly as I moved slowly up the harbor between them; I was nearly back in civilization. All of the strains of the last few days started to melt away. I went into the cabin and brought out the lantern, lighted it, and brought the radio out to listen to. Miraculously, the outboard continued to purr on.

It took another hour to reach Nhabe, and I turned in the Rach Roi and brought the *Linda Niña* to rest alongside one of the barge piers next to the Nhabe launch. I cut the motor and tied her up. The silence was lovely after listening to that splutter for the last eight hours. I cleaned up a bit, made the bunk, then sat outside in the cockpit and cooked up a can of spaghetti *with* meatballs (a bit of high living was in order), which I had with a can of Coca-Cola and a roll. I sat chewing reflectively, looking at the sky, listening to the water against the hull, and thinking over the last few days. *Choi oi*, what a weekend. I was awfully glad to be back.

The next day I cleaned up the boat in the morning, and toward noon, when it was again flood tide, I began the run upriver to the

Nautique and home. It took a few hours, and I arrived about three in the afternoon, just as the French cruiser was returning from Cap St. Jacques. I coasted into my mooring at the Nautique as they waved, and tied up the *Linda Niña* to her mooring stake, fore and aft, and—*Voilà!*—I was back.

A few friends were on hand to greet me, including an army buddy who had loaned me a Thompson submachine gun and two clips. After considering the pros and cons I had finally decided not to bring it along. It was just as well; I had not needed it, and it would have gotten wet.

We all admired the dragon, and got him safely unloaded and stashed away in the car. It was good to get back to my living room and relax in a soft chair with a gin and tonic. It had been a long weekend.

I got the dragon cleaned up on subsequent days, removed the cement, and mounted him atop my chiffonier, where he looked most attractive. He sits there now, dark green highlights shining off his scales, glaring down at me as I write.

6 / The Linda Niña II

Although the *Linda Niña* had seemed large enough when I had built her, as time went on I increasingly felt the need for a larger boat. The twenty-four-foot length and crouching headroom of the *Linda Niña* was obviously unsuitable for long-range cruising of any sort. As spring of 1966 approached, I started thinking about what I would do on long vacation (due again in 1967), and what sort of boat I would need to carry out these plans.

By now I was sold on trimarans, and after further correspondence with Art Piver, I decided on the *Herald* model as my next project. The Herald was thirty-two feet, six inches LOA, with a beam of nineteen feet, and with full standing headroom. Possibly the thirty-foot *Nimble* would have sufficed, but there were several features of the *Herald* that I preferred. First, she had a ketch rig, as opposed to the sloop rig of the *Nimble*. Within the limitations of my sailing experience (admittedly, practically nil!) I preferred a ketch rig, for I felt that it would afford more flexibility for the single-handed sailor, particularly in rough weather, when you can simply furl the mainsail and maintain balanced headway with the jib and mizzen. Another thing I liked about the *Herald* was the reverse sheer, both longitudinally and athwartships, which gave her a rakish look. In April I wrote away for the plans; they soon arrived, and I spent an absorbed week or so studying them, and making up plywood and lumber lists.

Again I thanked the Fates for giving me a garage of such monstrous proportions. After laying the strongback for the *Linda Niña II*, the end of the strongback just protruded out the back doors of the garage. Once the hull was complete, the transom was about a foot from the front doors, and the tip of the bow protruded about two feet, like a surrealistic wooden sculpture of a large nose, out the back.

The lumber problem was solved similarly to the previous boat. For framing I used local *"bang lang"* lumber from Vietnam; the marine plywood I ordered from Singapore. They make it there from a mahogany-type wood called Meranti, and it seemed of good quality, although rather heavy. The local Vietnamese lumber was heavy and very strong, and sanded well; but it used to drive me out of my mind trying to plane it, for the grain changes direction every foot or so.

Construction was held up by several unexpected business trips, including one to New York, and by local vacation, which was two weeks in May. The work had really been a grind during the early part of 1966, due to the rapid growth in military fuel requirements and the associated headaches. Hence, when my vacation came in May, it was a relief to get out of Vietnam. I went to Japan, revisiting old haunts, and spent a leisurely two weeks traveling down to Kyushu and back. In Yokohama I stopped at Nakamura ship chandlers and ordered some things for the boat, including fittings, marine head, rope, fenders, and a large variety of all the miscellaneous junk that you suddenly decide you must have when faced with it on the shelves.

By the end of May the strongback was complete, the framing lumber was on hand, and I was ready to start. I had ordered the plywood, which didn't arrive until July; however, this was no bottleneck, since it took me that long to get all the framing for the main hull done.

Construction progressed similarly as for the *Linda Niña I*, except that everything seemed much bigger. Once all the frames were in place on the strongback, and the temporary battens laid on to hold them in place, the main hull seemed enormous in comparison with the earlier boat. As before, I spent a lot of time putting internal framing in prior to planking the hull. As a matter of fact, I put nearly all of the framing for the settees, chart table, and galley in place while the hull was still upside down. This enabled me to install all the shelves, settee top, galley top, and miscellaneous other surfaces that I wanted to match perfectly with the hull prior to planking.

The Linda Niña II

Frames being mounted on strongback—front view.

Mounting the frames for the Linda Niña II on the strongback.

Frames and transom installed in place, held together with temporary battens, preparatory to notching for chines and stringers.

Rolled out into the driveway and ready for turning over. Note two supports which have been temporarily bolted in at crossarm locations to take the strain off the sheer stringer when hull is turned over. Six temporary tension members along sides prevent the cradle from slipping off during the turning-over operation.

The Linda Niña II

I spent about two months on this, and just as I was starting to slow down for lack of work, the plywood arrived, in three large crates. I had about 110 sheets of 3/8-inch ply, plus a number of sheets of 1/4-inch, 1/2-inch, and 3/4-inch for other purposes. It all came to quite a pile of plywood, a few tons of it. We put it in a back storeroom, where it made a pile nearly four feet high!

Planking of the main hull proceeded rapidly, and by October, I was ready to begin fiberglassing. This took another few weeks, and

A fork lift truck makes short work of the turning over. Note the manner in which the hull is resting on the supports at the crossarm locations; sheer stringer does not touch the ground.

then I was ready to paint. Finally the big day came when we turned the hull over.

I had spent a week or so just in constructing an elaborate cradle for the hull. The cradle had to be strong, for it would eventually sustain the entire weight of the boat, and would have to hold up under the joggling of the trip to the water and the launching. In November, assisted by some friends from Esso and a forklift truck, we trundled the main hull into the driveway and turned it over. It

Up, and over...

was a sweaty job, but otherwise went smoothly. We got the cradle onto sections of two-inch pipe, and rolled the whole thing, this time right-side up, back into the garage.

It looked great. I sat drinking a cold beer with the boys and eye-

...and ready to roll back into the garage for a few more months of work.

The Linda Niña II

...while the other was taking shape in the back patio.

One float was built in the garage...

ing it with satisfaction. The first step was complete; the worst was over. There was still a lot of work to do, of course, but the main hull was done.

For the next few months I worked on the internals of the main hull, finishing up everything inside, and constructing the roof, or at least that portion of it which covered the main hull. Later, when attaching the floats, I would make the extensions on either side of the roof. But for the time being, I could at least get this part of it done while the main hull was in the garage, and it would serve to keep the rain out when we moved it into the yard.

In February we moved her into the yard, and I installed the crossarms. The crossarms on trimarans are box spars, maybe eighteen inches across by a foot thick, made from 3/8-inch plywood. They were nineteen feet long; the floats are connected at the outer ends. The crossarms must be put in place before the framing for the floats is constructed, in order to guarantee that the frames at the bulkhead locations (which bolt onto the crossarms) are spaced exactly to match the ends of the crossarms. Needless to say, these box spars do not bend much, and if you are only a quarter-inch off when trying to mount the floats on the ends of the crossarms, you

The main hull has been moved out in the front yard, along with the central portion of the cabin.

The Linda Niña II

Main hull after installation of crossarms.

have a difficult time. Actually, the best way to construct them is to make the hull and float framing all at the same time, mounted on the crossarms, and then turn the entire boat over in one piece. This requires a fair-sized building area, though, plus a muscular crane.

After getting the crossarms installed, I took careful measurements between the outer ends and adjusted the locations of the bulkhead frames on the floats accordingly. I made two separate strongbacks for the floats, and built them at the same time. The two strongbacks were end to end, and I had just enough space to accomodate them. The whole thing stretched over fifty feet, meandering out from the garage and into the back corridor. I had made the frames for the floats at the same time as I had made the main hull frames, so it was only a matter of mounting them on the strongback, installing keels and stems and stringers, and planking. It went pretty fast, and I had the floats fiberglassed and ready for installation by March.

Putting on the floats was a bit of a chore. I borrowed a half-dozen coolies from a nearby contractor, and one spring day we wrestled them into place, and glued and bolted them. It was a fine

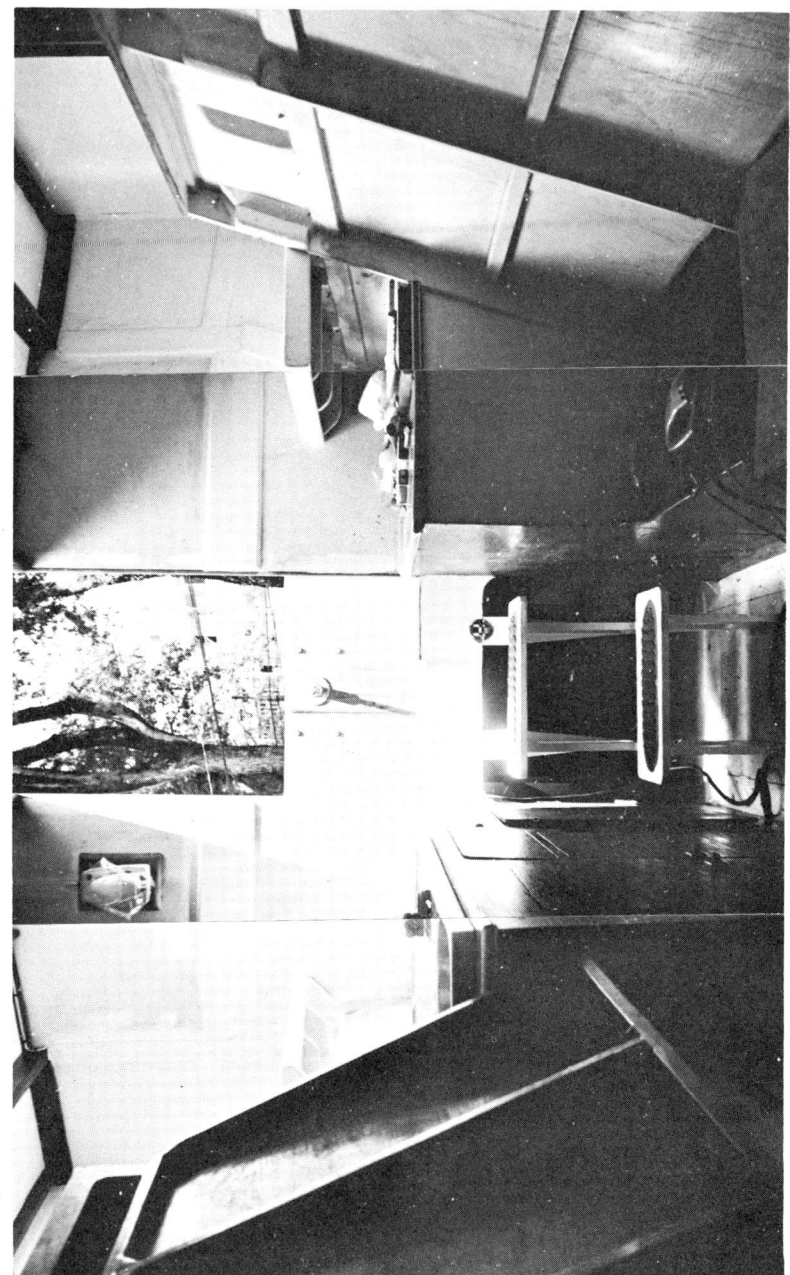

View from interior. At left foreground, fold-down table; background is galley. At right is settee and battery table. Steps swing up to permit access to shelves under cockpit.

day, and I felt considerable satisfaction to see both floats in place. This was the beginning of the end.

Construction proceeded rapidly thereafter, and soon the roof was complete and fiberglassed, and then the bunks and wing fairings. By June the boat was essentially complete. She looked graceful, out in the yard, like a big white bird, with wings half-spread.

As the day of launching approached, considerable planning was required as to how we were going to get her out of the front yard and down to the river. First, it was obvious that the front wall would have to go. There were several trees bordering the sidewalk outside, but measurements revealed that if we got her slewed about at a certain angle, she would just pass out and onto Rue Pasteur with about a foot to spare. Some of my friends at the airport got hold of a trailer that they felt would take the weight, and one Wednesday afternoon we got her ready to go. About half a dozen of us huffed and puffed all afternoon to get her slewed about to face out onto Rue Pasteur, and then we jacked her up with big railroad jacks to the point where we could slide the trailer, without wheels, under the cradle. We then switched the jacks over to the trailer bed itself, and jacked it up enough to be able to get the wheels back on. We left the jacks with just enough pressure to keep the weight off the tires.

I had a contractor come early in the week to tear down the wall and replace it with a tarp, and by the following weekend we were all ready to go. Curfew was from twelve midnight to four in the morning; I had made arrangements with my friends to come just at three-thirty (they all had curfew passes), and promptly at four we would start moving the boat down Rue Pasteur. We made arrangements with the local police to give us an escort in a jeep.

Everything went without a hitch. Fortified with hot coffee at four in the morning, we backed a pickup truck onto the front lawn, lowered the jacks, and took off.

What an odd sensation to be walking alongside a boat at four in the morning down the nearly deserted main street of downtown Saigon! The nineteen-foot beam took up two-thirds of the road. It was a strange sight. There was fortunately little traffic, and the police were fairly efficient, racing ahead in their jeep to divert an occasional early morning truck off onto a side road as we passed.

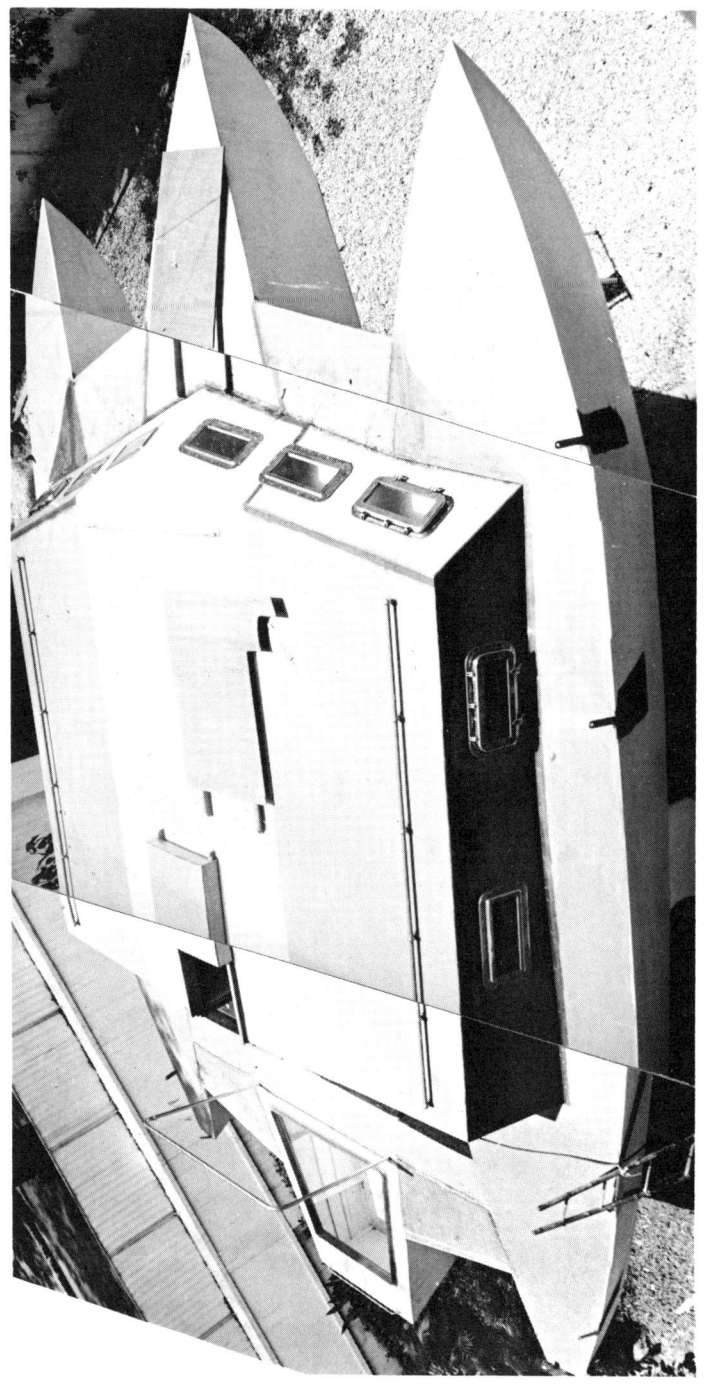

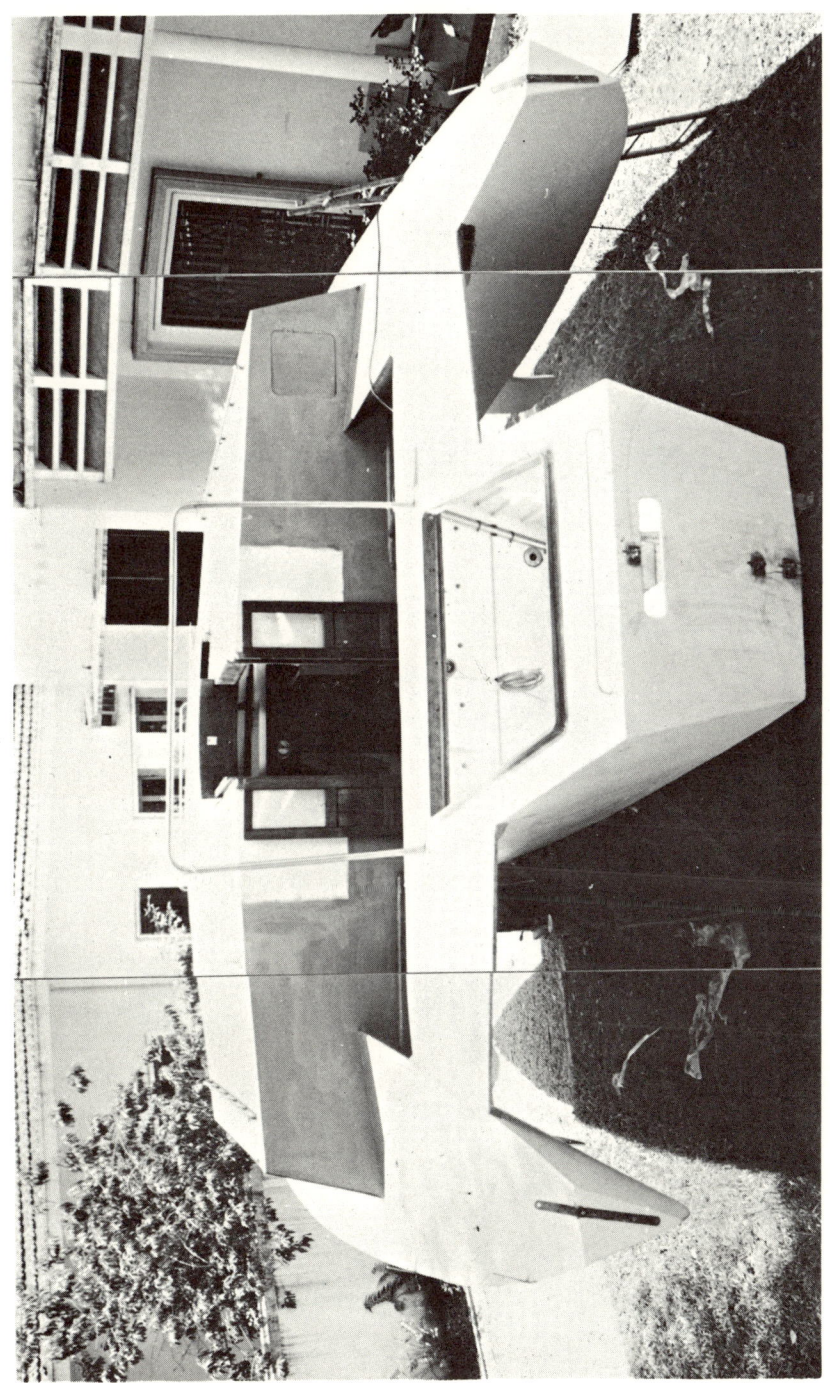

The Linda Niña II

Launching of the Linda Niña II.

I had occasional horrible notions of getting a flat tire and being stranded with this boat smack in the middle of Tu Do. It would have been the traffic jam of all time, come next morning.

But all went without mishap; we trundled her slowly down Pasteur, then turned down Thong Nhut past the cathedral, and finally turned down Hai Ba Trung and headed toward the river. We got her there without incident, parked by a ramp that we had previously selected, and settled down to await high tide at eleven in the morning. My friends went home to catch a few more hours of sleep, while a friend and I maintained vigil at the boat. By ten o'clock a number of people from Esso showed up, and at high tide we backed her down into the water. The wife of a close friend wielded a champagne bottle over the bow, and the *Linda Niña II* was launched!

We got her towed around to the bay in front of the Club Nautique, where I had made arrangements to use an unoccupied mooring, and tied her up. Later in the week we brought the masts down to the club and took them aboard, and still later we stepped and rigged them, one memorable day in the pouring rain.

By now my vacation had started, two and a half months of it, and I spent the next couple of weeks completing the fitting out of the boat. She floated well in the water, although a bit heavy toward the bow. I mounted the sails, and after the usual adjustments to a few balky slides, everything seemed to work well. I borrowed a dinghy to get back and forth. It was always a thrill of pleasure to set out from the Club Nautique dock and row out towards my boat, gracefully perched atop the water, sails furled, bobbing in the current. I had painted the hulls white, with a stripe of blue boot-topping, and the upper surfaces a light tan anti-skid deck paint, and I had left the sides of the cabin in mahogany stain with transparent fiberglass over it. The trim and the masts and booms were all stained mahogany and varnished. She was a rather nice-looking boat, I thought.

By now, my transfer to Singapore at the next posting after vacation had been confirmed, so I got all my household goods packed and consigned, and then moved aboard the boat with those belongings that I was going to take with me on the trip.

It was a pleasant place to live, out there in the bay in front of the

The Linda Niña II

Nautique. In the evenings I would row ashore and have supper on the terrace of the Nautique, overlooking the bay, and sit there sipping beer, chatting with friends, and looking out over the bay to where the *Linda Niña II* perched on the water. Sometimes some of my boating friends would come aboard in the evening, and we would sit in the cockpit, drinking cold beer and smoking and discussing the problems of the world. There are few things more pleasant than sitting in the cockpit of a boat in the evening, feeling the breeze and the slight rocking with the tide, and looking at stars overhead.

The bay of the Club Nautique is a little harbor formed where a small river empties into the Saigon River, in downtown Saigon. Just at the entrance to the bay is moored the floating restaurant My Canh, which had been the scene of several disasters, the worst of which occurred several years ago, when the Viet Cong terrorists exploded several Claymore mines and killed and wounded a large number of people. Coincidentally, this happened on the very day that I set off for Manila on my first ill-fated trip. A friend told me about it when I got towed back to Nhabe the next day, and as I rode into town on a tank truck we passed the My Canh. It was frightening to see the extent to which the shrapnel of the Claymores had ripped into the side of the restaurant. It seemed every square foot had at least one hole in it, and it was a wonder that more people were not killed.

A number of boats were moored in the Nautique bay besides mine, and there was a small crowd of boating enthusiasts who lived aboard these boats and met frequently at the Club in the evening.

My best friends were Warren Blake, Tim Milner, and Tom Henry, a well-balanced threesome who kept things hopping around the Nautique. Warren was a Kiwi—a New Zealander—who had come to Saigon a few years previously on the *Edward Bear*, a thirty-foot *Nimble* trimaran, after spending a few years cruising about the South Pacific. Warren stayed on in Saigon, and eventually founded his own maintenance company, specializing in boat repairs. He apparently got enough contracts with the U.S. Military to make a comfortable living. Warren was one of the most pleasant people I have ever run across. In his late twenties, he had seen a fair amount of the world, and had done a lot of sailing. He was generous, had a great sense of humor, and was always ready to do anything.

Tim was a South African, who had sailed about the world in a variety of vessels and finally settled through some circumstance in Saigon, where he got a job with Page Communications. He was always enthusiastic about everything, particularly boats. Tom Henry was a college graduate from the West Coast of the United States, who came out to Vietnam as a naval officer. Upon discharge he remained in Saigon to work with Pacific Architects and Engineers, and later went into business with Warren. For awhile all three of them lived on the *Thalia*, a thirty-foot-long keel ketch that Tom had bought in Saigon; then Warren went to live ashore. The *Thalia* was moored only a few yards from my *Linda Niña II*.

Now that the boat was launched and fitted out, only a few chores remained prior to departure. I had all my stores aboard by then, including several cases of C-rations garnered from friends in the Military, and about twenty gallons of water in one-gallon plastic containers. During the last week or so I had my friends with commissary privileges buying great bagfuls of stores, which I stashed aboard the *Linda Niña II*. The chronomoter was ticking away, and the clocks were set and running. The generator had fuel, and several jerry cans of outboard mix were stowed aft. I had a viable boat, ready to go.

During the year of construction, I had of course given considerable thought to where I was going on this vacation. Originally I had intended to sail across to Manila again, and then up Luzon and over to Hong Kong; thence to Taiwan and up the Ryukyus to Japan, to spend a few weeks on the Inland Sea. I had hopes of being able to arrange to ship the boat back to Singapore by ocean tanker, since Esso has a number of large tankers plying back and forth between the Persian Gulf and Japan, carrying crude and fuel oil.

As time went on, however, and I started eating into my vacation to complete the fitting out of the boat, it became apparent that I was not going to have time to do all of these things. I finally decided to travel up the coast of Vietnam to Danang, which would give me a week of sailing experience before setting off across any large bodies of water; thence to Hong Kong; and then I would come back down the coast of Luzon to Manila and return to Singapore. It was a more modest cruise than my earlier ambitions had envisioned, but seemed more practical.

Since I had never been at sea before on a boat, I prevailed upon Warren to accompany me as far as Danang, to get me squared away on the practical aspects of sailing at sea. I didn't have to twist his arm very much, since after two years ashore he was eager to get back aboard a trimaran, if only for a week. Tom could handle the business in his absence.

It was agreed that we would leave early Sunday morning, August 6th. A few days before departure, Warren moved his gear aboard. On a Saturday night we all went out and toured the bars of Saigon, drinking immense quantities of beer and toasting a successful trip.

7 / *Saigon, Adieu*

We were awakened by shouts from Tim Milner and Tom Henry, aboard the *Thalia*, which was moored about ten yards off our port side. It was four-thirty in the morning and we dragged ourselves groggily out of our bunks and emerged yawning into the cockpit.

The bay was quiet at this hour, and there was a pleasantly cool morning breeze. The tide was still coming in, lazily slowing down toward slack water which would occur at high tide in another hour or so. The *Linda Niña II* floated well off the bank, pulling gently at the taut bow line, facing into the flood current. The lights from the bridge and from the Club Nautique reflected across the surface of the black water. The other boats showed no signs of life. There were sounds of early morning traffic, and a few lights tentatively moving along the roads, after the end of the curfew at four.

Tim and Tom were clowning about over on the *Thalia,* and after a bit Tim got into the dinghy and rowed over. We chatted for a few moments, and then decided to get moving. The big day—how long I had waited for it!

Warren handled the stern mooring, while Tim rowed over and freed it from the after mooring buoy, and then pulled up the kedge anchor, which I had laid to the starboard quarter on a two-point mooring to keep the *Linda Niña* from swinging into the *Thalia* on the ebb tide. I primed the outboard, and it started on the first pull. I left it idling while we gathered up the stern mooring lines. Tim went forward to the mooring at the bow and freed it up; I put the outboard in gear and revved it gently to make headway against the current and, as Tim freed the line, we proceeded cautiously into the river between the *Thalia* and the mooring buoy.

We made a wide turn in the Saigon River and headed back to buzz the *Thalia* prior to leaving. There were cries of farewell and wishes of good luck; and then we were off on the great adventure.

It was with elation that I pushed the throttle lever on the outboard, and the boat picked up speed, heading downriver. I thought back over all of the work and assorted problems of the past year, sustained by the thought that just such a moment as this would come some day, and now it had indeed arrived, and it was as glorious a sensation as I could have imagined. There was an overwhelming feeling of satisfaction at having completed the boat, and now setting off on the trip that I had dreamed about for so long. I was filled with a pleasant anticipation of things to come.

Once out in the stream we relaxed a bit and leaned on the roof, looking ahead down the dark river. The cockpit was of such size that I could just lean comfortably on the roof while steering the helm with one foot.

We proceeded downriver at about five knots, at three-quarter throttle. I had found, after a bit of experimentation, that the eighteen-horsepower Evinrude would push the *Linda Niña II* along at about six and a half knots maximum at full throttle, and about five knots at three-quarter throttle. I figured the additional gas consumption at full throttle wasn't worth the extra knot, and usually kept the motor throttled back a bit. This was not so much in the interest of gas costs, but rather in order to conserve maximum cruising range with the jerry cans I had aboard.

The Saigon River was very quiet this Sunday morning. I had thought work went on around the clock unloading the ships along the piers, but things appeared to be slackening off now that the new pier facilities had cleared away the log jam. The river was pretty. In the commercial port, ships were strung along the piers and anchored in the stream; their lights reflected out over the water. Aside from slight ripples of the flood tide here and there, the water was very calm, and the breeze was soft in our faces and cool at this time of morning.

Small boats started to appear, crisscrossing the river on a variety of early morning errands. These were mostly small sampans without lights, and were very difficult to see until we were almost on top of them. We nearly ran one down, and then Warren decided to sit up in the bow for awhile, occasionally crying out instructions for evasive maneuvers, until we were clear of the commercial section of the river and the sampan traffic dwindled down.

In about a half-hour we had passed the main section of the river, and the lights dimmed once we had passed the anchored and lighted ships. There was barely enough residual light to make out the banks of the river. The sky was clear but moonless; there were many stars.

"How about some hot cocoa?" I proposed. Warren agreed that hot cocoa sounded good. He always agrees that anything sounds good, and is very easy to cook for. This apparently stems back to various cruises he has had on which they were down to eating nothing but rice and water, and a species of gastronomic sportsmanship developed where it was considered bad form to gritch about the chow. Warren took the helm and I went below to fire up the gas stove and heat water for the cocoa. It was the first cooking under way, I thought happily, not counting the occasional meals prepared aboard at the Club Nautique mooring. I made a couple of cups of hot cocoa, with plenty of sugar, and we stood leaning on the roof (which makes a dandy table), listening to the muffled grumble of the outboard, feeling the slight motions of the boat as she surged through the water, and feeling the breeze in our faces. It was one of those top-notch moments in life. Again, I felt a vast surge of anticipation as to what the next month would bring.

By six o'clock we were nearing Point de Feu Rouge, a few miles upstream of Nhabe. The main river branches at this point, one branch to Saigon, the other up to Bien Hoa. As we approached, we passed a dim gray shape to starboard, a mine sweeper, engines idling, waiting to begin the routine early morning sweeps on the Saigon River. Since the rash of Viet Cong incidents along the Long Tao in early 1966, security measures have been highly intensified along the river, with helicopter coverage, mine-sweeping, patrol boats, etc. They run across mines with some frequency. Over in Naval Operations, where I occasionally had cause to visit in connection with tanker security matters, they have a variety of primitive—and some not-so-primitive—devices that they had fished out of the river in the past. I blithely assumed we wouldn't run into any on this trip, since as far as we'd heard no one had gotten

Saigon, Adieu

blown up lately. It added a bit of spice to the trip downriver, though.

We rounded Point de Feu Rouge and headed downriver towards Nhabe, where the oil terminals are located. The sky was growing lighter now. Warren had made a tentative rendezvous with an LST at seven-thirty off Nhabe, which would give us a tow to Cap St. Jacques. This had been an informal arrangement made with some buddies at the MSTS office, and I was not overly confident that an LST would show up at the appointed time, or give us a tow if it did, but adopted a wait-and-see attitude.

We arrived off Nhabe in another half-hour, and cut the engine in mid-stream. It was slack water now. The silence was welcome after the roar of the outboard for two hours. We utilized the spare time to mount the self-steering gear on the rudder. We got it fitted to the rudder to check the location of the brackets, and then took off the rudder. It was a longish job, due to the need to disconnect the steering cables and remove the tiller arm. The bolts that the shop had given us turned out to be too short (and ordinary carbon steel to boot!), so I mounted the brackets with bronze wood screws instead. We fired up the little Honda and took out the electric drill, and had the brackets installed in no time. It was about eight when we finished, and still no sign of any LST's on the horizon, so we fired up the outboard again and took off downriver.

By this time we were starting to feel hungry, so I went below and fixed breakfast, the first real meal of the voyage. It was fairly lavish, consisting of C-ration chopped ham and eggs, a bowl of fruit cocktail, C-ration bread sliced in three and coated liberally with peanut butter, and coffee. Warren couldn't handle it all, being apparently one of those types who get by on skimpy breakfasts. It all went down well, though, and Warren said that if all the cooking was going to be to this standard he might come clear to Hong Kong with me. I told him this would depend fifty percent on him because I had news for him: we were going to share the cooking chores on this voyage! (Actually, Warren is the kind of guy who does a lot more than his share of the irksome jobs, to the point where you have to tell him to desist.) At any rate, we stacked the dishes bachelor-wise in the sink, and settled down to enjoy(?) the run downriver.

Toward midmorning the ships started passing by, going up and down the river. They were hurrying to get over Coral Bank, the low spot in the Long Tao River, about halfway between Cap and Nhabe, which limits ships' draft to about twenty-eight to thirty feet. The pilots like to bring vessels over this stretch during slack water, so during these periods there is a lot of traffic up and down the river. We did a lot of rocking for the next hour or so; those 10,000 to 15,000 ton freighters throw up a hefty bow wave, coming up the river at twelve to fifteen knots! The flat-fronted landing craft are the worst; they really push the water aside and generate a tremendous bow wave, which made the *Linda Niña* bob and pitch like a cork. After awhile the traffic died down, and we were alone on the river except for an occasional patrol boat and the minesweepers.

A pair of the latter passed us, coming upriver. Warren informed me that they usually travel in pairs, sweeping both sides of the river at the same time. It must be ticklish work. They tow porpoise-shaped paravanes, which appear to be about six feet long and are painted white. One of them passed us, about fifty feet to starboard, throwing up a jet of water as it shot by. For a moment it rolled in the water and appeared briefly, like a mechanical porpoise, exposing to our startled glances a big red eyeball painted a few feet aft of its snout—a bit of wartime whimsy.

The patrol boats would also go by every so often, roaring upriver and downriver, and armed to the teeth. They eyed us casually in passing, but no one seemed particularly interested in a thirty-two-foot trimaran. We were obviously round-eyes, and although we had prudently left the American ensign down while traversing the Viet Cong-infested section of the Long Tao, the boat was obviously not smuggling enemy supplies, so no one stopped us. The patrol boats were thirty- or forty-footers, manned by Vietnamese and Americans in about equal proportions.

We reached Ganh Rai Bay about noon, and headed out into the Bay, feeling a bit relieved now that the Long Tao had been passed. One potential hazard was behind us, at any rate. There would be no problem with Viet Cong along the coast, since we planned to cruise sufficiently offshore to be beyond the range of any casual marksmen ashore.

There was a nice ten-knot breeze blowing, so once out in the bay we decided it was time to put up the sails. We turned the outboard off and wrestled them up without much trouble. The breeze caught them and billowed them out, and we proceeded across the bay at about five knots. I put up the American ensign on the backstay, where it fluttered colorfully in the breeze.

It was pleasant to sit back and hold the helm, and listen to the water gurgling past the hulls and the chop of the waves. The bay was calm, and the day was bright and sunny. I recalled the times I had been through here before on boats. The first time had been during my trip to Manila, and had been disastrous, since this was just about where my mast had come down. I shook my head, remembering. The second time had been during the search for the dragons, and it had been about here, too, where I had been moored when they opened up at Fort Can Gio with all the artillery that Tet evening. It seemed long ago already, and now I was traversing the bay again. If I ever get to be an old man, I reflected, Ganh Rai Bay will always hold poignant memories for me.

En route to Cap, Warren washed the dishes, and I went below and cooked some lunch, with the usual C-rations, accompanied by warm Budweiser. We reached Cap St. Jacques about two in the afternoon, and turned southward into the strait between Cap and Fort Can Gio, out into the South China Sea. There were several ships anchored at Cap—a few freighters and a medium-sized aircraft carrier. The last time I had been down this way I had counted about thirty ships waiting for clearance to come upriver, but pier improvements since had corrected this situation to a great degree.

We spent a few minutes with the binoculars as we went by the beach at Cap, but few bikinis were in evidence. You can't have everything.

Then we were out into the sea, heading south to get well clear of the land. By late afternoon we were about twenty miles offshore, and then we turned east, setting a direct easterly course for Poulo Cecir de Mer Islands, which was to be our first landfall on the trip up the coast. These islands lie about thirty miles off the Vietnam coast, and are about a hundred miles to the east of Cap St. Jacques.

Warren rigged up preventers on the main to leeward and on the jib to windward, as we shifted course to the east. Since the wind was on our quarter, this was required to prevent jibing in the event of a shift in the wind. We now had a good breeze of fifteen to twenty knots from the southwest, or on our starboard quarter heading east. The sea had a mild three-foot swell, which increased to four or five feet as the evening wore on.

We ate early, and night came on. We had decided to split the watches into four-hour periods, with a sort of dog watch around the afternoon of two hours each, so that the next night the watches would be shifted. It worked well. The only problem was that on the eight to twelve watch we would both have to be up from about nine to nine thirty so that Warren could take the helm while I copied the weather forecast out of Hong Kong, which came in coded.

I took the eight to twelve watch this first night out, and Warren hit the sack about eight. It was very pleasant, sitting at the helm as the boat scudded along doing about six knots to the eastward. The evening was clear and the stars twinkled overhead. There were long five- or six-foot gentle swells from the southwest, and as they overtook the boat on the starboard quarter she would accelerate and approach the point of surfing for a moment, until the swell had passed beneath. Steering with the wind and swells on the quarter requires constant attention, for as the swells overtake the boat there is a tendency to broach, and a lot of helm is required. The swell passes beneath, and suddenly the helm is slack and must be spun back the other way to keep the boat on course as she sinks back into the trough of the following swell. It kept me fairly busy.

From time to time my attention would wander, and once or twice the boat shifted sufficiently to backwind the mainsail. Had it not been for the preventer, the sail would of course have jibed. When this happened I felt like an ass, and I could only do my best to keep her on course until another shift of wind, coupled with the motion of the boat on a swell, would bring the wind over to the right side of the sail. I would resolve to pay more attention from then on, but it happened several times. Occasionally it would backwind the jib, but this was little problem, for with the main there was of course sufficient control to correct the course and get the wind back on the right side of the jib. Needless to say, this awkward boat handling did not leave me feeling like Chichester, but at any rate I felt I was starting to learn.

Saigon, Adieu

Sailing alone in the cockpit of a sailboat at sea, at night, is a pleasant and heady experience. The cockpit is shrouded in a comfortable darkness, relieved only by the ethereal glow with which the mizzen light illuminates the mainsail and a light reddish glow from the compass light. There is enough residual light from the stars and the boat lights to dully illuminate the seas alongside and cast twinkling highlights on the white froth that leaps and breaks atop the swells as they go by. Like fire, the sea is a never-changing pattern of motion, and you can look at it for long periods without becoming bored.

There was little sound except for the slapping of waves against the hulls and an occasional rush of watery sound as she tried to surf down the face of a swell, dwindling to a low rushing gurgle as the swell passed under the bow and she fell back a bit. There was the most subtle of airy noises about the rigging, broken by the occasional flap of sails as a change in wind or course would cause a momentary luffing. It was all most pleasant and relaxing, and I sat happily on the seat above the aft crossarm, puffing at a cigar, my thoughts now here, now there, far away and entering distant ports.

And then *bang*! the main would backwind again, and I would suddenly recall the course and bring my attention back to more practical matters at hand, like steering a boat!

Shortly after nine I woke Warren up by gently banging a few times on the ship's bell. He presently emerged, yawning, to make coffee and take the helm while I went inside to copy the weather. We fired up the little Honda on the port seat and put on the lights. I got VPS-60 out of Hong Kong with no trouble and spent about fifteen minutes copying the forecast. It appeared there was an ominous trough of low pressure developing to the east of the South China Sea, but there was no other news of interest, so I returned to the helm and Warren to his bunk.

At twelve I woke him again, this time more nautically, eight bells gently on the bell. It sounded more seamanlike and seemed more appropriate somehow than yelling "HEY, WARREN!" through the hatch. We had another round of coffee and I hit the sack.

This first night at sea was not the best night's sleep I've ever had. Bunks in trimarans going from seven to ten knots are just too noisy until you get used to it. The plywood structure of the boat and the hollow floats combine to form one huge and complex sounding board, and as the boat surges through the water all of the sounds are magnified. There seems to be a great crashing and banging as the boat pounds into the swells; waves smack against the floats with resounding booms, and there is an intense gurgling and rushing of water past the hulls. It sounds as though you are on some kind of watery express train.

I tossed and turned, and half dozed, but real sleep was impossible. It was all too exhilarating! The hours passed slowly. Suddenly, I was brought fully awake by a great bath of water that came in through the port hole, sloshing through and soaking me from head to foot! I came up, spluttering and roaring, now wide awake, just in time to hear Warren banging on the ship's bell, calling me for the four to eight watch.

I got up and went dripping back to the cockpit, with a few things to say about his highly effective technique for waking up the next watch, and reminded him with some exasperation that I had mentioned earlier the need to dog down the hatches before we got out to sea. He went about ruefully dogging them shut, but this was strictly a case of closing the barn door after the horse has disappeared, and it was nearly a week before the mattress dried out.

We had some coffee. The sea was now fairly active, and there was a strong breeze. Warren advised that on the midwatch it had really picked up, and the boat had been making a good ten knots at times, and surfing on the larger swells. When I returned to the helm, it was more exciting steering than before, and almost frightening for the first time. The swells were indeed bigger, and the boat was really tearing along! Overtaking swells would go by with a roar and a crash of spray as they broke under the transom, and the boat would suddenly pick up speed.

The four to eight is a good watch. The first two hours go by fairly fast, awaiting the dawn, and then the rest of the watch goes rapidly too, watching the colors changing gradually in the sky.

As we sped along in the early morning hours, I felt a high sense of exhilaration, having passed this first night at sea and now awaiting the next day out. The steering had kept me busy, what with the higher seas, and I was pleased that I seemed to have picked up the essentials, for the sails did not backwind anymore on this second watch. It was a feeling of satisfaction, tearing along on this dark ocean, hearing the crash of the waves alongside, and looking at the big sails taut against the sky.

By now Orion had appeared in the heavens, and I soon found it a handy device to steer by. Using the stars is much more pleasant and easy than peering at a compass every few minutes. I got the three stars in the belt lined up between the diamond stays and the mast, and found that this put me just about on course. After awhile I could watch them out of the corner of my eye, and steering became almost automatic.

Sunrise at sea from the cockpit of a sailboat is one of those things that everybody should do at least once in their life, I reflected, as six o'clock came and went and the sky started changing color. It gets lighter to the east, and changes through successive shades of dark gray, becoming flecked with purple and blue, then shades of russet and orange and red, and finally the first rays of the sun start breaking over the distant horizon, and dawn has come. I sat, completely fascinated and completely happy, watching this most memorable dawn from the *Linda Niña II*, my boat, beating along on the South China Sea, and felt that deep and exhilarating feeling that goes with the conviction that at this moment you would change places with no one, and would want to be nowhere else in the world.

By seven the morning mist was clearing off, and land became visible in the distance to port. In another hour the land had advanced to a northeast bearing, and I got Warren up to go forward and change over the preventer on the jib, and we shifted course to a broad reach to the northeast. We ate breakfast and sat in the cockpit, watching the land approach. By ten in the morning we were close enough to get a position on the higher hills with the pelorus. They were, of course, the Poulo Cecir de Mer Islands (they could hardly have been anything else), and we got a good position and checked it on the chart against the previous afternoon's position off Cap St. Jacques. The results were encouraging; we had made an average of 7.2 knots all night, which seemed pretty good, and had totaled about ninety miles. The course line showed the effect of the leeway with the current and the southwest wind; we had deviated two to three degrees while steering a true easterly course all night.

The seas were quite high this morning, with about a six-foot swell

—some larger—topped by a two- to three-foot choppy sea. It was rough going, relatively; the *Linda Niña* jounced and banged about, and we took a lot of water over the forward decks, although the cockpit stayed dry enough.

We reached the islands in another hour or so. Poulo Cecir de Mer consists principally of two islands, a big one and a small one, separated from each other by a narrow strait of about 500 yards. We decided to thread our way through it. As we approached closer, we could see that the islands were green, but without much in the way of trees; mostly shrub and grass, with a lot of rock showing. There was some cultivation, and a few smallish habitations here and there. Flocks of screeching white sea birds were swooping about the promonitories. There were no people to be seen on the island, but several fishing boats were about, and the fishermen waved as we went by. By now we had the American ensign flying, so we presumed they were on our side. We sailed into the strait and noted a string of rocks ominously stretching down the shoreline of the larger island and disappearing into the water in the direction of the smaller one. Warren climbed the mast to spot any incipient problems, but it appeared there was plenty of draft in the strait, as the charts had indicated. We passed through without incident, and then into the lee of the other side of the big island. There were a number of junk-like fishing sampans about, and we got a few good photos of them. After pleasant sailing for the next half-hour or so, we got out into the open sea again, setting a northerly course for Cape Padaran. The sea had become higher yet, and waves were continually breaking over the bow; one big one splashed all the way back to the cockpit and soaked us both.

We had lunch, and a few hours later Cape Padaran came into sight. We arrived in the late afternoon, and got a position from landmarks. Another position check revealed that we had averaged 7.1 knots from early morning, which was good time indeed, considering the time we had wasted threading our way through the strait and loafing along in the lee of the big island.

We had made a total of 170 miles since the previous afternoon. At this rate, we could be in Danang in three days!

8 / The Vietnam Coast

As it turned out, the first day's run appeared to be due to a lucky combination of weather and seas; for the rest of the week we proceeded at a considerably more sedate pace.

After reaching Cape Padaran we started north up the coast, a few miles offshore, heading for Cam Ranh. The rest of the day passed uneventfully, and toward afternoon the wind began visibly slackening off. By nightfall we were down to three to four knots. Warren had the eight to twelve watch, and woke me up at nine to get the weather report. There was nothing particularly new. For the remainder of the week, despite the slackening wind and occasional mirror-smoothness of the sea, VPS Hong Kong continued to give forth unvarying reports of force three to four winds all up the length of the Vietnam coast. I wondered wryly where they were getting their meteorological data from.

The days along the Vietnam coast passed slowly and pleasantly. We worked our way up the coast, about a few miles offshore, to discourage casual snipers. The sea was uniformly pleasant, and the sun shone most days. It was a lazy life spent in sitting around the cockpit soaking up the sun, or in the bunk snoozing, or writing letters at the fold-down desk in the cabin, or reading. About the only thing lacking was cold drinks.

We saw surprisingly few vessels on the run up the coast. An occasional freighter would go by, and an occasional patrol boat of some kind. At night a few lights could be seen out to sea, presumably offshore patrol vessels of some type. On the whole run up to Danang, we were challenged only once, if it could be called that. Off Cam Ranh, a Navy patrol boat came up alongside to see what we were. After a brief conversation it became reasonably apparent that we were not Viet Cong, and we exchanged pleasantries with the crew. The patrol boat was a forty-footer, and it idled alongside the *Linda Niña*, motors throbbing, a powerful-looking craft. We asked whether they had any cold drinks and they obliged promptly, tossing us four cans of assorted soft drinks from the refrigerator. They sure tasted good! After a few more minutes the patrol boat took off in a wide circle back toward the base at Cam Ranh.

Tuesday night we passed Cam Ranh, and I had the eight to twelve watch, an uneventful stretch, doing no more than three knots. I went yawning to bed, leaving Warren with the mid-watch. The hours passed, and the night turned gray with approaching dawn. I suddenly awoke about six-thirty wondering why Warren hadn't awakened me for the four to eight watch. All was silent, and there was no rush of water at all past the hulls.

"Warren?" I called. There was no answer. I leaned out of the bunk and peered back toward the hatch, but the cockpit was empty! No sign of Warren!

This woke me up in a hurry, and I leaped out of my bunk and dashed back into the cockpit, assuming that he had fallen overboard. But no, there he was, curled up asleep in his life jacket on the port side of the cockpit, snoring away.

"You clown!" I snarled, half in exasperation, half in relief. Warren stirred awake and yawned, and I told him of my apprehensions. Apparently about two or three in the morning the wind had dropped to the point where the sails just kept flogging listlessly, so Warren took them down, let the boat drift, and curled up to sleep in the cockpit. What a scare, though!

Falling overboard at sea is a sobering thought, particularly when you're alone on watch. Whenever we were out in the cockpit, alone on watch, it was *de rigeur* to have our life jacket on and a safety belt fastened to some convenient point in the rigging. We were only a few miles off the coast, so I suppose if one of us had fallen over we could have made it to shore eventually. There were few stories of sharks in Vietnam waters. They were around, of course, but either they were not overly aggressive or they didn't like to eat Vietnamese. Perhaps there just hadn't been enough bathing along the beaches to build up any statistics as yet.

The Vietnam Coast

By Wednesday morning the wind was still slack. The sails were furled, and the *Linda Niña* floated placidly on a low swell, some twenty miles southeast of Nhatrang. After breakfast we decided to get some use out of the outboard and motor in to Nhatrang to get a bath, a good night's sleep, and some cold beer, and to await more favorable winds. We fired up the Evinrude and headed initially toward a small island shown on the chart about halfway into Nhatrang, called Con Son, also known as Swallow Island, and arrived about ten in the morning. It was a hot day, with blue water and bright sun, and the white beaches on the small island looked inviting. We dropped the hook in about eight feet of clear water a few hundred yards off the beach, and swam ashore.

As we swam, we felt odd little prickly sensations against shoulders and neck, and we discovered that there was a large number of very small jellyfish about! After taking a bath at the beach with salt-water soap, we wandered about for awhile collecting seashells. There was a small hut back on the beach, with a few oldish men sitting about. They seemed to be the only inhabitants of the island, which was only about half a mile long. We greeted them and I asked whether they were fishermen but it appeared not. Within the limitations of my Vietnamese, they seemed to be a sort of caretaker committee for the island, and performed various odd jobs for the frequent spearfishing and swimming expeditions that came out from Nhatrang, for the local servicemen.

After awhile we swam back to the boat. It was pleasant to stand on the beach for a moment and view my *Linda Niña II* rocking placidly on the blue water of the lagoon, sails furled. With her three white hulls sitting lightly on the water, she looked like some bizarre species of multi-bodied sea bird about to launch into flight! She *is* a beautiful boat, I thought happily.

We fired up the outboard and headed into Nhatrang, arriving about one. We motored about the commercial pier area for awhile, looking for a place to moor, and then veered over to what appeared to be an American patrol boat dock to one side of the commercial area. There were a few servicemen walking about on the dock, eyeing us as we approached. The American ensign fluttered prominently from the backstay of the *Linda Niña*. We asked whether we might be able to moor at the dock for the night. The noncom in charge advised us that the patrol boats would be coming in to moor later in the day, but said we might use the mooring buoy located a few hundred feet from the dock. This solution turned out to be ideal, since not only was there a mooring buoy, but a small plastic dinghy was attached to it with a painter. We had all the comforts of home.

We moored up promptly and went ashore in the dinghy with the gasoline jerry cans. Fortunately, the dock area was located just half a block from the new Esso terminal at Nhatrang. We walked the few blocks past the port area and up the hill behind the Oceanographic Institute. I had been there once or twice in the past on business trips to Nhatrang; they had a remarkable collection of saltwater fish in the Aquarium, rather unusual for a country such as Vietnam. Perhaps Madame Ngu liked fish.

Fortunately Mr. Diem, the area representative for Esso, was at the terminal, and we enlisted his assistance. We got into his car and set off for town. On the way, since it was about lunch time, we stopped at the Beacon Restaurant and had a pleasant lunch. It was nice to be sitting at a table with a tablecloth and cutlery again, after a few days at sea on C-rations. We drank cold beer endlessly with our grilled lobster, which is a Nhatrang specialty. After a drive into town to pick up gasoline we returned to the boat.

We offered Diem an outing, and motored up the coast along the beach at Nhatrang. Someday that beach will be a big tourist attraction in the Far East, I think. It stretches for over a mile, with clean yellow sand, and the swimming is good. Boats can be hired for trips to the nearby offshore islands, where the water is crystal clear and fine for skin-diving.

There were not many people on the beach except for a couple of dozen off-duty American G.I.'s and their Vietnamese girlfriends, and the usual bunch of kids. We pulled up to the beach and got the kids to hang onto the mooring line while Diem went ashore to get a few beers for Warren and me, and a Coke for himself, since he was still technically on duty. He was wearing a bathing suit under his pants, however, which was a bit surprising. The Esso executive is always prepared.

After awhile Diem had to return to work, so we motored back to our mooring. The wind was still completely dead, so we decided to

The Vietnam Coast

stick around and have supper ashore, spend the night at our mooring, and take off the next morning if the wind was good.

After getting cleaned up we went ashore and had supper at the only other good restaurant in Nhatrang—the Frigate Restaurant—and walked through town. We stopped for a few drinks in the Nipa-Hut Bar, which had a big sign downstairs that read "COLD BEER—HOT GIRLS—STEREO MUSIC—SORRY 'BOUT THAT." It seemed a likely combination. The beer turned out to be cold; the music possibly stereo, although it was hard to tell above the din. The girls were of dubious quality.

Vietnamese bars are all much the same. You walk in, eyed by various sets of feminine eyeballs as you take a seat. Eventually a petite female separates herself from the rest and sidles over. She grins, gamine-like. The conversations follow a set pattern.

"Hello," she says. "This first time you come here?" From here on a number of subcases develop, depending on whether you have been here before and, having been here, whether you have developed some previous liaison.

Case I "Yes, this is the first time I've been here."
"You buy me one Saigon tea?"

Case II(a) "No, I've been here before."
"You have girl-friend already?"
"No."
"You buy me one Saigon tea?"

Case II(b) "No, I've been here before."
"You have girl-friend already?"
"Yes."
"What her number?"
"Twenty-three."
"She not here tonight."
"I know."
"You buy me one Saigon tea?"

And so it goes. Saigon tea is, of course, just that, but goes under the guise of some supposedly alcoholic beverage for the girls. It is peddled under a variety of names, such as "whistea," and prices range from 80 to 160 piastres, depending on the quality of the bar; in nightspots with dancing, it can be as much as 300 or 400 piastres, which is about three bucks a throw. It can become an expensive evening.

Purchase of Saigon tea entitles the purchaser to the companionship of the young lady for from twenty minutes to a half-hour, by which time they are getting thirsty again. If you are a well-heeled mark, they can slug them down every ten minutes, and it gets very expensive indeed.

About eleven Warren and I took off, leaving the girls moaning piteously for one more Saigon tea, and caught a couple of local motorcycles back to the boat. Young Vietnamese cowboys hang around the bars at night with their motorbikes and motor-scooters, and offer you a ride to wherever you are going, to pick up a hundred piastres or so. We went tearing back along the seafront road to Cau Da pier, bouncing and raising all sorts of dust. It required all my fatalistic philosophy to cope with it, but I hung on for dear life and finally arrived in one piece. We rowed the dinghy out to the boat, and went to bed. It was the first good night's sleep I'd had in days, and I slept like a log.

After breakfast the next morning we left, and motored around the big island off Nhatrang and out into the sea. We got a few miles out and turned north, but there was little wind. About nine we picked up the weather report, which announced the formation of an ominous-sounding "tropical disturbance" to the north, and advised as to force 3 to 4 winds all along the Vietnam coast.

Thursday and Friday we crept up the coast, past Cape Varella, and then Quinhon late Friday night.

On Saturday the sea was calm as a mirror. There was no wind at all; just the hot sun, and not a cloud in the sky. There was the faintest of swells. We decided to motor awhile just for something to do. At dawn we were about twenty miles south of Culao Re, the big island off the coast where the coastline starts to change direction and head inward toward the west.

We still had about four cans of gasoline left, which was not quite enough to reach Danang. We passed Culao Re, and about noon an LST approached us from astern, heading towards Danang. It was LST 532, flying the American flag, sailing for MSTS, apparently manned by a Japanese crew. We waved them down in hope of a tow. They stopped amiably enough and threw us a towline,

The Vietnam Coast

which we affixed to the large turnbuckle on the forestay. The LST picked up speed, and we were under way.

We proceeded in this fashion for an hour or so, doing about ten knots. It was very pleasant, the *Linda Niña* scudding along at a good rate in the wash of the LST. After awhile Warren went forward and came back perturbed; it appeared that the towline was bending the turnbuckle. I went up to look, and sure enough, there was a noticeable bend in it. We hailed the LST again and disconnected the towline, indicating that thanks, we had had enough for one day. They waved cheerfully and took off for Danang.

We started the motor again and headed for Culao Cham, a big island just to the south of Tien Sha peninsula by Danang. About six in the evening we passed the island, motoring in close. There were several fishing villages along the shore of the island—very pretty little villages, with white sandy beaches, groups of thatched huts set back from the beach, and fishing boats moored in the little inlets. Palm trees were all about. They waved at us as we motored by. We spent a fair amount of time with the binoculars, trying to spot some of the better-looking village girls, but the crop was discouraging. I guess they were all hidden indoors. We also passed a few of what appeared to be Vietnamese military training camps along the shore, and heard one or two shots as we went by. We thought perhaps someone might be throwing a few our way just for kicks, so we motored more prudently further offshore.

We passed the island and had supper about seven; then the wind picked up a bit. I had the eight to twelve. By midnight we had come abreast of Tien Sha and had reached the opening into Danang harbor. I woke Warren up for the mid-watch. We turned into the harbor, and it was apparent that we were going to have to tack back and forth into the wind to get into the harbor. The chart we had was not very good, and the lighting in the harbor left much to be desired. It was rather blind tacking. Finally I left Warren with it and hit the sack.

After about half an hour I was awakened by a big spotlight shining in the window. I jumped out of the bunk and went back to the cockpit, and found that it was a Navy patrol boat coming alongside to investigate.

We told them our story, and they radioed back to the base for instructions. Apparently the base was called "Negotiate," and our patrol boat was "Negotiate 14." The base told them to give us a tow back into anchorage in Danang harbor, which was fine with us. They threw us a tow rope, and we fixed it about the base of the mast.

I almost got into trouble with that patrol boat. It backed up to the point where it looked as though it was going to bang against my port float. I ran out on the float and pushed at the transom of the patrol boat. At just that moment, they shifted forward to idle, and the boat pulled away, leaving me there dangling in midair like Mr. Magoo when he walks off buildings in the cartoons. I fell forward against the transom of the patrol boat. Fortunately it had a grab strip running along the back, and I grabbed at it for dear life as I fell down between the two boats, scrabbling with my legs against the back of the transom. I let out a great bellow as I went down, to attract attention. Warren rushed over to the port side.

"Drop into the water!" he was yelling. Looking down into a pair of churning screws about three feet below my drawn-up ankles and curled-up toes, I wasn't about to do any dropping into the water at that point. I finally managed to claw my way up onto the deck of the patrol boat. My shins were scraped and bleeding from the barnacles on the transom.

Finally, we got under way and proceeded into the harbor. We reached the anchorage about four in the morning and dropped the hook in about thirty feet of water just about one week to the dot from the time we had left Saigon. I let out 150 feet of line, and fell into bed.

We emerged onto deck the next morning to encounter a beautiful day. We were anchored smack in the middle of Danang harbor, which was full of ships. At the west side of Tien Sha peninsula were large piers with a variety of large vessels tied up. There were a lot of junks, and one aircraft carrier, presumably the one we'd seen earlier at Cap St. Jacques. LST's and patrol craft were scattered about. The bay was calm, and there was little traffic this Sunday morning.

We upped anchor after breakfast and motored to the Navy base wharf, looking for a place to tie up. There did not seem to be much chance of getting permission to tie up at military facilities, so we

The Vietnam Coast

motored on into Danang. I remembered from previous visits that there was a beach not far from the Esso office where pleasure boats had been kept. Perhaps we could moor there.

It was a good idea. The beach was there and had apparently been turned into a sort of recreation center for the G.I.'s. They had built a nice little dock and had set up some structures along the beach, and as we approached there were some G.I.'s tinkering with a pair of water-skiing boats. We motored up near the pier and asked the sergeant in charge whether we might moor there for a day or so. He amiably agreed, and we brought the *Linda Niña* alongside the pier out of the way of the T-head of the dock and the water-skiing boats, and tied up. It was an ideal location, secure and close to the Esso office, which lay only a half-block away. I reflected how lucky we had been. At both Nhatrang and here, the Esso office was a five-minute walk!

We tied up loosely at the dock, and then Warren put out the bow anchor near the beach and swam out with a stern line to an unused buoy off the port quarter. We hauled up tight on both lines until the *Linda Niña* was about three feet off the pier, so she wouldn't bang with the waves.

The next two days in Danang were mostly dedicated to relaxing and trying to dig up a few cases of C-rations to see me through to Hong Kong. We got the gasoline cans topped up, and the water containers, and made the boat shipshape for the forthcoming journey. After various visits to innumerable military installations, I finally found a friendly chief warrant officer in the Supply Corps who donated two cases. I was all set to go.

After breakfast on Tuesday, Warren got his gear together and waved from the dock as I took off on the great adventure. Warren would return by plane to Saigon, while I continued alone to Hong Kong. It was quite a sensation, motoring away from the dock, this time alone and in anticipation of a long journey. I felt no apprehensions to speak of, only a wonderful sense of anticipation. The boat had performed well, so I had few fears on that score. I felt that in the week we had come up the coast I had learned enough about handling her to take care of myself reasonably adequately. So now I was off to Hong Kong.

The morning was beautiful, and the bay was calm. By ten in the morning I was rounding Tien Sha, and by early noon I was well off the coast. I shut off the outboard about two and let the *Linda Niña* rock on the swells while I fixed lunch. There was little wind, and I drifted about for a few hours until the late afternoon breeze blew up from the southwest. I got the sails up, and after awhile got the self-steering rigged to hold an easterly course, which was about the best it would do with the southwest wind. This seemed all right, since I had to go east anyway to get to Hong Kong. Considering the fact that I had to rely on the wind, it seemed inevitable that there was going to be a certain amount of zig-zagging involved.

By nightfall I was making fairly good time. I cooked supper and sat smoking a cigar and watching the stars come out. I went to bed about eight.

It was a fair night's sleep, considering that it was my first night afloat alone. I kept waking up every hour or so and checking the compass, but the course held fairly steady on east to southeast all night. It was not nearly so bouncy as the first night out.

Wednesday morning, August 16th, I awoke, alone at sea. The boat was still on an easterly course. The Vietnam coast was out of sight.

After breakfast, I took out the chart and figured roughly where I was, allowing four knots during the night and assuming a course about east southeast from Danang. The result put me about forty miles east southeast of Danang. Later in the morning the sun came out through the clouds and I managed to get a good sun position, which LOP indicated me to be about ten miles further east than I had calculated. This was all to the good, and indicated that my speed had been nearer to five knots than the four I had roughly and conservatively assumed for the previous night's run.

By midmorning the wind had shifted ominously to the west northwest, which was an unusual direction for wind in the South China Sea at this time of year. I got the 9:18 weather report out of VPS and, sure enough, there was a storm warning! *Choi oi*, I thought, the story of my life, the first day at sea and already I'm running into storm warnings! These broadcasts start with the words "storm warning," when there is one, and you copy anxiously until you find out where the storm is. This one, named Iris, fortunately appeared to be well to the northwest of Hainan. Good, I thought, this may get it out of its system, so that statistically perhaps I could hope for good weather from then until I reached Hong Kong, since two storms should not be expected to follow each other closely. As it turned out, I was quite wrong. At any rate, this did explain the odd shift in the wind direction.

By noon the seas were increasingly rough and were up to six-foot swells with a two-foot choppy sea superimposed. It was getting bouncy, and the boat commenced to plunge and buck her way into the seas, taking a considerable amount of water over the port float and throwing up all sorts of spray. The swells were coming from the west northwest, driven by the wind, which was now up to about twenty knots. I sat back in the cockpit all afternoon, holding the helm and ducking spray, as the *Linda Niña* surged on to the north.

Toward nightfall I put on the self-steering, holding a northerly course, and went below to fix some supper. The night came, starless and black. I sat in the cockpit, smoking an after-dinner cigar and looking out into the blackness. The boat surged on into the night, with a crash of spray and the pounding of waves against the floats.

9 / *Mayday, Mayday*

It is a fitful sleep at best, alone on a small boat in a heavy sea. Throughout the night you are continually being jolted half-awake as the boat plunges into the trough of a particularly heavy swell.

Consciousness returns, and a few random thoughts swirl about. You are on a boat; you are out on the South China Sea somewhere; the weather is a bit rough. Background noises permeate through the sleepy haze. The waves are jostling the hulls, an occasional breaking whitecap pounds against the weather float. There is a random rattle of crockery from the general direction of the galley.

You stretch, yawn, and fumble for the flashlight tucked behind the head of the mattress. The boat shudders over another swell and lurches into the following trough. There is a jar as the float bangs into the next approaching swell, and spray rattles down on the roof.

You roll over, peer over the bunkboard, and aim the light in the general direction of the compass. Pressing the button, you open your eyes for a few squinting moments, just long enough to spot the reading. A few points off NNW. A brief mental appraisal; close enough. You grunt, realign yourself for sleep, and drift off again.

How many times does this happen during the night? Ten, twenty? But you are half asleep, and the next morning it is difficult to remember.

On Thursday, August 17th, after the tenth or maybe it was the twentieth jolt, it grew light outside, and after the usual check of the compass I rubbed enough sleep out of my eyes to read my watch as well. Nearly seven o'clock, and dawn. I lay for awhile, arms behind head, enjoying the softness of the pillow and eyeing the underside of the roof philosophically.

What is there about sailing, I wondered, that makes one morally obliged to leap up at the crack of dawn? The self-steering was doing fine, and there was no reason why I couldn't remain comfortably in the sack until nine or so, arising to a leisurely breakfast. But it did not seem traditional; I could never look Chichester in the eye. So after a few minutes of reflection, I resignedly clambered out of the bunk and went aft to yawn out the hatch and see what August 17th was going to be like.

It was a Masefield type of morning, with "...a gray mist on the sea's face and a gray dawn breaking." The sky was overcast with that uniform dullness that presages a long gray morning, and the horizon was obscured by mist. The sea had moderated since the previous evening and was now down to about three-foot swells, still out of the northwest, with little chop. There was no sign of land.

The *Linda Niña* was still on a northerly heading, dipping gently over the swells, surging steadily ahead at perhaps four knots. The wind was holding at fifteen knots out of the northwest. I stood in the hatch for a few minutes, enjoying the coolness of the morning breeze and appreciatively watching the operation of the self-steering gear. It was primitive, but it worked. The boat would slowly come about to a few points east of north, and then the wind would take hold of the vane, which would swing slowly over to starboard. After a moment or so, the rudder would start moving to port; the wheel would rotate, as though swung by ghostly hands; and the *Linda Niña* would slowly come back—north northeast, then north, and gradually a few points further west, until the wind would catch the vane again, a bit short of northwest, and the procedure would reverse itself. The whole cycle would take several minutes. It makes for a slightly ragged course, due to the time lag in the wind vane overcoming all the friction in the steering cable system; it is undoubtedly far more responsive when mounted directly on a free tiller. But it sure beats sitting at the helm all night, I reflected.

Awake by now, I rustled up some hot water for coffee, and thought about navigation while breakfast was heating up.

The sky was obviously not going to allow any morning sun shots, so I calculated a rough seven o'clock position based on the D.R. position from the previous evening. The heading during the night had been reasonably constant, varying from north northeast to north northwest, with the oscillations of the self-steering, but averaging roughly north. Speed was, as usual, something of a guess-timate, but I felt that four knots would not be too far off, and calculated accordingly. The result of these machinations, which took only a few minutes and did not quite leave me feeling like Bowditch, placed the *Linda Niña* at about 17°40' North, 109°20' East. In more prosaic terms, I was about forty miles south of the island of Hainan. Reviewing my earlier theoretical course to Hong Kong, it was evident that I was zig-zagging somewhat. (In retrospect, it would appear that I *zagged* a bit too much, but of course one never knows these things at the time.)

By the time I had finished breakfast, cleaned up the debris, and emerged into the cockpit for a morning smoke, it was nearly eight-thirty. The morning mist was clearing by now and, rather suddenly it seemed, land materialized over the horizon to the northeast.

As the mist continued to dissipate and the distant mountains became clearer, I judged them to be roughly thirty miles away. All things considered, the dead reckoning estimate had not been too far off after all. I felt mildly pleased. It's always nice, navigating alone on a boat, to come out more or less where you'd thought you would be, irrespective of how questionable the navigation procedures are. At any rate, the land was undoubtedly Hainan.

The sudden appearance of Chinese territory, which could conservatively be considered in the category of a "hostile lee shore," gave grounds for a reappraisal of the situation. Should I sheer off to the east immediately, or continue on the present course for a bit longer? I mulled over this question as the *Linda Niña* surged northward. I was reluctant to turn east, since my headway would be considerably reduced with the wind on the quarter, and the course downwind would require constant attendance at the helm. On the other hand, I was presently making good time to the north under self-steering. I finally decided to let things lay for awhile, and to beat closer to Hainan before changing course.

By about ten the mountains over the horizon had become ominously clear, and it appeared to be about time to start heading east, to keep a minimum of twenty nautical miles between me and the People's Cultural Revolution. I went back into the aft cockpit and freed up the wing nut on the self-steering gear, and then went forward to set the jib to windward with a preventer. With the self-steering disconnected, the *Linda Niña* headed into the wind and rocked on the swells while I tied down the jib. I got back into the cockpit and, after a bit of jiggling with the mainsail, headed her around to the east. The northwest wind was now on the port quarter and had eased off to about ten knots. The seas had gone down a bit further, to about three-foot swells, and the *Linda Niña* settled onto her new course at three to four knots.

I fiddled with the self-steering for awhile, in hopes of getting at least a modicum of control from it, with little success. The relative wind from astern was inadequate to hold the vane downwind, and as the boat wallowed in a swell, tipping to one side or the other, the vane would flop uselessly in the direction of gravity. The need for a counterweight became painfully obvious, since the weight of the plywood alone was more than sufficient to overcome the slight wind pressure. I doubted that it would have been effective even with a counterweight, however. If it was to work at all on a downwind course, it seemed that I would need a rather large, light, and well-balanced windvane, with minimal friction in the system. Even then perhaps it wouldn't work, with light winds and with any kind of sea running. I finally gave up, and returned to the helm.

Shortly before noon I spotted two ships in the distance to the northwest. They appeared to be running together in tandem, heading westward, and were about five miles to the landward side of me. Patrol boats? Fishing vessels, towing a net? I felt the first tinges of apprehension. As they passed to the north of me, I put the binoculars on them, but they were too far away to spot any details. They appeared to be a few hundred feet long, with unremarkable fishing-trawler-like profiles. Not warships, at any rate, or official-looking patrol boats. Both vessels continued on to the west, apparently ignoring me, and eventually disappeared over the horizon. I relaxed again.

(Looking back on it, about this time I should have set my course due south, set the self-steering, fired up the outboard full blast, and started paddling with my hands! But again, one never knows these things until later.)

By noon I was passing south of the southernmost point of

Hainan Island. I scanned the chart carefully, and tentatively identified a few of the more recognizable peaks. I got out the small hand pelorus, took sights on several of the peaks and a few high islands that fringe the coast, and got a fairly good fix on my position. Although I didn't check the exact distance with the dividers at the time, I roughly eyeballed it as being somewhere between fifteen and twenty miles from the coast. Certainly well outside of Chinese territorial waters, which I understood to extend for twelve miles.

I passed the southernmost point of Hainan and continued toward the east. The coastline of the island started to recede to the northeast; by noon we were at least twenty miles from the coast, and widening the distance with every additional mile we made good to the east. I went in to heat up lunch in fits and starts, climbing back into the cockpit frequently to adjust the helm. I had it lashed down with an adjustable slipknot, but the fixed setting would not hold the boat on course for very long going downwind. As soon as the wind varied a bit or a heavy swell was broached, the *Linda Niña* would rapidly swerve off course. The arrangement would work for about thirty seconds, though, which was ample to permit me to duck into the cabin, open a can of C-ration boned chicken, dump it into a saucepan, and jump out into the cockpit again in time to grab the helm. After five or six such forays into the cabin I was starting to feel like a jack-in-the-box, but lunch was about ready. It's surprising what you can do in thirty seconds if you're hungry.

I ate in the cockpit, using one foot to keep the helm on course, and took another look at the chart. We would continue on about another 120 miles to the east, then alter course to north northeast for another 280 miles or so, and we would be entering the Fragrant Harbor, as the Chinese somewhat euphemistically refer to Hong Kong. It would take about five days, with any kind of winds and no typhoons. Mentally I enjoyed a light Chinese supper, five courses or so, and a stroll along Nathan Road in the twilight, admiring the bright lights and well-filled cheong sams. It would be pleasant to get to Hong Kong after a week at sea. I would moor at the Yacht Club, take a cool shower, get into some clean clothes, and then have a cold beer....

These pleasant meanderings were interrupted by my sudden realization that the vessels that I had seen previously were in sight again, this time traveling eastward, and this time ominously further offshore! *Choi oi!* I squinted into the horizon, and got out the binoculars again, but there was no question about it—they were coming east, and this time they'd be coming a lot closer to me.

My earlier apprehensions returned, only partially offset by a slight optimism based on the fact that they had seen me earlier and had not bothered me. Also, I was now no closer to Hainan than I had been the first time they spotted me, and was widening the distance every moment. On the other hand they were definitely coming a lot closer, and their return in tandem seemed to spell "patrol" of some kind, although I still nourished faint hopes that they were trawlers hauling a net between them. Well, there wasn't much I could do about it at this stage. Perhaps they would again ignore me and go away.

By two in the afternoon, however, they not only showed no signs of going away, but had drawn a few miles astern, and were steadily closing on me. They appeared to be doing about ten knots. As they drew closer, I found myself looking over my shoulder with a species of forced casualness, like the driver edging the speed limit on the parkway looking back at the approaching motorcycle cop in the rear-view mirror.

As the time went by, I felt a growing feeling of apprehension. The outer vessel had now drawn directly astern of me and was cutting over to seaward in order to come up on my starboard side. It drew slowly abreast only a few hundred yards away. I was starting to mentally sweat; things were not looking up at all. I could see the vessel clearly now. It was about 150 feet long, of general fishing trawler shape, and painted black. Splashed all over the pilot house and along the sides of the ship were gaudy red posters, covered with yellow Chinese characters. Quotations from Chairman Mao, I presumed.

For the next few minutes, developments occurred with startling rapidity. The ship suddenly slewed in closer—a few hundred feet, then a hundred feet, and soon no more than fifty feet off my starboard side. They had slowed down to match my pitiful three or four knots, and were now almost alongside.

All of a sudden the deck seemed to be swarming with men! There were probably not more than a dozen or so, but at the time it looked like the Jubilee Year crowds in St. Peter's Square. They were all gathered against the rail, shouting and gesticulating at me. We were eyeball to eyeball for a few long minutes. Well, I thought, there goes the old Hong Kong trip. What did they intend to do? Who were they? They were a rag-tag looking lot, and bore no apparent stamp of officialdom. Fishermen? Pirates?

In one of these gestures that later make you think you must have been a bit mad at the time, I picked up my camera and took a picture of them crowded against the rail, shouting.

Things suddenly became warmer. A lot of armament appeared, including several submachine guns, and a number of rifles were pointed my way. This was starting to get serious. By now the vessel was even closer, and the crew were waving their arms angrily and making motions with their hands in the general direction of Hainan. Our two vessels were now proceeding closely together, no more than twenty feet apart, at a placid four knots, and I could hear their angry shouting above the muted throb of the trawler's idling engines.

I had thoughtfully taken down the American ensign that morning, realizing that I was in the general vicinity of Hainan and feeling that some discretion might be indicated in these quarters. Since the *Linda Niña* had a Latin name, I decided to try one more expedient before giving up. I ducked into the cabin and rummaged through the flag box, coming up with a Singapore flag. I had been looking for the Philippines, but I guessed Singapore would do. I came back on deck, waving the flag in the air, and shouted in Spanish:

"Hombres, qué quieren? Porque me están fregando la vida? Voy para Hong Kong en mi bote..." pointing hopefully eastward, *"... de modo que dejen de ser idiotas y déjenme en paz!"* This was all roughly equivalent to *Why the hell are you bothering me?* and delivered in somewhat vulgar Spanish on the assumption that nothing would be understood anyhow. I will have my little joke.

Well, it all went over like a lead balloon, as the saying goes. The shouting went on; the gestures became, if anything, more emphatic; the rifles were aimed more pointedly, to create a Tom Swiftie. I was obviously getting nowhere with this Spanish bit. Perhaps not surprising; after all, who ever saw a Spaniard with a crew cut? I couldn't think of anything else to come up with, and meanwhile they were growing more frenetic in their motions and I was afraid that at this rate there would be a couple of rifles popping off before long. So I stopped playing dumb and gestured questioningly towards Hainan.

"*Ustedes quieren que vaya hacia Hainan?*" There were emphatic gestures—*YES!*—and angry nods of assent.

Well, I thought, I guess that definitely does it. Towards Hainan. After a moment of reflection, mentally bidding adieu to Nathan Road and well-filled cheong sams, I went forward to free the preventer from the jib; the *Linda Niña*, helm freed, swung into the wind and stopped. I came back to the helm again and got her headed back on a northerly tack. The wind had shifted to a bit south of east, and she picked up rapidly to about five knots on her new heading. I trimmed the sails, steadied her on a northerly course, and sat back to await developments. After a moment I ducked in the cabin and got a cigar, and came back to the helm and lighted it up. When it's inevitable, you might as well enjoy it. I puffed away philosophically.

The trawler had meanwhile swung around and was following a few hundred yards away on my starboard quarter. The sister ship had come up and stationed herself on my port quarter. In this manner, a somewhat incongruous troika, we headed back towards Hainan.

I had some time to think, and spent it in dismal reflections and speculations. If I had only turned south when I had first spotted the trawlers earlier in the morning! If I had only gone to Manila after all! If I had only... but these were pointless reflections, water under the bridge, and I was mildly annoyed with myself for spending even this much mental effort on such thoughts. The past was definitely water under the bridge; the question now was, what would happen next? Even this was somewhat fruitless speculation, but at least marginally more worthwhile than useless reflections as to where I would be now if I had followed some happier past alternative.

I reviewed what I knew about Red China, which wasn't very much. In a previous year, an American yachtsman had gone off course on the Manila to Hong Kong race and had run aground in

China. As I recalled, they had treated him reasonably decently, and had released him and his boat after a week or so. For all the ideological excesses of the Red Chinese, I could not recall any instances where they had been accused of inhumane treatments or atrocities to Westerners. Of course, there were those brainwashing stories from North Korea—but were those Chinese or Korean in origin?

I mulled it over for awhile, with no conclusive results, finally settling into a wait-and-see attitude tempered with a reasonable degree of optimism. Since I was obviously not a spy and had no aggressive intentions, I could not really bring myself to believe that they would do more than interrogate me for a few days before turning me loose. As a matter of fact, it bore distinct possibilities of becoming interesting, providing I didn't get myself shot.

About this time, things got a bit warm again. The trawler on my starboard quarter drew close by, and the crew were again shouting and pointing rifles. I noted the vessel had no name; only a number —212—painted on the bow. The other vessel was numbered 203.

There were more gestures. Apparently I was not quite on the right course. I altered course a bit more westward, but they continued to make angry motions. As far as I could see, I was following the course being indicated. After about five minutes of this, punctuated by nerve-wracking pointing of rifles with intent, I got exasperated and frustrated and finally dropped the helm, climbed up on the roof, and shouted at them:

"For Christ's sake, what do you guys *want*? I'm already going the way you're pointing!" There was understandably little reaction to this outburst, aside from a more enthusiastic chorus of angry gestures and more rifle waving. I climbed angrily down into the cockpit again, and wrenched the helm even further to westward. Apparently I got onto the right course, since the commotion subsided and Trawler 203 dropped back to station.

Hainan was still a considerable distance away—perhaps fifteen miles—so I settled in for a long ride. I ducked into the cabin again briefly and got a can of fruit juice and a C-ration packet of cigarettes, and sat in the cockpit drinking the juice. I was going to keep the can but then thought to hell with it, and chucked it overboard, speculating whether I would later be indicted for cluttering up the clean waters of the People's Republic of China with imperialist garbage.

Mayday, Mayday 129

    I suddenly thought of the little emergency radio that I had in the cabin. The present circumstances might reasonably be considered an emergency. Would it have sufficient range to reach the Gulf of Tonkin from here? I felt sure that it would; the Gulf was only 100 miles away, and it seemed likely that the radio was designed to cover that range. I ducked into the cabin again, took the radio out of a locker, and returned to the cockpit holding it concealed against my leg. I brought out some cookies at the same time, and sat munching for a few minutes, to give an excuse to anyone watching with binoculars for my entering the cabin. The trawlers had by now dropped back an appreciable distance astern, perhaps a quarter of a mile or so.
    I pulled out the antenna surreptitiously, held the radio out of sight against the mizzenmast, and keyed the transmitter button.
    "Mayday, mayday, mayday!" I said. "Does anyone hear me?" I repeated this several times, and turned the set to Receive. There was no response, aside from the dry crackle of static.
    I keyed the transmitter and tried again, with the same results. I wondered how the battery was. There was a spare in the locker, but I was reluctant to stretch my luck by going into the cabin again to get it. Could it be that they could hear me, but that the receiver was not strong enough to pick up the response at that distance? Since the radio was, after all, designed to bring help, and not to engage in friendly chats at long distances, I thought it at least possible. I keyed the transmitter again, and reported:
    "Mayday, mayday, mayday! This is Dave Steele, an American, on the thirty-two-foot sailboat *Linda Niña*. I am near the south coast of Hainan, in position approximately eighteen degrees, zero minutes North, one hundred nine degrees, thirty minutes East. I have been captured by the Red Chinese, who are forcing me to go to Hainan. I am being forced to go to Red China. If anyone hears this, will they please report to the American Embassy. Mayday, mayday, mayday!"
    I repeated it twice for good measure, more or less along the same lines, and switched back to listen again on Receive. Again, no luck. I set the radio for beeping transmission, and laid it on the seat, hoping that someone had monitored the transmission. It seemed unlikely that F-105's would come roaring in over the horizon within the next half-hour, like the Cavalry rescuing the settlers from the

Indians, but at least those concerned might know what had happened to me in the event of undue delays in my arrival at Hong Kong.

About an hour after I had been forced to change course to Hainan, the trawler came abreast again. This time it appeared that they wanted something else, and after a long exchange of gestures—angry on their part, perplexed on mine—I finally gathered that they wanted me to take down the sails and put on the outboard engine. Maybe they thought we would go faster? I obligingly let go of the helm and let the *Linda Niña* come up into the wind and rock placidly on the swells while I went forward to drop the main and jib. I furled them up, and lashed them carefully to their respective booms. The Chinese could wait, and I certainly wasn't in any big hurry to get anywhere.

I climbed back into the aft cockpit, pumped the gas bulb, and yanked on the cord, and the Evinrude started at the first pull. We were soon under way again. I wondered what improvement they had expected. Either under sail or on the outboard, we made about five knots, so it was six of one, half-dozen of another. We continued to the northwest.

By four in the afternoon, Hainan was well in view, perhaps ten miles to the north. It was obvious that I had been a good twenty miles off the coast when apprehended. I wondered what the Red Chinese considered "territorial waters." I had assumed that these extended twelve miles from the coast, but it appeared that they were flexible in this respect. Maybe they considered territorial waters all the way to the Paracels. Or, more likely, territorial waters were any place that a Chinese vessel happens to be at the moment and there aren't any other big ships around.

About this time, the trawler came abreast again, closer yet, and I saw that they were now beckoning me to approach them. I turned the *Linda Niña* towards the trawler, which was now on my port side, a few hundred feet off to one side and a bit forward of my beam.

Glancing again at the Chinese vessel, I got the shock of my life! The crew were all lined up along the starboard rail, pointing rifles at me with intent. There were no gestures now; just a bunch of rifles resting on the gunwales, taking careful aim as I approached. On the afterdeck, a .30-caliber mounted machine gun was being slowly swiveled about to bear on me. Up at the prow, a man was carefully detaching a hand grenade from a string of a half-dozen grenades.

All of this I took in with one heart-stopping horrified sweeping glance as I approached the trawler from the starboard side. The vessel was closer now—eighty feet, seventy feet, sixty—as the *Linda Niña* approached at a shallow closing angle, making about five knots.

I felt, with solid certainty, that I had less than a minute of life remaining, and it was one hell of an unpleasant sensation! The realization transcended mere fright; it went into a wholly different category of emotion, which is difficult to describe and which I hope I never have to experience again.

In retrospect, alive and well and comfortably distant from China, I have often looked back at that scene—it was indelibly etched in my mind—and asked myself whether I was justified in the feeling of certainty I had at the time as regards my impending demise. And yet, I think no Westerner of sane mind could have drawn any other conclusion. I was obviously alone, a single-handed sailor in an innocuous thirty-two-foot sailboat. On the Chinese vessel, there were at least a half-dozen rifles aimed carefully at me, plus a .30-caliber machine gun, plus grenades held ready. It could point to only one conclusion: they had drawn me safely within Chinese territorial waters, and were now going to riddle me and destroy my boat. With what rationale, I could only dimly speculate. The rationale seemed a bit academic, in the circumstances. I only knew, to the very depth of certainty, that I had less than a minute to live, as my boat slowly approached the trawler.

I had idly wondered from time to time what people think about as they are about to die, and now I was finding out the hard way. I expect the thoughts must vary considerably with the individual and with the circumstances, but they probably all come down to the same basic theme. *What the hell am I doing here?*—at this time and in this particular place, about to die? What horrible and inexorable chain of events has led up to this moment? It doesn't seem right or reasonable, that my life should be ending in this meaningless, ignominious way. There was a lot left that I wanted to do.

Around the foregoing basic emotions flitted a host of other

thoughts, as the *Linda Niña II* slowly but inexorably approached the trawler, and what I believed to be her own demise as well as mine. I fleetingly recalled occasional past nightmares and how relieved a feeling it had been to wake up. This time I knew it was no nightmare, and there would be no waking up to safe reality in a warm bed. I remember, too, feeling a distinct annoyance that I would be disappearing and that no one back in my Western world would ever know what had really happened to me. It would be assumed that I was lost at sea.

One small corner of my mind considered briefly the merits of diving over the side, but it seemed pointless. So I remained rooted at the helm, staring at the trawler as I approached and waiting for the guns to start winking. What does it feel like, I wondered, when bullets start thudding into you? Is there any pain, or only a numbing shock, which quickly fades away into unconsciousness?

Closer, closer, and still no shots, and dimly out of the haze of awaiting execution I realized that they had indeed not yet shot me; that they were starting to make increasingly urgent gestures to the effect that I was going to collide with the trawler; and that, by George, I bloody well *was* going to collide with the trawler!

CRUNCH!

I had come slowly out of the haze and belatedly swung the helm hard to starboard, but too late; the port float of the *Linda Niña* collided with the steel hull of the trawler with about three tons behind it moving at five knots. The front tip of the float forward of the first frame snapped neatly off with a grinding rasp of sheared plywood, and dropped off into the water. The *Linda Niña* slewed up alongside the trawler, losing headway, bumping against the hull of the larger vessel in the heavy sea. Jets of water shot up between the two hulls as the *Linda Niña* rose and fell on the swells.

I was still in a sort of mental shock. I had been absolutely certain that I would be dead within a minute, and this does something to one's mind that it takes a little while to snap out of. I doubt very much that there has been much medical research done on the subject. It would be rather tough on the volunteers, and impractical to stage realistically.

Four or five Chinese swarmed aboard from the trawler, dragging ropes, and several of them grabbed me. One in particular I will never forget—he had a mean brown face, topped with hair sticking up wildly in the air, and had one wide-open milky *glass eye*! It gave his face a lopsided insane look. The others were no models for cigarette ads either.

They clutched me and hustled me toward the trawler, bundling me over the rail. The freeboard of the trawler was about four feet higher than the *Linda Niña's* deck. Hands reached down over the gunwales to haul me up and over onto the deck of the trawler. Meanwhile, the *Linda Niña* was bumping and banging against the hull of the trawler in the heavy sea. Thinking of that $3/8$-inch plywood, I half-automatically turned to push against the mainmast shrouds, to get the boat away from the side of the trawler. However, angry hands grabbed me away from the gunwales, and pushed me forward onto the foredeck to an open space next to the main cargo hatch. Several men stood surrounding me, with rifles and submachine guns trained on me.

They were a nondescript lot, dressed in ragged clothing. They were all fairly quivering with emotion and rage, although what I had done to provoke this display had me puzzled. I was kind of emotional myself, in the circumstances. They made gestures for me to put up my hands, which I did, clasping them over my head to ease the strain on my arms. I was dimly aware, out of the corner of my eye, that men were boarding the *Linda Niña* and making her fast to the side of the trawler with ropes.

After a moment or so the excitement seemed to subside a bit, and the men gestured for me to sit down on the cargo hatch. Several men then approached cautiously and searched me, coming up with a meager haul: a handkerchief, a few cigarettes, and a pack of matches. Somewhat surprisingly, they carefully wrapped the cigarettes and matches in the handkerchief, and one of them made gestures to the effect that these would be held safely and returned in due course. Happily, they didn't take my watch.

I sat on the hatch for a few more minutes. The emotional temperature went down by a few more degrees, and I was permitted to put my hands down. Four or five men continued to guard me closely, while others boarded the *Linda Niña* and started carrying objects aboard the trawler. I noticed a number of recognizable items being shuttled in this manner—sextant case, tape recorder, life preservers, charts—before being prodded to my feet again and led forward to the forecastle in the prow of the ship.

They indicated that I was to enter the forecastle and remain there. I went through the hatch and descended about five steps into a triangular compartment in the bow, and sat down on one of the bunks. A mean-looking Chinese sat on a box outside the hatch to keep guard, armed with an equally mean looking submachine gun.

Things quieted down for awhile, and I could relax momentarily and take stock. I was still alive, at any rate, although the incidents of the last ten minutes had left me extremely shaken up, and with my heart thumping.

But I was still alive.

10 / *Trawler 203*

I took a long breath and looked about the forecastle.

I was in Red Chinese hands, unquestionably. At the front of the forecastle was a large picture of Mao Tse Tung, benignly waving a hand to the grateful masses below.

The forecastle was triangular in shape, about twelve feet long by ten feet wide at the after end, where the central hatch opened onto the cargo deck. Along each side of the compartment were four wooden bunks, two pairs upper and lower, end to end, built against the side of the hull. Along the side of each bunk were painted what appeared to be quotations from the Great One, and on the hull behind each bunk there was at least one picture of Chairman Mao plus several posters covered with Chinese characters that I took to be more quotations.

At the left end of the forecastle, flanking the hatch on either side, were wooden lockers, painted bright red and imprinted with yellow characters. More quotations, I assumed. They were really gone on quotations.

The forecastle was floored with rough boards. Overhead, bare wires crisscrossed the ceiling to several bare light bulbs hanging at random locations. An electric fan was mounted in the forepeak, just under the picture of Mao. Overall, it was reasonably clean.

I sat for awhile on the bunk, mulling over the situation. What a scare they had given me! My pulse was still pounding along at a good clip. But I had not been shot after all; I was here, still alive. *Je pense, donc je suis.* I wondered by what margin I was still here, thinking, instead of floating lifeless in the South China Sea amid the ruins of a shattered trimaran.

From time to time I could get a glimpse of the mast of the *Linda Niña* through the open hatch. After awhile I stood up cautiously, as if to stretch my legs, and moved about the forecastle a bit. The guard shifted his feet, freshened his grip on the machine gun, and eyed me warily, but made no objection.

Standing, I could see out the hatch. By now they had taken the *Linda Niña* in tow, and she was heeled over at a steep angle. I remembered with a sudden shock that I had knocked a piece off the bow of the port float when I had collided with the trawler; I had forgotten all about it in the excitement. The float was of course filling up with water. I wondered how she would take to towing in that condition. The starboard float was already well out of the water, and the *Linda Niña* was heeled over a good thirty degrees. It was something of a shock to see the starboard float completely out of the water, indecently out of her element and exposing the bright red antifouling paint, with the keel fin waving in the air above the water.

Although still more concerned about *my* immediate future than that of the boat, I reflected ruefully that for the moment things were not going well for my *Linda Niña* either. A year of back-breaking effort and a substantial investment in money, and I had gotten to sail her, how much, two weeks or so? And now here she was, one float waving out of the water, the other wallowing drunkenly in the swells of the South China Sea. How long would she last?

These reflections were interrupted by the arrival of several of the crew, who came down into the forecastle. The air of belligerency that had existed a half-hour before had dissipated, and now they busied themselves with minor errands about the forecastle, either completely ignoring me or at most glancing from time to time with no particular animosity.

The Foreign Devil seated on the forward bunk must have presented an uninspiring example of Western culture. Not having expected company at this stage of the journey, I was still barefoot and clad in an old pair of shorts and an ancient sport shirt. The shorts had originally come into existence as a pair of khaki pants, the legs of which had later been amputated roughly with a pair of scissors. All in all, I cut a rather unprepossessing figure.

After awhile one of the men offered me a half-full pack of cigarettes and indicated that I could keep them. Another got down a thermos bottle hung on a rack by the bunks, and poured a cup of hot water for me. He gave it to me with signs that I should drink. It seemed odd to be drinking hot water. I had always thought the Chinese to be a nation of tea drinkers. Maybe they thought I didn't like tea? Emboldened by the somewhat friendlier—or at least more neutral—atmosphere that seemed to be developing, I leaned over and wrote the character for "tea" on the floor with a finger: 茶, accompanied by a questioning glance.

It just goes to show you never know when something is going to come in handy. For the last year or so I had been studying Japanese in my spare time, and in the course of so doing had taken the trouble to learn the Hiragana and Katakana syllabaries and, to date, about three hundred Kanji. Since the latter are essentially identical to those used by the Chinese, a fair amount of written intercommunication is possible. (A reasonably well-educated Japanese could not read a Chinese newspaper, but could certainly get the gist.)

My calligraphic effort on the floor of the forecastle evoked some spirited discussion. After a bit one of the crew left the forecastle and returned a few minutes later, carrying a handful of tea in a piece of newspaper, which he unceremoniously dumped into my cup of hot water. I made appreciative noises, and spent the next half-hour sifting tea leaves through my teeth, wondering whether perhaps I shouldn't have left well enough alone.

Meanwhile, however, another man had dug a piece of chalk out of a locker, and he now squatted by my side and wrote on the floor in careful Chinese: "What nationality are you?" They all huddled about, awaiting my answer.

I mulled over the implications of my response for a moment, weighing the pros and cons of an honest answer. I doubted that American stock was very high in the People's Republic at the moment. On the other hand, they would eventually find out anyway. Finally I thought to hell with it, and wrote the characters for "Beautiful Country" on the floor: American. There was no particular reaction.

One of them then wrote what appeared to be "How old are you?" but when I wrote "39" they looked puzzled, so I figured we'd reached the end of our rope, vocabulary-wise. They tried one more sentence, but this one was well outside of my modest fund of Kanji, and after poring over it for a moment I had to shrug and give up, so we abandoned the game.

After awhile I looked out the hatch again to check the status of the *Linda Niña*, and this time my spirits really fell; she had overturned completely! The red hulls were bottom up, awash in the sea, and several men in life jackets were clinging to them. This really dejected me, and for the first time I began to seriously face the possibility that my boat was truly lost and gone. I stared glumly out of the hatch, mentally visualizing the time spent, the construction problems encountered and solved, the long building process, board by board. It was a substantial investment that I had put into that boat, physically, financially, and emotionally. And here she was, bottom up, in unfriendly hands, in the South China Sea. Well, perhaps it was a more vivid demise than rotting away years hence in a boatyard somewhere.

Through the hatch I could see the crew members accumulating on the foredeck to turn in their weaponry. Rifles were unloaded, shells carefully replaced in bags and bandoleers, and all of the arms and grenades were carried aft in armfuls, presumably to be stored until the next American came along in a trimaran, or some equivalent international incident. A couple of men appeared to be having problems getting the shells out of their rifles, and solicited assistance. The arms appeared for the most part to be of elderly World War I vintage, although the submachine guns looked lethally modern.

I mentally shook my head, wryly, reflecting on the use of all of this armament to capture one lousy thirty-two-foot sailboat and one man. By the time the crew got back, the whole thing would undoubtedly be magnified into something approaching a major encounter with the Seventh Fleet. I could imagine the reports flowing into Peking from Kwangtung Prefecture. The valiant coastal militia of the People's Republic has triumphed again. *Choi oi.*

The late afternoon wore on, and the trawler continued cruising slowly off the coast of Hainan. After awhile the *Linda Niña* was no more to be seen, and I wondered whether she was still afloat and being towed, or what. Later a crewman came down into the forecastle and made gestures to the effect that she had sunk! I found it difficult to believe, and continued for a long time to hold out hopes that she was still afloat and repairable. For the time being, however, I gave her up provisionally and turned my thoughts to what was likely to become of her owner.

The call of nature finally asserted itself, and I indicated to the crewmen that I had to urinate. They discussed this development for awhile, Committee-fashion, and eventually reached a favorable decision in my behalf. I was allowed to go out the hatch onto the foredeck, and was carefully herded (if one man can properly be "herded") over to the starboard rail near the cargo hatch where I had been sat shortly after capture. The gunwale looked a bit high to squirt over, but as I was about to have the old college try at it they gestured that I should kneel down and aim through the scuppers. I did so; and it sure is awkward, kneeling. Also, the presence of a submachine gun a foot behind my head was psychologically uncomfortable, giving persistent rise to mental images of kneeling to receive the coup de grace. It was not the most pleasant relief I've ever had, by far.

I returned, sans ballast, to the forecastle, and sat to await nightfall. The trawler continued to motor about, from time to time slowing down, and I could hear shouting from the deckhouse, apparently to the sister ship. It appeared they had no radio communications. Once they stopped for awhile to haul in a large net, and then continued on patrol. During this period I briefly spotted another vessel, which appeared to be forty or fifty feet long, and looked like an official patrol boat of some type. This gave rise to momentary hopes that, in spite of the rag-tag appearance of my captors, there was some official backing underlying it all.

Toward nightfall I grew more pessimistic, however, as to my chances of surviving the night. By the time it got late, I had convinced myself that it was only a matter of time, and lay on the bunk waiting for them to come and get me. If the prospect of violent demise on short notice is unnerving, perhaps it is even worse when you have a lot of time to sit around and think about it.

After the initial numbing shock just prior to capture, the next few hours had buoyed up my spirits appreciably, if only for the simple fact that I was still alive at all. But after this initial period of optimism over heaven-sent reprieve had worn away, I grew increasingly convinced that the reprieve was only temporary.

I spent a lot of time considering the pros and cons and weighing probabilities. The debit side of the ledger seemed to outweigh the credit side by an uncomfortably substantial margin. I wondered: Were these people official, or were they fishermen-cum-coastal-militia, or were they just plain fishermen addicted to a bit of casual piracy on the side?

The first alternative was rejected almost immediately; they wore no uniforms, and there seemed rather little of the disciplined atmosphere that is normally associated with official organizations.

Although I hopefully tried to convince myself of the second alternative, there appeared to be too many things that militated against it. First, why did they overwhelm me with such a degree of angrily brandished armament, far out of proportion to the incident? It seemed to betoken spot piracy rather than organized and disciplined militia action. Second, why did they start carrying items off my boat as soon as she had been brought alongside? Third, why did they show such a lack of concern for my boat, which was certainly a substantial bit of property, and could easily have been maintained afloat with any effort at all? And last, why did they not bring me to shore and turn me over to the proper authorities rather than cruising about into the night? Even more basically, why hadn't they simply continued to drive my boat on into port in the first place, where I could be taken in hand by the shore authorities, rather than having initiated the pointless encounter and boarding at sea?

There were a few factors on the credit side, but at the time they seemed irrelevant compared to the cumulative weight of the foregoing. They were not unkind to me, once captured, and provided hot water (complete with tea leaves), cigarettes, and food. However, I could readily rationalize this as being final acts for the condemned man. Hence, as night wore on, I sweated in my bunk, ever more convinced that at any moment a hard-eyed little contingent would arrive, haul me purposefully out onto deck, and chuck me to the sharks.

Supper arrived shortly after nightfall. A generous plate of food was brought down into the forecastle, consisting of a cooked flounder-like fish floating in a grayish pasty sauce, accompanied by several hard-boiled eggs sloshing about alongside. The tail of the fish drooped tiredly over the edge of the plate, and one eye stared listlessly up at me. It was enough to make you flip your lunch just to look at it, much less eat it. I picked at it, nonetheless, and managed to nibble away half an egg. The fish was absolutely unapproachable. The men made encouraging gestures for me to eat, but I rubbed my stomach with a wry look to indicate that I was not in the mood. Carrying the charades a bit further, I pointed to the machine gun in the hands of the guard by the hatch, and made sign language to indicate that if I were going to be shot in a few hours, it wouldn't make much difference whether I ate or not.

The men appeared to understand the point and shook their heads emphatically: *No, we won't kill you.* Slightly encouraged, I made a final effort at Kanji, and wrote on the floor: 我們行中国不行？ —*We go China, not go?* One man wrote back "go," or an affirmative answer. However I had worked myself into such a mood by this time that I really didn't believe it, and spent the next few hours on an empty stomach, awaiting the worst.

The mind is a remarkable instrument. It is amazing what you can talk yourself into, and the manner in which you can interpret circumstances in the light of preconceived conclusions. Having convinced myself of imminent demise, every little thing became interpreted in such a way as to bear out this belief. When loud voices were heard on deck, they were obviously arguing about the best manner in which to do me in. Clanking metallic sounds on deck were undoubtedly the weights being prepared for my feet, or other alternative and unimaginable arrangements.

Several men came down into the forecastle from time to time to light up odd-looking water pipes and suck at them for a few moments before going back out on deck. The water pipes were made of wine bottles, with a mouthpiece set into a cork in the top. A sort of pipe was mounted in a hole about a third of the way from the bottom of the bottle, which in turn was about half-full of water. The procedure was to put a pinch of rough tobacco into the pipe and light it, while sucking on the mouthpiece at the top. The smoke bubbled through the water and filled the bottle. The whole process lasted only a few minutes, through several pinches of tobacco, each of which had to be lighted individually, before the man went back on deck. Not having seen a device like this before, I started thinking in terms of opium, and wondering whether they were working up enthusiasm for an execution. I was really in a state.

Apparently they worked late on Trawler 203. Eight, nine, and ten o'clock came and went, and there seemed to be no diminishing of activity. Men came in and lay down in their bunks awhile, before arising again and going out on deck. About eleven they finally started settling in for the night, after washing up and brushing their teeth at what sounded like a pump on deck near the hatch.

The brushing of teeth gave me a ray of hope. Everybody knows only good guys brush their teeth.

If I can get through this night in one piece, I thought, maybe everything will turn out all right. I sweated for another hour or so, but there were no further developments, and finally about midnight I fell into a restless sleep.

11 / Red China

I awoke about seven in the morning. For a few moments I stared uncomprehendingly at the dusty underside of the bunk above and felt the unfamiliar rasp of rattan matting against my shoulder. Then the memories rushed back with a jolt as I realized where I was. No dream indeed; instead of the familiar comforts of my double bunk aboard the *Linda Niña II*, I was in the forecastle of a Red Chinese fishing trawler. *Mi madre*!

I sat up cautiously on the bunk. It was a pleasant morning. Sun filtered through the open hatch, and a light breeze was evident. I felt an overwhelming sense of relief. I was still alive and, having lasted out the night, the prospects were excellent for my remaining so.

The forecastle was quiet. One or two men were still asleep in their bunks; the others had departed. Another guard sat outside the hatch, machine gun cradled on his knees, eyeing me impassively as I arose, stretched, yawned, and took a few tentative morning steps about the forecastle.

The trawler had evidently come into a harbor during the night, and it was now quietly moored, engines silent. Land was visible nearby, and a number of vessels could be seen at anchor in the harbor, including what appeared to be several large freighters a half-mile or so off in the distance.

As I stood watching, a large ocean-going junk went sliding majestically by, a few hundred yards to starboard, under full sail. It was one of the very big ones, three-masted, which are seen only in China: a colorful Terry-and-the-Pirates type of junk. In other circumstances, how interesting it might have been to board it, explore it, and inspect the rigging. But at the moment, unfortunately, my tourist status was uncertain.

Presently several men came down into the forecastle, bearing breakfast, which consisted of a cup of hot water and the identical fish from the previous evening, warmed over. It had the same glassy-eyed stare, the same tail drooping despondently over the edge of the plate.

It was a measure of my buoyed spirits that I actually had a go at it this morning, in spite of its discouraging demeanor. I got about a quarter of it down before my enthusiasm flagged. Actually, it wasn't anywhere near as bad as it looked.

Shortly thereafter, a smallish launch pulled up alongside the trawler and tied fast. It appeared to be a local launch for ferrying crew members ashore, and at the same time appeared to be selling various sundries. Several of the crew returned shortly with soap, cigarettes, and other items. One of them gave me a pack of cigarettes, which I received gratefully.

Breakfast, such as it was, over, I sat smoking appreciatively, feeling surprisingly optimistic about life in general, while awaiting further developments. My own mental attitude surprised me slightly. Only the day before, I had lost my new boat and had had the wits frightened out of me; this morning I was unshaven and relatively scruffy, without much to eat, and looking forward to God knows what sort of reception in Red China and some species of imprisonment for an indefinite period. And yet, I did not feel at all bad, and was looking forward with some interest, if not outright anticipation, to what the future would bring. Perhaps it was mostly euphoria brought on by relief over simply still being alive.

Analyzing my mood further, it occurred to me that much of one's mental attitudes at any given moment can be directly related to an awareness of present position as compared to possible alternatives. You can always work yourself into a state of mind to be quite grateful for who you are and what you are doing at the moment, if you put your mind to sufficiently horrible alternatives. Compared to a life sentence in Ossining, the most dreary office trap becomes a welcome citadel of liberty. The concept of a slow and agonizing end by cancer makes the trip to the dentist seem relatively pleasant. And an unexpected reprieve from a sudden and violent demise bathes all subsequent events, I concluded, in a sort of golden light.

And so I sat smoking philosophically, awaiting the morning's events.

Presently a group of people came from the launch and looked down into the forecastle at me. There was a lot of animated discussion with the crew members. It appeared that they had come to take me ashore. Several of them came down into the forecastle and motioned me forward. They seemed reasonably pleasant about it, or at least neutrally impassive. One of them had a long red blindfold, which they discussed at some length, folding it in various ways and trying it out on themselves to see whether it was peek-proof. It was an odd-looking blindfold—of irregular shape, red with white stripes criss-crossing it—and then it came unfolded for a moment, and I realized it was from the ship's flagbag—the Number 4 Numerical Pennant! I was to be blindfolded in fitting nautical manner.

Before being blindfolded, I felt the call of nature again, and made indications to this effect. A crewman brought a wooden bucket and some toilet paper. I squatted over it, resolutely ignoring the audience, and left a final offering for the crew of the good ship 203. It seemed an appropriate parting gesture, the final word, so to speak, and left me in even more improved spirits.

They tied the blindfold in place and led me, not ungently, up the steps of the forecastle and across the deck. I stumbled my way past the cargo hatch and over the gunwales, and carefully guided, felt my way down onto the deck of the launch and forward to what apparently was a cabin. A chair was procured and placed against the back of my legs; I sat. Presently the launch cast off and the engines revved up.

Being blindfolded is an odd sensation. I had played at it as a child, but this was something else again. I sat quietly, listening to noises about me, trying to picture the scene. I was aware of a feeling of utter helplessness, like a hooded falcon, subject to the whim of my captors.

The launch ride took about fifteen minutes. Then we were docking, and I was guided up onto a wharf and across a gravelly patch of ground to a waiting vehicle. Around me I could hear voices of people, including children. I reflected that I must have been an interesting sight. *Guess what we saw at the dock today, mommy.*

The vehicle appeared to be a small bus. I was helped in, and to a seat. The vehicle took off and drove for about fifteen minutes, honking continually. We went around corners and up hills, with the horn going all the time. It didn't sound as though there was much other traffic, so I wondered what they were honking at so much.

The vehicle stopped, and everyone got out, leaving me alone. I sat for five minutes or so. They came back and got me down. We walked for a few yards, and then onto a concrete floor and into some sort of room. A wicker chair was pushed against the back of my legs, and I sat down again.

For the next half-hour or so things were relatively quiet, although I could hear people moving about, low murmurs of conversation, and the occasional squeak of furniture. I could hear a woman's voice. It was all turning quite social. There were sounds of shuffling furniture. Then there was a sudden brief pregnant silence.

"What is your name?" a disembodied voice spoke out of the silence. It was a sort of shock to hear English, and to be communicated with directly after so long a time.

"David Steele," I said clearly. There was a silence, while they mulled it over.

"What?" my interrogator asked. "How do you spell?" I repeated my name, and spelled it out. There was some discussion in murmured Chinese.

"Ah...that is your fully name? Your complete name?"

"Well, actually my *full* name is David Joseph Steele. Joseph, that's jay,oh,ess...." It looked as though it might be a long day. There was a further exchange of Chinese as they passed this information around.

"Where did you come from in you boat?"

"From Vietnam."

"What was your last port?"

"Danang. Some people call it Tourane." There was a pause, and more conversation in Chinese. I could hear the woman's voice again, and the voices of at least two other people. It appeared that my interrogator was only a translator, and that someone else was posing the questions in Chinese.

Over the next half-hour or so they asked a bewildering variety of questions. Had anyone else been with me on the boat? Where had I commenced my voyage? What had I been doing in Saigon? Where had I built the boat? Who had helped me build the boat? How long had it taken? What kind of boat was it? Why was I sailing it to Hong Kong? Why had I come into Hainanese waters?

After awhile they found out that I could speak Vietnamese to some degree, which demonstrates how far-ranging their questioning was. As luck would have it, one of the men there spoke Vietnamese, and before I knew it I was fielding questions in Vietnamese as well as English.

"How long is your boat?" one interrogator would ask. "Thirty-two feet," I would say. Then the other would chime in: "*Ong, tai sao chung nao di Hong Kong, khong co cai visa?*" and I would answer in Vietnamese. Not infrequently his questions would exceed the bounds of my modest Vietnamese, and I would have to answer *khong heo*—I don't understand—and then there would be further chit-chat in Chinese and the question would be repeated in English. All in all, it was a rather odd interrogation.

After about half an hour of this, I got a little fed up with the blindfold, and asked them to take it off. This evoked a long discussion in Chinese. Finally they agreed, and carefully relocated my chair, presumably so I would be facing away from something highly strategic, which later turned out to be no more than the dusty compound outside the room in which I was. Then they removed the blindfold.

I found that I was in a smallish room, maybe ten by fifteen feet, with concrete walls and ceiling. To my back was a door in one of the narrow sides of the room, with a window on either side. In front of me was the back of the room, with a single window. The windows had wooden grills and screens, but no glass. Under the rear window were two small desks, back to back. At each desk sat a scribe, apparently transcribing the gist of what was being asked and answered. Peering in the back window were several wide-eyed urchins.

Along the side of the room to my right were two cots, with mosquito nets suspended above. On each cot were seated about four or five people, among them my interrogators. To my back I could feel, rather than directly see, the door, with windows at either side. There seemed to be people peering in the door and in the windows.

The people seated on the bunks were, for the most part, youngish, say, in their mid-twenties. They were dressed in a fairly uniform manner: unpressed light-colored shirts with long sleeves, unpressed cloth pants, and plastic sandals. About half of them had socks. Most of them had a Mao button prominently pinned to the breast pocket of their shirts: about the size of an I-Like-Ike button, but with the head of Mao cameo-like in gold, on a red background. They did not look either particularly friendly or particularly antagonistic.

My interrogator was a smallish clerk-like man, with balding head, glasses, and an unctuous look. He had an oily way of smiling after each sentence that made me detest him on sight.

Next to him sat a plump young woman, the one whose voice I had heard. She was the only female present, rather shapeless, and with rimless glasses that gave her a somewhat intellectual, prim look. She had cropped hair, and when she smiled she displayed small neat teeth with spaces between. I later learned her name was Miss Wu. There was something indefinable about her that made me think of her performing vivisection laboratory experiments, or playing opposite Vincent Price in an old horror movie. Perhaps it was my imagination in the circumstances.

At their side was a medium-sized Chinese of strong features, but otherwise unremarkable, who appeared to be the power behind the scenes, asking most of the questions in Chinese. I was to see a lot of him, subsequently.

At the onset, and several times during the questioning, the oily man counseled me to tell the truth, the whole truth, and nothing but the truth.

"If you tell the truth," he would say earnestly, "you will be treated leniently. But you must tell the truth! You must be..." he would pause, searching for the word.

"...frank," Miss Wu would chime in. "You must be frank." She would smile, with small neat teeth, spaces between, one frank soul communicating with another. I would assure them that I had every intention of being frank, which was quite true, since I had nothing to hide.

The questioning went on for another hour or so, and finally they got up to go to lunch. I had asked once or twice whether I could shave, take a shower, and get a change of clothes, and now reiterated this request. The translator said that my request "would be considered," which phrase I was to hear often in the future.

I also asked whether there was a British consul in the vicinity, or some other diplomatic representative that I could get in touch with, but got no firm response. They had a very shifty way of answering such questions; either they did not know, or would have to look into it, or it would be considered, etc.

They blindfolded me carefully before leaving for lunch, and left me sitting on one of the bunks alone, feeling a little ridiculous. These people were really neurotic about security. There wasn't a thing to be seen, but they like to play the 007 game to the hilt.

After awhile a man came in with food, and took off my blindfold. I sat at one of the desks and had a bite to eat. This consisted of heavy buns and a thermos full of hot milk—sickeningly sweet—apparently condensed milk in water, which I understand goes over big in China. The combination was enough to turn my stomach. I managed to get down one of the buns and about half a cupful of milk. I had a few cigarettes, dawdling over my milk, hoping that I could drag it out for awhile and avoid having the blindfold put back on. Happily, my guard (sans machine gun) was in this case a sensible fellow, and since there was absolutely nothing of any interest to be seen he kindly left the blindfold off. After awhile he even left the room and sat on a chair on the porch outside, leaving me alone. I took the opportunity to survey my surroundings a bit.

The room appeared to be one of a number of two-man rooms in a longish one-story barracks or rest-house of some kind. The rooms opened onto a roofed-over corridor running along one side of the building. Outside, there was a courtyard, dusty in the sun, with occasional bushes and sparse grass. Other similar buildings were grouped about in the near vicinity. They all had red Mao quotations plastered up and down the outside walls and on the pillars flanking the entrances.

Out in back there was another dusty yard, and a fence. Quite a few people were crowded about behind the fence, mostly children, and when I momentarily appeared at the back window of my room there would be a big commotion, and hands pointed in the direction of the Foreign Barbarian. Every now and then one of the more courageous kids would sneak through the fence, cross the yard, peer into my window round-eyed (or as round-eyed as Chinese can get), and run off shrieking. This went on, with variations, for most of the afternoon, and though amusing enough at first, it got to be a bit of a drag as the afternoon wore on.

Presently Miss Wu returned with pen and paper. She wanted me to write out my personal history, apparently from time of conception, in great detail. I told her I would be pleased to write up the history, but would appreciate the chance for a shave and a bath first, to get into good writing spirits. She smiled, gently insistent that I write the history first. I smiled and remained gently insistent on the shower first. Wu finally tired of the game and bugged off, after assuring me that my request for a shower and clean clothes "was being considered."

Later in the afternoon the group returned, and we went into further interrogation for an hour or so, before they left. My oily friend wanted to "borrow" my watch for "checking." I guess they thought I had some secret C.I.A. codes stamped on the balance wheel. I was most reluctant to release it, pointing out that I didn't want to lose it; that it had been (untruthfully) a present from my old Dad, since departed from this world, etc. They were quite patient about it, and promised that it would be returned to me. By when? I persisted. After a bit of conversation among themselves, they said it would be returned to me "before I slept" that night. Finally I gave it to them. (True to their word, it *was* returned to me that evening, still ticking.)

Toward evening, another small group came back, this time led by a newcomer, a small intense man who spoke English fairly well. "We will be *kind* to you," he assured me fiercely. I told him I was most appreciative. They brought toothpaste, a toothbrush, soap, and a safety razor. After awhile several more men came in and measured me for clothes. Presently they returned with an armload of them. Things were looking up.

Miss Wu returned briefly and had another go at the history bit. I still wanted a bath. We batted it about for awhile, ending in a draw. Before she left, a photographer came in. Miss Wu told me smilingly that they wanted my picture.

I was pleased to oblige, and tried to look as stalwart as possible in my scruffy state, waiting for him to ask me to say "cheese" or something. He was a strange photographer, though. He just stood, an embarrassed-looking young man, shifting his feet and fiddling with the camera. After awhile I gave up looking pleasant and relaxed for a moment, looking down at the floor. *Flash!* and he had taken a picture of me.

I looked up, startled, wondering why anyone in his right mind would waste film on a lousy shot like that. What kind of bum photographer was he?

After awhile I yawned, covering my mouth politely with a hand. *Flash!* another picture. I finally got the idea. I could now imagine my pictures in the *Peking Review*, the American Sea Pirate looking dismally down at the floor (in guilt) and covering his face (in shame) when confronted with the enormity of his crimes against the People's Republic.

I was careful to look pleasant and wide-eyed for the rest of the time. After awhile the photographer got frustrated and left, along with Miss Wu.

Presently the call of nature asserted itself, and I told my translator of the moment that I had to go. They led me out the door and down the corridor to a privy near the fence. I could hear people crowding against the fence and expected to see heads pop up over the wall of the privy at any moment, to watch the Foreign Devil urinate. But the guards chased them away.

Night fell, and they brought some more buns and hot water. After eating, I was escorted between the buildings to a sort of fountain in the courtyard, where I was allowed to bathe. I came back and put on the clothes that they had brought: a pair of underpants, blue cloth trousers, white long-sleeved shirt, and black plastic sandals. Someone brought a bucket of water, and I was allowed to shave. I felt like a new man. I brushed my teeth as well. The toothpaste was named *Guangdung*, after one of the Chinese provinces, and tasted appropriately like a blend of *guana* and *dung* until I had gotten used to it.

The small fierce man (actually not an unpleasant fellow) said we would be moving to another place, and apologetically advised that they would have to blindfold me again. They put on the same nautical blindfold, and led me out to a car in the yard. They put me in the back seat, and the car took off. We proceeded for a half-hour or so, honking. The blindfold got cocked over to one side at a sufficient angle so that by tilting my head a little I could see under it. There wasn't much to be seen. We seemed to be driving mostly through the countryside, and there were few street lights.

We finally arrived, and I was helped out of the car, and the blindfold was removed. We stood on a graveled path in front of a long villa. The building appeared to be about a hundred feet long, one story, and had a roofed-over corridor along the front onto which the rooms opened. There appeared to be a central conference room, or community room, opposite the steps in the center, and about three or four rooms on either side in the wings. They brought me to my room, which was the second to the right of the center.

After the previous accommodations, I immediately dubbed this the Hainan Hilton. It was not bad at all—a fair-sized room with two beds, a small table and chairs, and a desk; with an adjoining bathroom with washbasin, toilet, and bathtub. It was screened in, and the beds were fitted with mosquito nets. On the wall was a large picture of Uncle Mao, flanked by two posters in Chinese, presumably quotations.

I sat in the room for awhile, and then was summoned to the Conference Room in the center. Before I went, they asked me to put my old clothes back on again. Apparently they wanted more pictures.

Sure enough, our friendly photographer was there, fiddling with his camera. This time I was bright-eyed and bushy-tailed, and ready for him. I apparently looked too fresh to suit them. The oily one looked unhappy.

"You do not look tired enough," he complained. I heard it, and didn't quite believe it, but that's what he said. I shrugged regretfully.

I was careful to look pleasant, and not look down. When I yawned, I held it in and sort of choked it down under a wide-eyed open grin. The photographer shifted his feet and looked harassed. Finally he went through the motions of taking one or two standard poses, and left. I returned to my room, feeling as though I'd come out ahead on that round.

I turned out the light and climbed onto one of the bunks. It sagged, but otherwise was not too bad. I realized that I was quite tired. It had been a trying day, emotionally if not physically.

How long would they keep me here? I drifted off to sleep, wondering.

12 / *Twenty Questions*

As on the previous morning, I awoke with something of a jolt, in unfamiliar surroundings. It seemed as though I was waking up in some rather strange places these days. Oddly enough I had slept like a log, although the bed was not quite up to Hilton standards. Also, the pillow was a bit scrawny. I would have to speak to the Management about this.

Sunlight streamed through the screen door and window, and I could hear birds twittering outside. I got up, washed briefly at the basin in the adjoining bathroom, and went to the door to get a better view of my new quarters.

The villa appeared to be one of a number of rural rest-houses nestled among the trees, each surrounded by a large yard and garden, the whole area studded with palm trees. Flowering plants abounded, and the asphalt paths that meandered about the area were shielded by high hedges. The garden in front of my particular villa extended perhaps fifty or sixty feet out to the road. Birds flew among the palms, and bees and butterflies were active all about the flowering bushes of the garden. All in all, it was a pleasant atmosphere, apart from its political connotations.

A few men were in evidence on the front veranda of the villa. My awakening had been closely observed, and after a little while one of them came with a tray of breakfast, which he brought in wordlessly through the screen door and placed on the desk. There was a glass of hot coffee, one hard-boiled egg, and a piece of bread. After the last day or so of relative fasting, I was famished, and polished it off promptly. It tasted great.

After awhile the small intense fellow showed up, with a couple of nondescript companions who I gathered subsequently were local tailors.

"How do you feel?" he asked. I told him I felt fine, thank you. "Did you enjoy your breakfast?" he asked. I assured him that the breakfast had been very good, and in response to his next question, that I had slept well. We exchanged a few more platitudes, heavily scraping at the bottom of the conversational barrel. Finally, after pondering for a moment, he got down to more weighty matters at hand.

"I give to you," he announced with gravity, "a copy of *Quotations* from our Chairman Mao Tse Tung!" He reverently laid a small red book on the desk.

"Chairman Mao is red sun in the hearts of Chinese people," he explained. "You should read carefully what he say, and apply it."

I thanked him for the book. Actually, I had been looking forward to reading it, to see what all this Chairman Mao jazz was about. I had heard so much about this little red book that apparently carried such political and emotional significance over six or seven hundred million Chinese, and was interested to have a look at it.

It was a small book—about three by five inches, and about a half-inch thick. On the front cover was embossed "Quotations from Chairman Mao Tse-Tung," with a red star beneath. On the inside page it got right down to business, with the stirring exhortation "WORKERS OF THE WORLD, UNITE!" It looked as though it might be lively reading.

After I had tucked Chairman Mao carefully away in a drawer, the two tailors came forward to take measurements. The small man informed me that they were going to make some clothes for me. They inquired as to my preferences: Did I want my shirts with short sleeves or long? Pants long or short? Back pocket in pants?

I opted for short-sleeved shirts and Bermuda-type short pants. Regarding the back pocket in the pants, I pointed out that I didn't have anything to put in it anyway, so there didn't seem much point. They chuckled dutifully as the small man translated, leaving me with an embryonic hope that perhaps they had a sense of humor after all.

This business transacted, paper and pencil were produced, and I was again asked to write my life history. I tried to get a little more specific guidance on just how much detail they wanted, but the answer boiled down to "everything significant." This was a rather broad mandate, so I anticipated that it would take quite a while.

After the small man and the tailors had left, I spent the rest of the morning writing up my life history, with "everything significant" back to time of conception. It ran about fifteen pages when I was through. They appeared satisfied when I passed it over later. Since I never got any feedback on it, I assumed that there had been sufficient detail for their needs.

Lunch was mostly inedible, consisting of a bowl of greasy meat. I spent the early hours of the afternoon lying about on my bed and thinking philosophic thoughts about my situation.

At about three they came and took me to the central conference room, which I came to think of as the Interrogation Room. A stocky, pock-marked, but otherwise pleasant fellow named Chin came to fetch me, telling me to come along and to bring my Quotations. I wondered what was coming.

The Interrogation Room was a few steps down the corridor, and was the central room in the villa opposite the front steps. On either side of this central room there were three rooms strung out in each wing, each room with an adjoining bath and with two beds, a desk, etc., similar to mine.

The interrogation room was about twenty-five feet deep by about fifteen feet wide. As I entered, I saw that a long table had been set up across the back part of the room, where a number of people, presumably my interrogators, were seated. At each end of the table sat a man taking notes, similar to the scribes I had noted in the previous interrogation. To the left of the table sat the Chinese whom I had previously observed as being the power behind the scenes; next to him sat two translators. Along both sides of the room were a number of chairs for interested observers, of whom there must have been a dozen or so. In the very center of the floor, facing the table, was a wicker chair: the seat of honor.

I was led to the chair and seated; I sat, clutching my little red book and wondering what was going to come next. I felt nervous, to say the least, although the people in the room did not look particularly hostile.

Mr. Chin, the translator, opened the proceedings by referring to *Quotations*, somewhat akin to the minister referring to the Gospel. "Please turn to page seventy-two," he said. I obediently turned to page 72, and Chin proceeded to read the first quotation from Section VI, entitled *Imperialism and All Reactionaries are Paper Tigers:*

All reactionaries are paper tigers. In appearance, the reactionaries are terrifying, but in reality they are not so powerful. From a long-term point of view, it is not the reactionaries but the people who are really powerful.

> "Talk with the American Correspondent Anna Louise Strong" (August 1946), Selected Works, Vol. IV, p. 100.

Chin stumbled over a phrase or so, but on the whole read rather well. I listened impassively. "Did you understand?" Chin asked. I said yes and nodded assent. Throughout the reading the rest of the room was silent.

"Now turn to page seventy-six," Chin instructed. We read another little gem, which I was to hear oft-repeated during the course of succeeding interrogations:

U.S. imperialism invaded China's territory of Taiwan and has occupied it for the past nine years. A short while ago it sent its armed forces to invade and occupy Lebanon. The United States has set up hundreds of military bases in many countries all over the world. China's territory of Taiwan, Lebanon, and all military bases of the United States on foreign soil are so many nooses round the neck of U.S. imperialism. The nooses have been fashioned by the Americans themselves and by nobody else, and it is they themselves who have put these nooses round their own necks, handing the ends of the ropes to the Chinese people, the peoples of the Arab countries, and all the peoples of the world who love peace and oppose aggression. The longer the U.S. aggressors remain in those places, the tighter the nooses round their necks will become.

> Speech at the Supreme State Conference (September 8, 1958).

After each reading Chin would ask if I understood, and I would nod and say "Yes." After the second reading, Chin turned to the Leader, who then began to speak in Chinese. After every sentence or so he would stop and let Chin translate. He spoke for ten or fifteen minutes, mostly about the war in Vietnam and about the situation in Taiwan. As regards Vietnam, the gist of it was that the

Twenty Questions 157

United States imperialists had forced their way onto Asiatic soil and were killing the Vietnamese people and preventing the people from establishing their own government, for various imperialistic motives. He got pretty warmed up on the subject, and then switched over to Taiwan, where he had considerably more to say about the Chiang Kai-Shek "bandit regime" and the interference of the imperialists in assisting Chiang to keep the people in a state of submission, etc. After every sentence or two, Chin would ask if I understood.

Finally, political polemics over, Chin invited my attention to one final Quotation on page 267 from the chapter *Criticism and Self-Criticism:*

Taught by mistakes and setbacks, we have become wiser and handle our affairs better. It is hard for any political party or person to avoid mistakes, but we should make as few as possible. Once a mistake is made, we should correct it, and the more quickly and thoroughly the better.

> "On the People's Democratic Dictatorship" (June 30, 1949), Selected Works, Vol. IV, p. 422.

Apparently this particular Quotation was supposed to give me a message, namely, don't tell any lies! It was frequently read during subsequent interrogations, particularly during periods when they had indicated that they didn't believe some aspect of my story. Whereupon, we would turn to page 267 and read the same paragraph again, apparently in the hope that the Divine Word according to St. Mao would get through to me somehow and make me realize the error of my prevaricating ways.

Chin followed this up by advising that if I told the truth, I would be dealt with leniently; but if I told lies, I would be severely dealt with. With this ominous preamble, we launched into the interrogation.

To detail the questioning would take many pages. Imagine all the conceivable queries that might be asked about your life, your job, your background, and why you happened to be on a boat at any given moment near Hainan. They asked every one of them, and a whole batch more that you would never think of.

Initially, the principal questions concerned the basic background of the trip and the details of how I happened to be in Hainan waters when accosted. The meat of the interrogation on this first day (Saturday) concerned what I had done from the time I left Danang until I reached Hainan. The procedure was fairly consistent throughout. Chin would ask: "And what did you do next?" and I would say something like: "Well, I left the self-steering set so that the boat would steer roughly north, and I went to bed about eight o'clock. I slept all night, and when I got up in the morning the boat was still heading north. I got up about seven o'clock, and had breakfast. Then..." and I would notice Chin starting to hold up his hand, and I would fall silent. Chin would then think a minute, mentally translating, and turn toward the leader.

"*Tadze...*" he would begin, and then launch into Chinese for several moments, amplifying with gestures. The room would be silent as they all listened. I would sit, sweatily clutching my little red book, listening, and watching expressions. Chin would turn back and say: "And what did you do next?" and the routine would continue. I later asked what "*tadze*" meant, because I had heard it so much, and it appeared that it signified "he says," which sounded reasonable enough. Occasionally the Leader would respond with a few sentences in Chinese, and Chin would turn to ask a specific question with regard to my story.

Time went amazingly rapidly, and before I would know it, four-thirty had arrived, time for the hot-water break. I guess it's cheaper than coffee breaks. Chin would say "We are through for now. You may go to your room and rest," and I would rise from my chair and return to my room for awhile, until they called again. We would start again in about fifteen minutes; someone would summon me, I would return to my chair, with my little red book, and we would start again. While I was in my room they would sit in the conference room sipping hot water and discussing the previous session.

This went on all week, with minor variations. They would come to get me at about three in the afternoon, and the questioning would go on until about six thirty, with a fifteen minute hot-water break in the middle.

Although I was somewhat nervous during these interrogations, they were not all that nerve-wracking. In a sense, they were actually a sort of break after an otherwise dull day, and it was interesting in a way to see what questions they would dream up next. Although there were long periods when the interrogation would take the simple form of having me recite just what I had done over a given period, there were other sessions in which they took the offensive, plying me with long series of questions about my life, my job, my background, and the circumstances under which I had built the boat and embarked on my ill-fated voyage. These were not overly trying, since I had nothing to hide.

The week of questions and answers got to be a daily routine. I would wake up about seven in the morning, and when they saw I was awake somebody would go to the kitchen and get breakfast. The dining hall was apparently a hundred yards or so away; they always returned promptly. I would spend the morning reading or preparing one of the write-ups they were forever asking me to submit.

The reading matter was strictly non-fiction, although looking back on it perhaps there was a lot of fiction at that. I started off on the little red book, reading it once or twice to see what it was about. Later they brought me copies of the *Peking Review*, the *China Pictorial*, and most of the Mao pamphlets on various essays or lecturers that he had written over the last thirty years. Although it was rather interesting at first, after awhile it got pretty dull. There is a tremendous amount of repetition of ideological clichés; and although there was at the outset a certain amount of common sense and pithy philosophy in some of Mao's early writings, as related to down-to-earth goals and correction of abuses of the existing political/economic system in China, the wheat was soon buried under the chaff of out-dated Marxist ideology and fanatic polemics against imperialism, revisionism, and various other assorted -isms.

From time to time in the mornings various of my translators would drop in to have "free discussions" with the Foreign Devil, and practice their English. Most of these discussions degenerated into one-way polemics on various American aggressive acts, the abuses of imperialism, and the wanton and criminal acts being carried out by the imperialist lackeys of the United States, including the bandit Chiang Kai-Shek regime, the fascist Ne Win militarist regime in Burma, the oppressive Suharto regime in Indonesia, the Saigon puppet regime, etc. It seemed they didn't like anybody.

Sometimes, however, there were some relatively non-political discussions concerning such innocuous subjects as the price of shoes in the United States, but these were in the minority.

Lunch hour was about noon, at which time everybody would take off for the dining hall, leaving me essentially alone except perhaps for one individual sitting on the veranda to casually check on my presence. Later they even dispensed with this, and left me completely alone, free to wander about the yard. Mr. Chin injected a bit of practical psychology into the earlier discussions, pointing out that there were Red Guards in the vicinity and urging me not to wander too far from the villa, since they were inclined to be "emotional," and my safety might be endangered. He didn't have to tell me twice; I was in no hurry to wander.

After lunch I would take a nap until two or so, and at three they would usually summon me to the interrogations. About six thirty these would be over, and someone would bring supper shortly thereafter. By eight it was dark, and I went to bed, but I usually tossed about until nine or so when I could fall asleep.

The second day, Sunday, they went into more details of the background of my trip, and questioned me closely regarding my plans for the voyage; where I had obtained my visas, and what had transpired along the trip up the coast. They wanted a blow-by-blow description of everything that I had done and seen on my voyage up the coast, excluding trips to the john.

On Monday we went into the details of what we had done at Nhatrang, including a description of the Esso facilities there; what restaurant we had eaten at; and even the name of the bar we'd gone to. That morning they also asked me to write up a long treatise on the manner of determination of commercial oil products. I dutifully prepared one of about eight or nine pages, describing all the basic tests for identifying products (API gravity, color, ASTM distillation, flash points, etc.) and all the supplementary tests (sulfur, olefins, octane number, lead content, vanadium, explosivity, and numerous others) that I could think of for testing a variety of petroleum products.

On Tuesday they wanted a detailed description of Esso worldwide facilities. This was a tall order, but I finally got them to bring a big world map, and spent several hours in tracing countries from it onto a big piece of paper and listing all the Esso affiliates I could think of, from Arabia to Zambia. There are quite a few, and I kept thinking of more, so the whole thing took several hours, thinking sessions included. That afternoon they wanted a detailed description of our activities at Danang, which took most of the interrogation session.

Wednesday morning I had to make up a rough map, by memory, showing the route of the *Linda Niña II* up the coast of Vietnam and to Hainan, giving the daily positions as well as I could remember. Also they asked me to make up organization charts of the Esso organization in Vietnam and in Singapore. That afternoon we spent a large portion of the interrogation session describing the detailed routine for handling an ocean tanker when it arrives, including all aspects from Ship's Agency work, to Customs declarations, shipboard tests, discharging operations, shore tank gauging, etc. They were really going into detail, apparently, to see whether I was an executive with an oil company or not. They also got a detailed description of the last leg of the voyage from Vietnam to Hainan.

Thursday we covered a miscellany of details, including a sketch of the boat and a complete list, from memory, of every item aboard. Surprisingly, I could remember almost all of them, and the list ran for several pages. They were particularly interested in any harmful weapons that I had aboard, and I had to make a special sketch of the boat showing where these had been stored. Aside from the .38 Colt that I had in a locker and a .25 Star automatic stowed elsewhere, they considered "dangerous weapons" to include the flare gun and flares I carried, plus the kitchen knives. The way Chin kept referring pointedly to my "dangerous weapons" made me sound like Captain Kidd invading the peaceful coast of Hainan for rape and plunder.

On Friday and Saturday (the last day of the interrogation), they spent a lot of time on what I did when accosted. From somewhere they appeared to have gotten the idea that I had thrown something incriminating overboard when captured—presumably my secret C.I.A. codebook. In retrospect I have never been able to figure out whether this resulted from some zealous fisherman reporting the fact that I had thrown an object (empty fruit juice can) overboard while under observation, or whether they just assumed it to be the logical thing a spy might do and were grilling me to see whether I'd admit to anything. They kept implying that I was lying, and we read page 267 from Mao *ad nauseum*. Chin warned me that if I continued to tell lies I would be "severely dealt with," and urged that when I retired to my room I give the matter "further thought." They really bore down on this point during the last few days, and they had me sweating a bit. I racked my mind for any items that I might have thrown overboard, but all I could come up with was an empty fruit juice can, an empty packet of C-ration cigarettes, and perhaps a cigar wrapper. This was not very satisfying, apparently, and they continued to press intensely for more incriminating material. Since I could hardly make up something incriminating just to please them, I had no recourse but to stick to my story. Abruptly, they dropped the whole thing and never mentioned it again. I suppose it is one of their techniques.

The interrogations on the whole were not too unpleasant except for a few occasions when they wouldn't believe something I'd told them. For instance they found it difficult to believe that we had not been stopped for a thorough search and inspection while proceeding up the coast, although I pointed out to them that we were flying the American ensign and that a thirty-two-foot trimaran was hardly a likely vehicle for Viet Cong contraband. They were also sceptical of our having seen very few vessels of any sort while proceeding up the coast. A third point on which they gave me a lot of trouble was the fact that I had not obtained a visa for Hong Kong when I left Vietnam. I kept explaining that Americans didn't need a visa for visits of less than two weeks to Hong Kong. This was a fact that could readily be checked, but they continued to bring it up nonetheless. I could only conclude that they were hopelessly lacking in communications with the world outside of China. The other point on which they were skeptical was that we had left the boat unattended at Danang for long periods while away on errands.

On this last item I nearly got myself into hot water. They kept demanding to know how I could leave a boat unattended alongside a military dock at the Special Services beach without someone coming aboard to take something. I told them that the only people about were American G.I.'s using the beach for water-skiing; that there was a sergeant in charge who would generally keep an eye on the boat; and that at any rate American G.I.'s would not normally think of going aboard somebody else's boat without permission. This went back and forth, and they didn't want to believe it, so finally I advanced the admittedly tactless theory that perhaps they were tending to judge American soldiers by their own standards.

The translator translated, and then it hit the fan, as the saying goes. The Leader got red in the face and barked out a short intense phrase in Chinese. After thinking a moment, Mr. Chin turned to me and seriously said "Nonsense!" He then turned back to see what further the Leader had to say. He said plenty! It appeared that I had insulted the Chinese people, and he went on at some length, growing redder in the face as he warmed to the subject. I squirmed in my wicker chair and sweated. He was really sore. I determined to be more careful in what I said from then on.

About eight people were involved in these discussions. The chief interpreter was Mr. Chin, a stocky fellow whose face was heavily pock-marked, apparently by some past bout with smallpox. In general he was a sensible and amiable fellow, and to the extent circumstances permitted I rather liked him. Perhaps he, more than any other individual, made me actively deplore an ideology that could produce a basically nice fellow in most respects except for the shuttered mind, politically. I would have discussions frequently with Chin and he was uniformly pleasant and cheerful, even when disagreeing with me. But get onto the subject of politics, and he was a classic victim of Communist double-think, believing what the little red book and the *Peking Review* told him. It seemed incredible that a pleasant and intelligent man, who had had a university education, could believe hook, line, and sinker all the malarky they had fed him about life in the United States. I tried to explain what life there was really like, as objectively as possible, presenting the bad points as well as the good. We discussed the racial situation, and I frankly admitted that this was a problem, and would continue to be for some time; but that, considering social inertia in any (except an actively revolutionary) society, and considering that the Negroes were only five generations away from slavery, they had come a long way since 1865, and that civil rights progress within the last ten years had been impressive. According to Chin, however, they were all in a desperate state of oppression, which only revolution could correct. It was necessarily a highly qualitative discussion, and I was on somewhat weak ground; undeniably, the racial situation in the United States is a most unfortunate social phenomenon, irrespective of the gains that have been made in recent years, and there are sufficient examples of Bull Connors and Watts to maintain a lively awareness of this in other parts of the world. It is a tough point for an American to argue with a determined opponent. As I say, quantitatively Chin had an image extremely on the pessimistic side, but since directionally there was a fair amount of truth on his side, and since I didn't have much in the way of economical or sociological statistics to back me up, I couldn't get too far on this item.

On the general subject of the American people, he was really out in left field. Although I would admit to five percent average unemployment and poverty extending to possibly fifteen percent of the population, certainly the median American standard of living is the highest in the world. I provided some rough statistics on this, but Chin was unconvinced. He knew absolutely that the great majority of the American people were poor and oppressed, and nothing I could tell him could convince him otherwise.

The other members of the team were equally adamant, but also equally cheerful and pleasant in the discussions we had. Most of them appeared to be university students who had been drafted from whatever jobs they had at the moment to serve as interpreters/observers in connection with my detainment. They appeared to have rather unprepossessing jobs for university graduates; Chin told me he was some type of clerk in a shipping company.

Mr. Chuan served as interpreter on one or two occasions, and like Chin spoke English very well. I never ascertained his background, but one would think that he had served a hitch in the U.S. Navy, since he liked to use terms like "affirmative" and "negative" instead of yes and no. He was in his twenties, slim, dark-complexioned, and a rather clever fellow.

The rest were a generally unremarkable lot. Mr. Choo was small and nearsighted, with buck teeth that made me always think of Bugs Bunny. Mr. Huang was tall and wore glasses, and looked more Japanese than Chinese. Mr. Cheong was medium and unremarkable looking; he was the one that spoke Vietnamese, and he seemed to have appreciable political power in comparison to the

Twenty Questions 165

rest, who were mostly average people (to the extent that university students in China can be called average), drafted out of their jobs for the emergency with the Foreign Devil. Mr. Hong was a tall, good-looking fellow, shy, who never said too much. The remaining characters included the Leader, the handyman, the waiter, and Shao Lee, a pleasantly ugly little Chinese girl who cleaned up the rooms and served as general factotum about the villa.

Various of these people would be about the villa at any one time, doing miscellaneous odd jobs, washing laundry, or reading the thoughts of the Maximum Leader. At times in the morning I would emerge from my room to find several of them seated on wicker chairs along the corridor, absorbed in their little red books, mouths moving silently as they read.

In general I was very loosely guarded. The first day or so I remained prudently within my room, but after that I ventured out to sit on a chair in front of my door. No one objected, and after a few more days I made more daring excursions, partway down the corridor to sit on the steps in front of the conference room, or even down to the brick walkway in front of the villa to inspect some plants. Eventually I had the run of the garden in front of the villa, but further afield was taboo.

I had shaved again a day or so after arrival at the villa, but the safety razor had apparently been stamped out of old steel plate or had been previously used on somebody's legs, and the results left much to be desired. Partly due to this, but mostly for something to do, I started to grow a beard.

I spent many hours of the day thinking, lying on the bunk and looking moodily up at the picture of Mao on my bedroom wall. I was frequently tempted to draw a mustache on it, but never quite dared. Other engrossing occupations included frequent forays to the bathroom mirror to check progress on my beard, sitting in the wicker chair in the corridor fanning myself and looking out over the garden, and dreaming up a variety of James Bond-like escapes.

In the evening I took a bath in the tub. The water was pleasantly cool. Frequently they would turn it off during the day, and you could tell when it came on again in the evening by the rustling noises in the pipes. Surf's up! and into the bathroom I would go, to grab a bath, brush my teeth, or use the toilet.

The food was uninspiring at first, but got a bit better once they found out by trial and error what I would and would not eat. Breakfast was usually one small egg, a glass of coffee, and a piece of partially toasted bread. Sometimes the egg showed signs of embryonic development, discouraging further inroads, and I would then be hungry by lunch.

Lunch would be a bowl of rice (which I grew to rather like after awhile), three fried eggs, bread, a thin soup with pieces of beef floating about, and a bottle of beer. The beer, a good quart, made my day. I would drink sparingly during lunch, and save the rest for leisurely enjoyment along with an after-lunch cigarette. Supper was roughly the same except that meat or fish would be served instead of the eggs. All in all it was not too bad. When I ultimately left China I had lost about fifteen pounds, but five of these had probably already been lost during the week on the boat eating C-rations, so only ten could be attributed to the China diet. Physically, I felt fine, except for a backache I suffered during the first week until I got used to the sagging beds.

I considered the beer with lunch and supper a minor triumph of psychological counter-offensive. Initially they had expressed some concern over the fact that I was not eating much, and I persuaded them to give me a bottle of beer with the meals. I managed to give them the impression that I and most other civilized Americans drank a bottle of beer with every meal back in the West, where it was felt to have strong nutritional value. Apparently they bought the story and, not to be outdone vis-a-vis the imperialist West, thereafter provided a bottle with every meal to show that Chinese could be civilized too. I didn't have the conscience to press for a bottle with breakfast. They never appeared to drink any beer themselves, whether because it was too expensive or because they had simply not developed the habit I never found out.

So at every meal I got a bottle of Wu Yang Pi Jiu, or Five Goats Beer. Chuan explained in a social moment that Five Goats were involved in a folk legend of the Canton area, where the beer was made. For some reason Shao Lee never brought back the beer bottles with the rest of the dishes, but placed them on a little ledge running along the outside of the concrete balustrade at the edge of the corridor. After awhile I had built up quite a collection—twenty-three bottles, as I recall—before they were finally collected when we switched to another brand.

Twenty Questions

After awhile the Wu Yang Pi Jiu ran out, and I was reduced to drinking regular beer-bottle-sized (12 ounce) bottles of Tsingtao beer. It was most discouraging. However, we finally ran through the Tsingtao stocks, and thereafter returned to the more healthy quart size of Pearl River Beer. Apparently I was progressively exhausting their wine cellar, vintage by vintage. Toward the end they must have replenished stocks, for I was back on Wu Yang Pi Jiu again for the last week or so. It was pretty good beer. That was the first word I learned in Mandarin: *Pi Jiu*, beer.

Shao Lee was the little worker who kept the place swept and tended to the garden. She was a small girl, five feet or so tall, dark of complexion, with a pleasantly ugly face, flat-chested as a board, and with a large gold tooth in front. She would frequently giggle when I said something in execrable Chinese, and cover her gold tooth with her hands. She wore shapeless cloth pants and unpressed shirts like the rest, plus the usual sandals. Apparently she was married, for from time to time in the evenings she would bring her little daughter, age two or so, around to the villa. The little girl was a real sweetie, and would stare with big black eyes, at the bearded *gaijin*. She would take care never to get too close, though!

Shao Lee had one priceless possession, a bicycle, which looked new. It was black and shiny, and she would ride off on it occasionally for some errand. When she returned she would put it on a stand by the door and spend considerable time assiduously polishing every part with a cloth rag, before stowing it carefully away in the storeroom. The bicycle had a Kwangtung license plate on the back and a neat red placard on the front with some Mao quotation. The bicycle cost 120 yuan or so, which was undoubtedly many months' salary for Shao Lee, since even the university students told me that they only made about 40 yuan (twenty dollars or so) per month.

From the standpoint of recreation, the Hainan Hilton was somewhat lacking. The principal spare-time sport appeared to be reading from *Quotations*. In the evening, however, things would liven up, and the group would get together for their nightly card game, played on a rickety table under a bare lightbulb in front of the conference room. After the interrogation sessions were completed, at the end of the first week, they became relatively cordial and used to invite me to sit down with them to watch the card game.

They had a real ball, and played with the enthusiasm of a bunch of sailors, slapping down tricks triumphantly and moaning over poor cards. Particularly cunning finesses were carried out with great roars of glee.

They had one game that they played continually, which they called "one hundred points." It was a bridge-like game, or perhaps more like a cross-breeding of bridge and pinochle. Each round a different card was the joker—one round all fours, the next round all fives, etc. In addition there were two regular jokers. The cards that were temporary jokers counted for five points each; the jokers ten each; and each of the face cards counted five, for a grand total of 100—hence the name of the game. As cards were dealt the players would look at them, and the first player who got one of the temporary jokers in a suit that looked like a good bet for trump would turn the card over face up on the table, and trump would thus be established. They would then bid, by point, and the one who won the bid would take all of his partner's cards, pick out the best, discard an appropriate number into the discard (including point cards, if desired, to bolster up the final score), and then play against the other two players. The bidder had to get sixty points or more to win.

The first time I looked at the cards I did a double take, because the jokers had in big letters "PUKE" along the sides. It seemed like an odd way to name cards. I asked Chin and he explained that "poo-kay," as they pronounce it, is Chinese for "playing cards." I told him what it meant in English, with appropriate gestures, and he was amused. It still seemed like a hell of a way to name cards.

In the evenings the other mode of recreation, if one could call it that, was to listen to Radio Peking—straight from the horse's mouth, although I was inevitably reminded of other extremes of the anatomy. Usually they listened to the Chinese version, but once or twice they called me over and put on the English broadcast.

The English transmission is invariably conducted by a young woman speaking excellent English with a tweedy British accent. It sounded odd to hear these dulcet tones, immaculately correct and prim, carrying on about the American war criminals, oppression of the workers in Hong Kong, the fascist provocations of the Ne Win regime in Burma, etc., in a highly cultured monotone. One would have expected at the very least a touch of indignant emotion. But

Twenty Questions

she would drone on and on, tabling the latest imperialist atrocities in the manner of a housewife's program outlining the latest recipe for lemon meringue pie.

An American pilot had recently been shot down over Kwangtung province, which information one of the group had passed on to me earlier in the day. When Radio Peking announced this triumph of the People's Air Force, they chucked me almost playfully in the knee and said "See? Didn't we tell you?" See, Radio Peking just said it; that proves it. I didn't know whether they expected me to say that's nice, or what. I felt sorry for the poor devil they'd gotten hold of, and wondered how he was faring at the hands of the local Red Guards. I later learned that they parade the captured prisoners around at rallies. It must be nerve-wracking; by comparison, I had it good indeed.

One evening Mr. Chin announced a special treat: we would go to see a movie. The title of the picture was *The East is Red*, starring none other than that personality of screen and radio, our own Mao Tse-tung.

The picture started about eight, and several of the group led me to the hall, which as it turned out lay only a few hundred yards away among the paths and palm trees. We proceeded with the aid of a flashlight and soon arrived. The hall was a sort of auditorium, utilized for various recreational purposes. Inside a number of folding chairs were set up with sixty or seventy people awaiting the big event. I had not seen so many people since I had arrived in China, and it was a bit overwhelming. Special seats were reserved in the first two rows and we proceeded to them, followed by the fascinated stares of sixty-odd pairs of eyeballs. I eyed them nervously, assessing the reaction, but there seemed to be little visible antagonism, just curious interest.

We sat down, and after a few moments the murmur of the crowd stilled and a man stood up in the front and barked out a few words, apparently a rallying cry of some kind. They all responded enthusiastically with a shout. He barked a few more words and everybody stood up and launched into three choruses of "The East is Red." It made the hair prickle at the back of my neck; there was something a little frightening about the fanatic strength with which they all bellowed out this Communist national anthem.

We sat down again, and as a warmer-up (apparently having no

Mr. Magoo cartoons on hand), they showed a twenty-minute slide show of cartoon-like pictures depicting various scenes of worldwide workers from various countries reading Chairman Mao, accompanied by spoken commentary over a loudspeaker. The commentator was apparently describing how these people's lives had been enriched by the revelations bestowed upon them by the gospel according to St. Mao. Then they played some music, and finally we got to the main feature.

The East is Red was apparently made at the October 1966 celebration in Peking, in commemoration of the October 1917 Russian Revolution. It was held in Tien Men An square in Peking. The film consists mostly of crowds roaring, people surging by the reviewing stand, waving their little red books, tears streaming down their cheeks in emotion as they pass the reviewing stand and see their beloved Leader. The camera switched around from crowd to crowd, with frequent cuts to the stand, where the Great Man himself stood, looking tired and waving benignly to the populace from time to time. Lin Piao, Mao's second-in-command, made a speech; he speaks funny Chinese, and sounds a bit like a frog croaking. This went on for half an hour or so, and I wondered when the plot would start, but apparently there was no plot. Practically the whole movie consists of views of people waving their red books and cheering, and Mao, and more people, and Mao again, *ad nauseum.*

"See," Mr. Chin pointed out to me, "they are crying because they are so happy to see Chairman Mao." I grunted. "Chairman Mao is the red sun in the hearts of the Chinese people," Mr. Chin explained. I said uh-huh. The picture went on and showed the Red Guards marching into Peking, tearing down the street signs and replacing the Old with the New. Later, they showed the firecrackers in Tien Mien An square and evening fireworks, and then Chairman Mao sitting on the grass and conversing with the common people. Mr. Chin pointed this out as an example of his great democratic spirit.

At first, every time Mao appeared on the screen people in the audience applauded, but after awhile they apparently tired and gave up, because he appeared so much. Finally the picture ended, and we rose and wended our way out of the hall, past the curious eyeballs, and back to bed. It had been interesting.

Twenty Questions

On Saturday the barber came around. Apparently they have one come about every two weeks to give haircuts, and one by one everyone climbs on the stool for a haircut and shave. They don't have much in the way of beards, so they get a dry shave at the same time, including what fuzz has accumulated on the forehead and around the eyebrows. They offered one to me too, so I said what the hell, and mounted the stool just to be one of the boys. It cost 26¢ of a yuan, which would work out to about 10¢ in United States currency. Considering the outrageous prices you have to pay in barber shops these days, this did not seem bad at all. This is what the U.S. economy needs, I thought, a good five-cent cigar and some Red Chinese barbers.

My beard was well along by this time, and they urged that I have a shave as well, but I desisted. It would probably be about the most work he'd have had to do for 26¢ in a long time if I had acceded. He started to cut off one sideburn in the course of shaving down the side hair and I caught him too late, and went around for the next few days with an odd empty space in front of one ear.

Then came Sunday, and the interrogations magically ceased. A noticeably more relaxed atmosphere started to prevail. I commenced to speculate about the possibilities of early release.

But as it turned out, I was to be around for a bit longer.

13 / The Thoughts of Mao

The next few weeks were a bore. I almost missed the interrogations, which at least had provided a break in the daily routine.

Every day seemed to be about the same, with nothing on Sundays worthy of note. I would rise about seven-thirty, eat breakfast, and amuse myself as best I could until lunch. After lunch I would usually take a nap, until two or so, and then await supper, which arrived about six. Bedtime would be about seven-thirty or eight, but I would usually kick and thrash until nine or ten, when I finally fell asleep, listening to the boys out in the corridor guffawing over the nightly card game, and to the rasp of Chinese music from the radio in the next room.

Meals were the high point of the day. Aside from assuaging hunger, it was something to *do*. The menu followed the standard established during the first week: coffee, egg, and bread in the morning; rice, eggs, and beer at noon; and rice, meat, and beer in the evening. Sometimes they introduced a scintillating note of variety by serving the meat at lunch and the eggs at supper. It was not up to Four Seasons fare, but it was edible. I don't know how the calories checked out, but on the other hand I sure wasn't burning up much energy.

Needless to say, I spent a lot of time just thinking, much of this in the form of speculative daydreams about James Bond-type escapes. I was by now very loosely guarded, and often not guarded at all, particularly when everybody was away eating. At night there was a sleepy fellow who sat about on a chair in the corridor, but I could easily have made it out the back window of the bathroom.

There was a single window in the wall about seven feet above the floor, accessible by standing on the edge of the tub. It was glass, and hinged at the top, with a simple locking device that could be opened from the inside. The screen over the outside appeared to be similarly hinged and closed with only a hook and eye. It would have been simple to climb out without making much noise.

The sea was not far away, apparently to the south. Occasionally I could hear the mournful sound of foghorns. If I were ever to get out of Hainan, it would obviously have to be by sea. My Walter Mitty-ish mental endeavors usually envisioned the getaway in two forms: by small boat or by ocean freighter.

In the small boat episodes, I would slide out the back window at night, shortly after midnight, to gain maximum time under cover of darkness to reach the coast. The coast was an unknown distance away, but I presumed it was reasonably close—a few miles at most. I would carry along a thermos of water and a supply of bread, hoarded from the daily rations. Once reaching the shore, I would search out and steal a small fishing boat. Hoisting sail, I would endeavor to get far enough away from the coast so as to be beyond pursuit by dawn. I would steer southwest until hitting the Vietnam coast. With any sort of luck, it could be done in about two days. Finally would come the moment of deliverance: the American patrol boat picking me up, clinging to the mast like a Virgil Partch character; bearded, tongue hanging out, etc. Alternatively, I would land on the coast somewhere near Danang, and come staggering dramatically into the Esso office.

With two weeks to sit and think, I really did justice to it, and worked out a multitude of complicated plots, hairbreadth escapes, and technical details, in Technicolor yet. The various routes traversed to the sea were beset with an array of human and natural obstacles; fishing boats were heisted under an admirable variety of adverse circumstances; and the perils encountered in the crossing to Vietnam were many and diverse.

All of these exploits were comfortably carried out from my wicker chair in the corridor, or lying in bed, but they made life interesting and occupied the time.

The ocean freighter alternatives were predicated on the assumption that there must be a fair-sized port in the vicinity, visited by international freighters trading with Red China but not necessarily hostile to Westerners. Two sub-plots developed, depending on whether the freighters were anchored in the harbor or moored to piers. Principal problems encountered in these escapes were getting aboard, requiring in the case of the harbor (Case I) theft of a suitable small sampan, and in the case of the pier (Case II) a means of getting past the dock guards and Customs controls undetected. In one of the latter I made it disguised as a coolie carrying a bag of wheat. Just the technicalities involved in getting to look like a coolie carrying a bag of wheat could easily take up half an hour of thinking time, although I don't recall how I ever solved the problem of getting rid of my beard. (They had taken back the razor blade once it became evident that I wasn't going to use it.)

Ultimately I undoubtedly would have made some sort of effort to escape, had it appeared that I was going to remain in China indefinitely, but I would probably not have arrived at this point of desperation until many more weeks or perhaps even months had passed.

A fair amount of pensive time was also dedicated to thoughts of what I might have done had I been able to foresee events, say, a day beforehand. This was, of course, thinking of the most wishful variety, but it occupied more hours. I also thought a lot about how it would be when I was finally released; how I would feel; and what the reactions of people on the Western side—particularly my friends—would be to my tale of capture, confinement, and release.

Opportunities for physical activity were limited. I started keeping a small calendar under the glass top of my desk, marking off the days as they passed. *Glass top of my desk*—it evokes images of executive suites, but the desk was a small battered thing, with a scratched-up piece of glass that more or less fit the top. The remaining furniture was of the wicker type, equally battered but serviceable. The beds—both of them—sagged disastrously.

Back to my calendar, I would make a mental goal of the following weekend, telling myself that surely before that time they would have finished their "investigations" and released me. When the appointed time had come and gone, I would take it ruefully and start thinking about the next weekend. I also had a small diary that I was maintaining on slips of paper, one for each day. They had left me a pencil and some extra paper, in the course of preparing the various write-ups that they had demanded, and had let me keep these for use in studying Chinese. Toward the end of each day I would surreptitiously scribble a summary of the day's events on a half-sheet of paper, fold it up, and add it to the growing collection that was accumulating. I kept these papers casually tucked away in a pocket of an old pair of pants hanging on a hatrack, and they escaped detection.

During the day I would spend a lot of time sitting out in my wicker chair, feet up on the balustrade, fanning myself idly and looking out over the garden. After awhile I developed an interest in the flora and fauna, and used to make daily rounds of the garden to see how things were going. There were many large land snails about, and I would watch them climb slowly about the plants and trees. There were also many birds, and occasional squirrels. The flowering bushes attracted a variety of insects and butterflies, of which there was one particularly common black variety that laid eggs on the bushes. After three days the eggs would hatch into $\frac{1}{8}$-inch long caterpillars, which ate voraciously. I followed a couple from little fellows to strapping youths of a half-inch or so, but then the rains would come and wash away my charges, and I would start following up a new batch. It was something else to do.

During the second week that I was in Hainan, most of the original group departed, and I was left with only two newcomers, the Leader, Shao Lee, the handyman, the waiter, and Mr. Cheong, the one who spoke Vietnamese. Mr. Cheong would occasionally drop around for a chat, but the discussions were never on a very sophisticated level due to the limitations of my Vietnamese. Our communications would therefore generally be restricted to comments on the weather, the food, how I felt, etc. I would ask him whether he knew when I was going to get out of there, but all I could get out of him was *"ong sap di,"* or "soon," which although directionally encouraging was a little too qualitative for satisfaction.

From time to time I broached the subject of representations to some sort of foreign diplomatic agency in Hainan, but without success. I presumed there must have been some sort of consulates in Hainan, whether Swiss or English or Scandinavian, I had no idea, but there must have been *something*. However, all my inquiries met with evasion in one form or another. I daresay it was all highly illegal, by international standards, but the Red Chinese seem to be well known for making up their own rules in this respect, as evidenced by their attitude toward international water limits. There was obviously nothing I could do about it.

Aside from the matter of diplomatic representation, I prevailed upon them to at least let my company know that I was alive and being held in Hainan. I pointed out that by now I was long overdue in Hong Kong, and people would be presuming me dead. Undoubtedly searches would have commenced by now. At the beginning of the first week they seemingly acceded to this request, and took down the names of the general manager and terminal superintendent in Hong Kong, both of whom were personal friends. They allowed me to write a short note to the general manager, informing him that I was alive and well, and being well treated, and would undoubtedly be released in due course as soon as the People's Republic (the use of the term "Red Chinese" is frowned upon in Red China) had completed their investigations. I was assured that these messages would be passed on. (Unsurprisingly, when I finally was released, no one in Hong Kong had ever received them.)

In the middle of the second week, two newcomers arrived: Mr. Yee, a small, prim man who spoke English well and wore rimless spectacles, and a tall beanpole-like man with a small head perched atop the longest neck I have ever seen on man or beast. Yee introduced himself to me and we even shook hands, getting off to a friendly start, although later he used to become sulky when I asked him leading questions. The thin man spoke no English, but appeared to have political influence, since he spent a lot of time talking with the Leader. Otherwise, he was pleasant and friendly.

Yee took to dropping by in the morning to chat, and at my request, for want of something better to do, started teaching me Chinese. After my previous battles with the linguistic intricacies of Vietnamese, Chinese was not particularly difficult, although it has a number of sounds that I had never encountered before, except perhaps in a fit of sneezing. Nonetheless, I could imitate them well enough to manage communication. By the end of a week or so, I had learned about a hundred key nouns and verbs (the grammar is negligible), and could manage basic and vital sentences like "When are we going to eat," or "Please bring some cigarettes," or "I'm going to bed." Similarly to when I had been in Vietnam, the local natives got a big kick out of the round-eyes' attempts to speak Chinese, and Shao Lee would break up and cover her gold tooth with her hand. On particularly hilarious attempts she would use both hands.

My discussions with Yee were not always pleasant, because I was growing impatient with the delay and would inevitably end up asking him leading questions, like when I would be getting out of there, and he would withdraw into his shell and become primly sulky. This in turn would annoy me, and we would sit for long periods in silence, looking moodily at our respective fingernails. Yee would always answer that I would be out of there "sooner than I expected" or that I "would know later," as if this gave me anything of value. I kept pressing him for information regarding the fate of the boat, and whether it was still afloat and repairable or not, but these inquiries would meet with the same evasive answers. He would say simply that "there was no chance of repairing the boat," which was information of a sort, but would refuse to clarify exactly what had happened to it, whether it had been beached, or what. It was all most frustrating, and I fear I took my impatience with the whole situation out on Yee.

In the evenings, I would usually watch the card games for awhile. The Leader had become quite sociable now that the interrogations were comfortably past, and he would invite me with gestures to pull up a chair and watch the cards. He seemed to be a rather pleasant fellow, after all.

With a few exceptions like Yee (whose attitude was perhaps an understandable reflection of my own), the Chinese who formed the group at the villa were not unpleasant people, ideology apart. I suppose it is the same the world over; once you get to know people a bit, they tend to be much the same. I think that what impressed me most favorably, relatively speaking, about this group was the way they all got along well together, despite what was obviously a substantial disparity in background and education. No one put on airs, no one seemed to dominate the conversations, there were no loudmouths, no wise guys. I never once saw what remotely appeared to be a real argument between them, although there were differences of opinion. Of course I may well not have had anything approaching a fair statistical sampling of Chinese as a whole; probably quite the contrary. Judging from what I have seen regarding the Red Guards, etc., there are obviously rowdies and hotheads, although to what extent this is a result of ideological drives overriding their usual social behavior is hard to say. At any rate, this particular group was fairly pleasant, once interrogation week was past, and I think most of them would have been considered reasonably nice people, once transplanted out of their ideological framework and into a less politically impassioned society.

And so the two weeks passed, slowly.

During this period I spent a fair amount of time reading the various pamphlets and magazines that were provided. All of them were of course rabidly pro-Mao and highly political, sometimes to the point of nausea. Looking back, there was quite clearly no attempt to "brainwash" me in any way, aside from an occasional casual lecture on how great the Chinese political system was. As regards all the Mao literature and periodicals, it would appear that this was about the only reading material they had around in English. Obviously, they felt that it was all very worthwhile reading, and presumably hoped that I would find it equally rewarding.

The Little Red Book was interesting, representing as it did the Bible of Red China, and I read it several times. It is an odd mixture, consisting of selected excerpts from Mao's speeches and writings over the last thirty years or so, obviously carefully chosen (much of it undoubtedly out of context) to present a relatively organized series of statements designed to cover the various phases of political ideology with which every young Marxist-Leninist is supposed to be familiar. You might call it a policy manual, and it is evidently intended to be used in this manner. Presumably, whenever any sort of problem arises for the politically oriented Chinese, whether with politics, economics, or an intransigent wife, the answer can be found somewhere in *Quotations from Mao Tse-tung*.

After the frontispiece, there is (inevitably) a picture of the Great One, looking benign. After that comes a page of what appears to be doodlings by somebody trying out a new ball-point pen, but which is in fact a short foreword written by Mao's second-in-command,

Lin Piao, exhorting the masses to "study Chairman Mao's writings, follow his teachings, and act according to his instructions." The foreword, also written by Lin Piao, is perhaps worth quoting, since it reflects well the general flavor of everything that I read while I was there:

Comrade Mao Tse-tung is the greatest Marxist-Leninist of our era. He has inherited, defended, and developed Marxism-Leninism with genius, creatively and comprehensively, and has brought it to a higher and completely new stage.

Mao Tse-tung's thought is Marxism-Leninism of the era in which imperialism is heading for total collapse and socialism is advancing to worldwide victory. It is a powerful ideological weapon for opposing imperialism and for opposing revisionism and dogmatism. Mao Tse-tung's thought is the guiding principle for all the work of the Party, the army, and the country.

Therefore, the most fundamental task in our Party's political and ideological work is at all times to hold high the great red banner of Mao Tse-tung's thought, to arm the minds of the people throughout the country with it and to persist in using it to command every field of activity. The broad masses of the worker, peasants, and soldiers, and the broad ranks of the revolutionary cadres and the intellectuals should really master Mao Tse-tung's thought; they should all study Chairman Mao's writings, follow his teachings, act according to his instructions and be his good fighters.

In studying the works of Chairman Mao, one should have specific problems in mind, study and apply his works in a creative way, combine study with application, first study which must be urgently applied so as to get quick results, and strive hard to apply what one is studying. In order to really master Mao Tse-tung's thought, it is essential to study many of Chairman Mao's basic concepts over and over again, and it is best to memorize important statements and study and apply them repeatedly. The newspapers should regularly carry quotations from Chairman Mao relevant to current issues for readers to study and apply. The experience of the broad masses in their creative study and application of Chairman Mao's works in the last few years has proved that to study selected quotations from Chairman Mao with specific problems in mind is a good way to learn Mao Tse-tung's thought, a method conducive to quick results.

We have compiled Quotations from Chairman Mao Tse-tung in order to help the broad masses learn Mao Tse-tung's thought more effectively. In organizing their study, units should select passages that are relevant to the situation, their tasks, the current thinking of their personnel, and the state of their work.

In our great motherland, a new era is emerging in which the workers, peasants, and soldiers are grasping Marxism-Leninism, Mao Tse-tung's thought. Once Mao Tse-tung's thought is grasped by the broad masses, it becomes an inexhaustible source of strength and a spiritual atom bomb of infinite power. The large-scale publication of Quotations from Chairman Mao Tse-tung is a vital measure for enabling the broad masses to grasp Mao Tse-tung's thought and for promoting the revolutionization of our people's thinking. It is our hope that all comrades will learn earnestly and diligently, bring about a new nation-wide high tide in the creative study and application of Chairman Mao's works and, under the great red banner of Mao Tse-tung's thought, strive to build our country into a great socialist state with modern agriculture, modern industry, modern science and culture, and modern national defense!

He becomes a little emotional toward the end, with that exclamation point.

I studied Mao's thoughts with care, and with a specific problem in mind, namely getting out of Red China, but I couldn't seem to find a pertinent Quotation.

Aside from the Little Red Book, other absorbing reading put at my disposal included six months' back issues of the weekly *Peking Review*, a number of issues of the monthly magazine *China Pictorial*, and a collection of pamphlets dealing with various essays and speeches by Mao Tse-tung.

The *Peking Review* is a particularly rabid little journal, averaging about thirty pages. The following is a random sample from August 25, 1967:

> Peng Teh-huai and His Behind-the-Scenes Boss Cannot Shirk Responsibility for Their Crimes
> Burmese People's Revolutionary Armed Struggle is Bound to Triumph
> Indonesian People Have Raised the Torch of Armed Struggle
> Basic Assurance for Consolidating the Proletarian Dictatorship
> U.S. Imperialism and Soviet Revisionism are Backstage Managers of Anti-China Farce
> Baring British Imperialism's Crafty Features
> Mao Tse-tung's Thought Lights the Whole World
> Ceylon Must Stop Anti-China Provocations

I had about two dozen issues, which over the course of several weeks I read from cover to cover at least twice. They were quite incredible.

The *China Pictorial* is Red China's answer to *Life* magazine. There is much less emphasis on rabid polemics, and the magazine is mostly dedicated to showing how peoples all over the world love Chairman Mao and read his *Quotations* and other works; how China is progressing in agriculture and technology; how generally happy and prosperous the Chinese have become; and the recent developments in the arts and the opera. It is full of pictures, many of them in color.

I spent much of the following two weeks reading the foregoing. Much of it was dull reading, but perhaps it was time well spent; I got an idea, at any rate, of the ideology currently in vogue and of some of the political developments in China that had led to the current situation.

The days passed, and the days crossed off on my little calendar continued to mount. I was beginning to despair of ever leaving.

14 / *Canton and Release*

By the time these two weeks of enforced leisure had passed, I was in a mixed psychological state of frustration, wondering when they were ever going to let me go, and philosophic resignation to my fate, whatever it might be. It was not wholly inconceivable that they would keep me indefinitely, if only through political inertia in deciding what to do with me.

Two weeks had now passed since the interrogations had ceased; surely they had had sufficient time by now to check all the essential details of my story! I wondered how far they would check. The more recent years in Vietnam could readily be verified. I wondered whether they had a pipeline through to their Viet Cong underground chums in Saigon, and whether even now some nondescript Vietnamese might be chatting with an acquaintance in the company, asking casually whether a supply manager named Steele had ever worked there, etc. How far back would they check? I could imagine a Chinese janitor in a Bronx hospital sneaking into the records room in the dead of night, thumbing through old records to ascertain whether someone named David J. Steele had indeed been born there on March 22, 1928, and if so what his parents' names were. If they wanted to be really assiduous, I could count on being in Red China until I had grown a long white beard.

Deliverance finally arrived, however, on one magic Thursday. It was late in the evening, and I had long since gone to bed, when I felt someone shaking the bed saying "Wake up!" I awoke groggily, and it was Mr. Yee, standing at my bedside. A tinge of apprehension jolted me awake. What in God's name would they be waking me up at this hour for?

Canton and Release

"Get up and prepare yourself for something." said Mr. Yee impassively. I arose, wide-eyed by now, speculating like mad. It was obviously something highly non-routine, and I wondered whether the time had finally arrived. I pulled on some clothes and washed my face quickly, and picked up Mao. (Whenever I had to go anywhere, it was *de rigeur* to bring Mao along.)

Yee looked down at the little crude penciled calendar I had been keeping under the glass of the desk and, inexplicably, giggled. What did *that* mean? My brain started clicking, trying to pin some significance to it. Was he amused because after all my questioning they were finally going to release me, and the ordeal was over? Or because I had been hoping for days for release, and he was waiting to see the expression on my face when they told me that for my crimes they were going to sentence me to ten years of hard labor digging wells in upper Honan Province?

Sometimes imagination can be a burden; you start speculating and run the gamut from the worst to the best possibilities, run up high blood pressure, and in the end are left as before—out the same door wherein you entered, as old Socrates was wont to say.

"Wait here until you are called," Mr. Yee advised primly. He left, and I remained in the room for another five minutes, mulling over the situation and wondering what would come next. He came back presently and summoned me to the Conference Room.

When I arrived, there were a small number of people seated behind the table: the Leader, Mr. Chin, Mr. Yee, the handyman, and the Thin Man. I sat down in my usual chair. I had entered somewhat informally smoking a cigarette; they indicated that I should put it out. It was apparently a formal occasion. I did as directed and sat impassively, waiting.

The Leader had a formal-looking Chinese document before him, and proceeded to read. It did not take long. Everyone listened without expression. When he had finished, Mr. Yee began to translate.

"Your request to be released to Hong Kong...," he began—my heart jumped; go on man, *go on*—"...has been approved by the authorities." Hot *dog*! "But first," he continued ominously, "there are certain formalities which must be completed." I wondered what these "formalities" would consist of.

Mr. Yee then read off a five-point list, summarizing my crimes

against the People's Republic of China, and including a number of other points as well. The summary was roughly as follows:
1. While sailing my boat on a pleasure cruise, I had illegally entered into the territorial waters of China.
2. While in Chinese waters I had collided against a vessel of the People's Republic, at which time my boat had become damaged.
3. While in Chinese waters, I had illegally taken a photograph of a Chinese vessel.
4. The Chinese fishermen had done their best to save my boat (Ed.—Ha!) and had retrieved a number of items from the sea, which items had been returned to me. For this I was very grateful.
5. During my stay in the People's Republic of China, I had been treated kindly. For this too I was very grateful.

The "formalities," it appeared, merely consisted of my having to write out all the foregoing in ink, in two copies, and sign them. Messrs. Yee and Chin read the first draft carefully, and after making a number of minor qualifications, I completed the required two copies and signed without demur.

Regarding the first item, I had unquestionably been outside of Chinese territorial limits at the time I was accosted. The mere fact of heading towards Hainan at five knots for two hours, and the coast still being a goodly distance off, was incontrovertible evidence of that. There was, obviously, no way in the world that I could prove it.

The second point was true enough, on the surface, although I ruefully reflected that they were omitting a few of the circumstances! The third point was again true, although the photo had been taken outside of their territorial waters; hence, there was no "illegality" involved.

The fourth point was ironic. They tried to save my boat, indeed! By towing it upside down at twelve knots! As regards returning items to me, I had not seen them yet. Later, they did return a few items, but not all of them. I had seen them ferrying my tape recorder onto the trawler at the time; I never got that back, and there were a number of other items that I am sure they took that never again appeared. The Leader advised that they were keeping my charts, for their own use, to which I assented gracefully. I had little

The last of the Linda Niña II—photos given by the Red Chinese to the author upon his release from China.

choice, and anyway, with no boat, they wouldn't be doing me much good for the foreseeable future.

As to the fifth point. I would have agreed to this readily enough. They did treat me reasonably well, within their limitations; I had no kick there, aside, of course, from the circumstances that put me in their hands in the first place.

The formalities over, the atmosphere became more relaxed, and they told me that I would be flown to Canton the next day, for release into Hong Kong. It seemed too good to be true. It was a wonderful feeling, the thought of imminent release!

They informed me that my boat had been irreparably damaged, and brought out a few photos to prove it.

My poor *Linda Niña II* was indeed gone. The photos showed several large chunks of the front part of the hull and one float, which had been dragged ashore. The hull section still had the identification numbers on the bow. I asked whether they could give me a print of each photo. I pointed out that when I arrived in Hong Kong I might have problems in obtaining a new passport and in getting my lost traveler's checks refunded, and the photos of the boat would assist in establishing my claim of shipwreck. They discussed it at length, and finally gave me the prints.

I returned to bed in a jubilant mood, and finally slept, after kicking about for a long time, savoring the thought of release.

On Friday morning I arose with unusual alacrity and gathered my stuff together. It was a beautiful day, psychologically and actually, and I felt absolutely on top of the world. Breakfast arrived, and it was obviously a sendoff of sorts, for there were *several* eggs, and a bottle of beer! They were really doing it up brown. Everyone seemed unusually friendly.

The morning passed, however, and there was no sign of the car. Toward noon they advised that the plane was having difficulties in arriving from Canton due to bad weather en route. Lunch arrived, and was better than usual, with a side dish of excellent meat.

By mid-afternoon it became evident that the plane was not going to arrive that day. It was most frustrating, being at the point of departure and having things held up because of the weather. That damned weather; it had gotten me into all sorts of trouble from the very start! The day passed, and supper, and then I was back again in my same bed, hoping for more luck on the morrow.

Canton and Release

The next day I again arose in anticipation, and after another good breakfast (with beer) the car finally arrived at about eight. There was a sort of parting ceremony. Everyone came up and made short speeches in Chinese, and one by one they pinned Mao buttons on my shirt. I felt like one of those Comrade Commissars in the Lichty "Grin and Bear It" cartoons, all covered with medals.

The thin man gave me a carefully wrapped package as a "going away present," and an extra copy of *Quotations from Mao Tse-tung*. I suspected that the "present" was the collection of pamphlets, *Peking Reviews*, and *China Pictorials* that I had been reading for the last two weeks. (It was!)

We all shook hands, smiling, and they packed me in the car for the sendoff.

The car was a somewhat elderly vintage of foreign make that I didn't recognize. On the fender it said "Warszawa." Warsaw?

I got in the back between Yee and the Thin Man; the handyman and Cheong sat in front with the driver. I gathered that the Leader had left by other means and would meet us at the airport. I asked Yee whether the car had been imported or had been made in China. He thought a bit, as usual, to assure himself that he wasn't giving away any vital state information, and finally admitted cautiously that no, it had been imported, but he didn't know from where.

After some further chit-chat between the members in the car and those remaining, we took off.

The sea was just a short distance from the villa after all—only about two city blocks. The car turned right and followed a pleasant road that meandered along the edge of the ocean, lined with pine trees. It was asphalted and in fair condition. We drove for an hour or so, passing few other vehicles. There were a few people along the road, with occasional ox-carts, and a number of cyclists. There was also an occasional foreign-looking jeep and a number of trucks, but no other automobiles. The driver did a great deal of honking.

Along the road by the sea there were frequent signs placed along both sides with Quotations from Mao; in some places these were every few hundred yards. They appeared to be printed on both sides, so you could enjoy them coming and going. I reflected that maybe we didn't have it so bad with billboards in the United States after all.

I commented on the pretty scenery along the sea, and Yee agreed and translated for the Thin Man, who then got launched on various analogies with the Socialist system. I gathered that the scenery was beautiful, just as the Socialist system was beautiful in a different way, etc. He went on for some time, warming to the subject, with Yee translating at intervals. I ragged him a bit to the effect that couldn't he admire a simple seascape without tying ideology to it, but was never quite sure whether Yee translated this or not, for the Thin Man kept on in the same vein for some time.

After awhile we turned inland, and the road became increasingly rough. I wondered what kind of airport we were going to, and for awhile entertained fleeting thoughts that after all this rigamarole I was being taken for a ride in some diabolical Chinese fashion. The sendoff had been amiable enough, and all indications were that I was indeed going to Canton, but after the previous few weeks I could believe that things were not what they might appear in China; they have funny ways of doing things to which the Western mind is simply not geared.

We finally arrived at the airport, however. From a distance no runways could be seen; it looked like a big field, but as we drove across it I could see that there were concrete slabs grown high with grass that sprouted up between the cracks. The runway was spotted with ox droppings. It did not appear to be a place where Boeing 707's would care to land, and had about it an air of disuse.

At the other side of the runway was a congeries of small stucco buildings, flanked by the old rusted skeleton of a hangar. A tired wind sock hung from a pole to one side. Parked in front of the buildings was a jeep, with several guards and perhaps half a dozen other people. I recognized the Leader among them.

Our car pulled up alongside and they all talked for several minutes. I gathered from Yee that the plane had not yet arrived and that we were to proceed further up the field to a waiting room at the far end.

We proceeded as indicated, alighted, and sat in a small room for the next hour or so, joined by the Leader. The room had a small table in the center with the usual thermos of hot water. On one end of the table was a small plaster bust of the Great One, with a red cloth banner below with the Chinese characters for *Mao Chu Shi Wan Sui!*—Long Live Chairman Mao! The walls were covered

Canton and Release   189

with posters and quotations. Having nothing better to do I counted them, adding a total of twelve pictures of Mao and thirteen Quotations. The thermos bottles also had Quotations written up and down one side, and the cups as well. When they smiled, one would half expect small Quotations to be engraved on their front teeth. I suppose the day will come.

After about an hour the plane had allegedly arrived, so we piled back in the car and returned to the runway, where a single-engined biplane was parked. The car pulled up alongside the plane and we boarded. There were about six seats for the passengers, and a jump seat in the cockpit for a total crew of three. However, they squeezed eleven people in, digging in the back compartment of the plane for a few small wicker stools to accomodate the overflow. It appeared that the sole purpose of the plane had been to get me, since no tickets were collected, and it was obviously not a routine commercial flight. The Leader, the Thin Man, Mr. Yee, and Mr. Cheong went along, in addition to three others whom I had never seen.

All was finally ready to go. The pilot and co-pilot boarded, somewhat dubious-looking types in greasy jackets and badly in need of shaves. However, they appeared subsequently to be able to fly well enough. The third crew member was a youngish man in blue coveralls. While the other two were fiddling with dials in the front cockpit, the third crewman stood up in the front of the cabin with the small Red Book and read out a few passages in an official tone of voice, to which the passenger section responded enthusiastically.

The Great Red Spirit thus propitiated, the flying machine was ready to go. They warmed up the engine, and the third crewman took his jump seat. For a few minutes they were all fiddling with dials, reaching across in front of each other to adjust this or that. I hoped they'd all learned on the same type of plane. Presently the craft began to move, bumping over the grass, gaining speed, and then we were off the ground.

From then on there was not much to see, since the curtains over the portholes had been thoughtfully pinned shut with straight pins. I was again impressed by their neurotic mania for security, and wondered what on earth one could see of strategic value from the window of a plane ten thousand feet in the air. Maybe they were building a bridge to Taiwan and hoping no one would notice?

From time to time one of the passengers would peek, but I felt it would be imprudent on my part.

After a two-hour flight, we came down to land somewhere on the mainland for refueling and lunch. They led me through the small airport building to a room behind and finally brought some food. The room appeared to be a part of transient living facilities behind the airport. After lunch we went back and sat in the waiting room for awhile, apparently awaiting a favorable weather report.

I wandered about the waiting room a bit, and went to the john, which had signs to indicate its function in Chinese, English, and Russian. I noted the last with interest; it was the first time I had seen Russian signs in China. There was a small stand selling various items, which I looked over out of curiosity. The stand sold toothpaste, soap, some canned goods, cigarettes, a brand of local wine, and Mao buttons. I reflected that it was a somewhat odd combination to sell at an airport waiting room counter. The Mao buttons were artistically displayed on a rack at one end, and there were nearly a dozen varieties of sizes and styles. The Thin Man came over and purchased a couple more to round out my collection, and presented them with a short speech. Everyone smiled.

The airport was relatively empty, but for ourselves and a few other people, including a group of small girls who came in with their mother. They clutched at her skirts in mock terror, giggling and looking sidewise at the bearded Foreign Devil. When no one was looking I stuck my tongue out at them. They emitted gratifying shrieks. Mother remained impassive.

Finally it was time to go, and we returned to the plane. I got on first. There was some delay at the door—they were playing Alphonse and Gaston with each other again—and feeling daring I took the opportunity to pull out two of the pins from the curtain on my window. The flight to Canton took about two hours, during which time I surreptitiously spread the edges of the curtain apart and sneaked a peek now and then. As I had suspected, however, there wasn't much to be seen from ten thousand feet, with a fair cloud cover to boot.

Finally one of them caught me looking and told me sternly to stop. I managed to sneak an occasional peek thereafter anyway, but there was nothing of interest to be seen.

Only the Leader had continued the flight from the second stop, but a few others had boarded. One of these was introduced to me as a Mr. Huang, who would be accompanying me to the border. He was polite enough, but appeared to be another of those prim types, like Mr. Yee.

We landed at Canton airport, and the plane stopped about half a block from the main airport building. It was a large modern-looking airport, although there were few aircraft to be seen and little observable activity.

We got out, and my companions milled about the plane for awhile, finally digging into the back compartment again and fishing out a variety of items. I recognized the sailbag as being from the *Linda Niña II*, and watched with interest to see what else there was. So these were the goods that were being returned to me! I recognized my sextant case, a plastic bucket, and various other odds and ends. It was quite an assortment, and appeared to be the booty from a nautical scavenger hunt.

We sat on the runway for awhile, apparently awaiting a car, but none appeared, so finally Mr. Huang borrowed a bicycle from someone and went pedaling off toward the main airport building. He reappeared presently and announced that he'd managed to book a room at the hotel, which was apparently the building adjacent to the airport building. By now the others had left, leaving me with only Mr. Huang and one other fellow. We had packed the odds and ends into the sailbag and the rest into the plastic bucket. We each picked up a portion of the loot and started trudging toward the airport building.

The hotel seemed to be new, and we proceeded up to the third floor, where I was deposited in a smallish room facing out onto a courtyard between the hotel and the main airport building. Huang showed off the room with evident pride, and got me installed. Eager to demonstrate the technological innovations of modern China, he mentioned that the room had an adjoining bathroom *with bath*, and flung open the door to demonstrate it, but there didn't appear to be one. Nonplussed and frustrated, he turned in confusion and started looking in the closet, but I silently pointed out the heretofore-unnoticed shower head protruding from the wall. Apparently it was one of those bathrooms where you take a shower and everything else gets wet.

Nonetheless, it was all much more modern than my quarters in Hainan, and looked quite comfortable. After the Hainan Hilton I felt I had to give this one a name too, so I dubbed it the Canton Inter-Continental, which had a pleasant rolling sound to it.

After I had gotten installed, Huang and I went down to the airport building for supper. We sat in the dining room, which is located on a sort of balcony above the waiting lounge. It felt quite luxurious to be sitting at a table with a tablecloth, and a menu, and presentable cutlery. I asked if there was beer, but Huang said no, so I drank three straight bottles of orange pop, topped off with a plate of chow mein. (I later discovered that there was *too* beer, which just shows you what kind of guy Huang was.) After supper I wandered over to the edge of the balcony and looked with interest at the passengers below, but it appeared to make Huang nervous, so I returned to the table. There appeared to be a number of Albanians, judging from the green jackets. I heard several of them talking English with a guide, and it sounded very good. I felt that I was getting back into civilization again.

The airport was quite new, and Huang informed me proudly that it had been completed in early 1967. On the wall above the balcony was a large Quotation in Chinese with the English translation below: "ARMED WITH MAO TSE-TUNG'S THOUGHT, GO AHEAD STEADILY AND COURAGEOUSLY!" This brave exhortation was somewhat marred in its effect since a very large chunk of plaster had fallen out of the ceiling nearby.

"My, your ceiling seems to be coming apart," I pointed out. I couldn't resist the opportunity to puncture his balloon. Huang acknowledged that the building was "just new" and said no more, leaving me wondering what that was supposed to mean. Did this imply that things might be expected to keep falling out, in a sort of teething process, until the ceiling was broken in properly? I did not pursue the matter further.

The next day we went down to breakfast to the airport again, but this was to be my last meal in this manner; from then on they brought me my meals in the room. I was anxious to find out just when we were leaving for Hong Kong, but it appeared that deliverance was not yet at hand. Huang advised that he would find out that evening, and that I "had to be patient."

Later in the day Huang came back to the room with two men, and they thoroughly searched every inch of my baggage, unfortunately discovering the notes that I had prepared detailing my experiences in Hainan. They also took my pages of Chinese lessons and a notebook that they had given me prior to departure in which I had been jotting down the events of the past few days. I explained that the notes were only a diary, and Huang promised that they'd look them over and give them back, but of course I never saw them again.

In the afternoon I separated out the things from the boat. There were a number of shirts, pants, and underpants that had apparently been fished out of the water; a few pairs of socks, handkerchiefs, a plastic bucket, a few cans of food, a can of ginger ale, two bottles of champagne(!), a package of soggy paper cups, the sextant case, the camera, one sailbag, and a tattered piece from the head of the jib sail. It certainly was an odd assortment. I kept out the better items, retaining the piece of the jib as a souvenir, and piled the rest in the closet for disposal.

That evening Huang came back briefly, and in response to my inquiries advised that I would have to spend "a little more time in Canton" while my story was being "completely checked." This was most disappointing, since I had been led to believe that I would be released immediately. There was, as usual, nothing I could do about it, so I settled in for another wait, and started another calendar.

The next week went slowly, perhaps even more so than in Hainan, since I no longer had the flexibility of sitting on the front porch and wandering about the garden. I was instructed to remain in my room at all times.

Similarly to Hainan, a routine evolved. I had breakfast in the room, usually coffee, toast, and an egg, but sometimes tea instead of coffee, and sometimes no egg. The service was rather erratic.

In the mornings I would generally read. In the course of the search they had opened the package that I had been given in Hainan, and sure enough it contained all the literature I had previously read. They were most thorough about it, thumbing through all the pages of the magazines to make sure there was nothing written in the margins, etc. So in the mornings I began to go through it all again, starting with the *Peking Reviews* and reading every word. It would take an hour or so to go through one *Peking Review* at this rate, and I figured I had enough for nearly a week; then I would start on the *China Pictorials*. From time to time I varied the diet with a few chapters from Mao. It was something to do.

After lunch I would take a nap, and in the afternoon I spent most of the time lying on the bed thinking. Towards supper I would take a shower. After supper, another hour of thinking, or sitting at the window watching the sunset, and then to bed. The bed was excellent, and I invariably slept like a log.

Huang dropped in from time to time to chat, but I had taken a dislike to him for the same reasons I had disliked Yee. He was secretive and petty, and had about the same reactions to my questions regarding my leaving. The visits were usually the same; we would exchange some banal comment about the weather, and I would spend most of the rest of the time studiously examining my fingernails and letting him carry the conversational ball. I would answer his questions politely enough, but that was all. After a short while he would become discouraged, look pointedly at his watch, and advise that he had to be leaving, which I would accept without comment.

When I first arrived I thought there was a sheet metal shop operating down below in the courtyard, but I later realized that it was Chinese music. If you think normal Chinese music is discordant, you should hear them when they are practicing. Apparently they had an incumbent orchestra in the airport, and when visiting planes arrived they would put on a short show in the waiting room to entertain the passengers. I could just barely make out the small stage through the windows of the airport building. Apparently once the passengers had gotten settled in the lounge, the orchestra would come out and play a few numbers and a small troup would entertain with folk songs and dances. Some of the sounds would filter through; it sounded somewhat like distant earthmoving equipment operating in need of oil. I wondered whether they would dig Paul Desmond.

Favorite numbers were "The East is Red" and "Sailing the Seas Depends on the Helmsman." The first one was the national anthem, and hardly a day had gone by since I had arrived in China that I had not heard it blaring out in some form or other. The second number was almost as popular; it starts off a little like "Yankee Doodle," and presumably chronicles the joys of sailing on a turbulent sea with Chairman Mao at the helm.

From my third-story window I could look down onto the patio and to a certain extent out onto the tarmac of the airport, where I could see planes trundle in to discharge passengers. Apparently 707's came into the airport, and once one came close enough to the airport building that I could make out the PIA insignia on the tail. In earlier conversations I had had with Huang, back in more social days, I had gotten the impression that some international airlines came into Canton and other airports. Apparently the only ones allowed to fly directly into Peking were those from other socialist countries such as Russia and North Korea.

I spent some Walter Mitty time dreaming about escape via airline, as a variation on the escape-by-boat routine, and managed to while away a number of pleasant if unproductive hours in this manner. I was apparently completely unguarded in my room, although it appeared that Huang and one or two others had a room on the same floor nearby. However, on several occasions I had ventured into the corridor unchallenged, and I had no doubt that I could make my way out of the hotel undetected if I chose the moment carefully. On one occasion I had even descended to the second floor, where the reception desk was located, unseen. On that particular occasion I had seen the waiter bringing my supper tray from the airport building; when he did not appear within another five minutes, I decided he'd left the tray at the reception desk, so I went down to get it. Sure enough, it was there, with the food getting cold. There was no one else around, so I bore the tray back to my room. Later Huang spoke sternly about this and reiterated that I was not to leave the room. At any rate, there was no doubt that I could have gotten out, had I wished to.

The planes parked a few hundred yards out on the tarmac, near the hotel. Getting aboard one of them would undoubtedly have presented problems, and stowing successfully aboard would probably have been almost impossible. It gave it a lot of thought, though, and worked out a number of interesting episodes, complete with details as to what I would do once arrived in Karachi, etc. As before, it occupied time.

After a few days a new man arrived on the scene who turned out to be the most pleasant fellow I had run across yet in Red China. His name was Shung, and he was well educated, had a good sense of humor, and was not nearly so heavy on ideology as the others to whom I had been exposed. From time to time I could even get him to concede a point or two.

Shung would drop by nearly every day, and we would spend an hour or so discussing various subjects. I would at times prevail upon him to give me some information as to when I would be leaving China, but could find out little more out from him than I could from Huang; however, he was nicer about it and seemed honestly regretful that he could not tell me more, so it wasn't nearly as annoying. Also he seemed more assured that I would be out of there very soon, and this left me feeling generally more optimistic.

Shung and I would have long discussions on Communism versus Free Enterprise, and although obviously I could not sell him on the latter and he wasn't about to turn me into a Communist, the discussions were interesting. I was ready to grant a few concessions as to some shortcomings of free societies, and occasionally I could get him to grant that Socialism had a few problems too, and on the whole the discussions were amicable and fruitful. Shung spent a lot of time explaining how communes work, with their "work point" systems for distributing proceeds. It did not sound wholly unreasonable, and presumably represented a vast improvement over the previous system in which a few rich landlords had squeezed the peasants unmercifully.

During my discussions with Shung, I tried to convey some of the image of the American way of life, but with somewhat limited success. He just didn't want to believe that so many people owned cars or went to college, or that the general standard of living was as I described it. For an otherwise well-educated man, he had an extremely distorted image of the United States.

We had one interesting discussion on advertising, which was amusing. Shung referred to American advertising as "pornographic." He had a pretty good vocabulary. I had to admit that he had a bit of a point, now that I thought about it, and reflected what percentage of American advertising seems to rely on the presence of some smiling and chesty bathing beauty to call attention to this brand of beer or that brand of deodorant, not to mention a miscellany of other items such as tractors, lawnmowers, tools, and other equipment with which women would not normally be associated. I felt that his use of the word pornographic was a bit strong, though. Apparently the modern generation of Maoists are being brought up with some very puritan views on womanhood and sex. They never tell impure jokes, I gathered, and it is generally considered bad form and unrevolutionary to talk about Girls.

Shung waxed eloquent for some time on advertising, and seemed to know quite a bit about TV commercials, billboards, etc. I argued somewhat weakly that advertising is generally thought to be one of the evils necessary to sustain a high rate of economic growth, but on that particular round perhaps I conceded more points than I won.

The week proceeded, and by the following weekend I was becoming discouraged. On Monday morning, however, Shung and Huang came unexpectedly to call, and told me to get my stuff together, since we were moving to a different place. It seemed like doubtful encouragement, but maybe any change portended for the better. They insisted over my objections that I lug along all of the junk that I had stacked in the closet for disposal.

We left the hotel and got into a car downstairs, and drove into the city of Canton. It was a most interesting drive of about half an hour, through tree-lined streets. We passed a number of well-tended large farming plots on the outskirts of the city, which Shung informed me were communal vegetable plots. As we got further into the center of the city, we passed numerous buses of somewhat ancient vintage, but not many other types of vehicles aside from trucks. As before, I saw few automobiles.

The new hotel was a large old-fashioned type, with a large garden in front, located on one of Canton's main streets. There was an open paved square in front of the hotel, which was painted up with Chinese slogans that I assumed to be quotations and other political matter. There were also a few succint phrases in English, such as "DOWN WITH THE INDIAN REACTIONARIES!" attesting to some previous rally. The front of the hotel was liberally plastered with old newsprint on which large black Chinese characters had been brushed. The lobby was large and empty.

We got on an elevator and creaked up to the fifth floor, where they installed me in a large room facing onto the square. It had two comfortable beds and an adjoining bathroom that was rather dingy. The tub had a ring.

"Here's where you will settle down," said Shung. My spirits dropped at his wording.

"Settle down?" I asked. "You make it sound very permanent!" But Shung laughed and assured me that I wouldn't be there long.

They left me in the room, and I had lunch and later supper, with nothing much to do except thumb through the *China Pictorials* again. From the front window I could look across the square and the garden, and across the main street to another large building on the far side of another square. I thought I could just make out Russian lettering on one side of the building. When I asked Shung about it later he advised that it was indeed a Russian-Chinese Friendship Building, put up a number of years ago by the Russians. In view of their present relations, I assumed it wasn't getting much use at the moment.

During the night I heard sounds of firing from a distance, or perhaps they were firecrackers; it was hard to tell.

The next morning Huang showed up about seven thirty. I was surprised to see him at such an hour. He had the copies of my "confession" in his hand, and informed me that they desired some alterations to be made. The changes were relatively minor, and included such things as adding the name of my boat and inserting a few additional details here and there. When he was finally satisfied, I had to make two new drafts of the whole thing and sign them, and he went away.

About half an hour later Shung appeared and summoned me to come with him. We went to a small conference type of room down the hall, and entered. There were two Chinese there in military uniforms, whom I had never seen. We nodded to each other somewhat coldly, and we all sat down. There was some discussion between them and Shung and Huang, and after awhile the two military types stood up formally. We did likewise. One of them read from a piece of paper, a short speech. When he was through, Shung translated:

Canton and Release

that I had violated the waters of the People's Republic of China; that the authorities had duly considered the matter; and that I was to be extradited from China, effective immediately.

I was amused at his use of the word "extradited," but it didn't seem like the right time to correct his English. Extradited, immediately; hot dog!

The formalities finished, we returned to the room, and Shung told me to get my things together again. This time they let me leave behind the junk I didn't want. I stuffed everything into the seabag except the sextant case, and we went downstairs to the square, where there was a military truck waiting. We all climbed onto the back and sat down on the floor, and the truck took off.

It was a fine feeling driving through the streets of Canton on the way to the station. It was a nice day, and the breeze was enjoyable. For the most part, the sections of the city we drove through were unremarkable: tree-lined streets, two- or three-story buildings of pre-war vintage, a moderate number of people in the streets. We passed at one point through a barrier crossing the road, indicating that there had been some civil disturbances in the recent past. I inquired about this, but Shung was reluctant to comment.

The only building of particular note was a large pagoda-like villa in a garden at the outskirts of Canton, which Shung informed me was a monument to Dr. Sun Yat-sen.

We drove for quite a while, and I was starting to wonder whether they were going to drive clear to the border, but it subsequently appeared that they were heading for a station on the outskirts of the city. Apparently the main Canton Station was temporarily closed for business.

We finally arrived at the station, a small local variety with a signboard that said "Tian-He." As we arrived in the station, a long column of people went by holding a demonstration, waving red banners, singing, and firing off firecrackers. They all wore red armbands, and I presumed these were the famous Red Guards. They looked like a bunch of fanatic rowdies, and were throwing the firecrackers to right and left, causing a number of people on the sidewalk to jump aside.

They parted ranks to let the truck enter the station. The train was already there, and Shung and Huang accompanied me onto the train, and we all got seats. We were apparently going first class. The train was fairly comfortable, with cushioned seats and old-fashioned mahogany woodwork. It must have been fairly elegant in its day, say, twenty or thirty years ago. Presently it pulled out with a hissing of steam, and we chugged off.

The train was a coal burner, and by the time we reached the border, five hours later, I was full of cinders, right into the roots of my hair. It was a real milk run; the train stopped at every station along the way, and there were a lot of stations. Shung bought me a couple of bottles of beer, quart-size, which I sipped along the way while smoking, and the time went by rapidly. In some respects it was easily the best train ride I have ever had in my life, and I felt in high spirits as we chugged toward the border and freedom. The scenery was pleasant—fields and rice paddy along the way—and I watched the people working in the fields with their water buffalo. There were many places along the way where they were pumping water over dikes with old-fashioned bucket-type devices, driven by leg power. Mechanization had apparently not progressed too far yet.

We finally arrived at the border, got out, and walked down the length of the station toward a covered railway bridge a few hundred yards down the track, and I suddenly realized with a thrill that we were *there*! The bridge spanned a small river, and there were barbed wire fences running along the banks of the river on either side. On the near side of the bridge was a large Chinese flag waving from a pole, red with a big white star and four smaller stars in the upper corner. On the other side of the bridge I could see the British flag waving from a similar pole. I reflected that the Union Jack had probably never looked so good to an American since 1776.

We stopped at the near end of the bridge and I stood for a moment looking at it. Outwardly I was impassive; inwardly I was grinning to myself at the random Hemingway-like thought that had suddenly crossed my mind: *Ay mi madre, truly this is a fine bridge. The mother of all bridges.*

Several guards stood on the Chinese side of this mother of all bridges, cradling their rifles. Not a soul could be seen on the British side, although I could see a train pulled up several hundred yards down the line, presumably waiting to return to Hong Kong. I turned to look back at Huang and Shung, and briefly considered

Canton and Release 201

shaking hands with Shung, who had been quite a decent sort, but he waved me on.

"Go ahead," he said simply, "cross the bridge."

I picked up the seabag and the sextant case and, not looking back at Red China, trudged onto the bridge. My sandals went clop-clop across the rough board walkway, echoing hollowly under the roof. Ten steps, twenty, and then I was on the other side, passing below the British flag waving warmly above. Mental strains of Rule Britannia filled the air.

I was back in the West.

15 / Hong Kong

There was surprisingly little activity on the British side of the Lo Wu bridge. I could see no one at all, although there were occasional vaguely seen motions behind the cyclone fencing that bordered the path to my left. Down the track stood a train, motionless. Where the hell *is* everybody, I wondered.

I finally arrived at an entrance a few hundred feet further on, marked Immigration, and turned in the door. There were quite a few people in the room. They looked up in some surprise as I came popping in the door, seabag over my shoulder. A pleasant Eurasian lady hustled forward.

"May I have your passport and health book, please?" she asked. I couldn't help but grin. Passport and health book were down somewhere at the bottom of the South China Sea. I explained all this, happily, in a few sentences.

The lady said "Oh my," and there was a brief reappraisal; then a number of people had crowded about, chattering, and I was led over to a desk to "fill out some forms." By then an English fellow had come up to see what was going on. He turned out to be a Mr. Frazier of the British Immigration Service. It was so good to see a Western face again and hear English spoken. I ran over the essentials of the story again for him.

"Right...well, come along to the back here, and we'll see what can be done about this," Frazier said in a friendly manner. First he asked to examine my bag, and I obligingly opened the sextant case and dumped the meager contents of the seabag on the floor. Frazier asked if I had any pernicious literature, and I told him boy, did I ever have pernicious literature; however, he glanced through the Mao pamphlets and *China Pictorials* with little interest. Apparently he was interested in more inflammatory fare; this was relatively mild stuff. He dumped it all back into my bag without comment. He was interested in my little package of Mao buttons and filched a few, whether for his personal collection, or because they carried particularly inflammatory slogans, I never asked.

Two more British Immigration people had arrived by this time, and we all went to an air-conditioned room in the back and had a Coca-Cola and a few smokes, while I told them all about my trip, capture, etc. They called into town and contacted the general manager of Esso and the American Embassy, and let them know that I was there and would soon be coming into Kowloon. The British Immigration people were most friendly. After we had talked a bit longer they took me out, bought me a ticket, and got me installed on the train for Kowloon. Mr. Frazier was going home about this time and rode part of the way with me.

The train started off, rolling through a vitally different type of countryside from that which I had been seeing *ad nauseum* for the past month, although perhaps much of the difference was in my imagination. There *were* differences, though: strings of new cars at the railroad crossings, as opposed to the few elderly vehicles that one saw in China, and signs in English (*English!*), and pretty houses, and more activity in general.

Frazier advised that at the next stop there would probably be quite a few reporters getting on. They interview the people coming out of China, to get some first-hand information on what is going on there. Frazier suggested that I not talk too much until I had had a chance to talk with the American Embassy people, to which I agreed. As it turned out, no one showed any interest in me anyway. With my beat-up clothes and month-old beard, I must have looked rather seedy. Frazier and I had a pleasant chat on the way in. Apparently he had lived in Hong Kong for some time, and liked it. I asked about the long-standing problems with the water supply in Hong Kong, but it appeared that the new reservoir was solving that. Currently food was becoming a bit of a problem, though.

I asked about border incidents, but there had been relatively little of this type of activity lately. "They always blow it up to a lot more than it really is," said Frazier, and I had to agree based on what I had seen of life in Saigon versus the sensational reports in the Stateside press. I had gone home for a few weeks during my vacation in 1965 and had been somewhat disturbed at the way the press exaggerated some of the goings-on in Saigon. Well, I suppose it sells papers.

Frazier got off a few stops before the end, leaving me to ride on into Kowloon alone. I sat there, watching the large new buildings of Kowloon come into sight, feeling that I was really back in the West again. It was a wonderful sensation.

The train stopped and I got out at the Kowloon station, the end of the line, by the Star Ferry pier. As I walked down the corridor toward the exit, I became aware of a small group approaching, one man with a camera clicking away madly. They greeted me, and I shook hands with George Belcher, the U.S. Consul, and Mr. Karl Shum from the public relations office of Esso in Hong Kong. There was also a reporter and a cameraman. We all piled into a car and they drove a few blocks to the Ambassador Hotel, where they had booked a room for me. The reporter was eager for all the details, but I told him I'd have to wait until I had had a chance to talk to the Embassy, and that I would give him the whole story tomorrow.

We had a pleasant drink in the hotel, and then Belcher left, after having made an appointment for me to be at the Embassy on the morrow at nine. I took a bath and changed clothes, and Shum took me out shopping. Esso had thoughtfully provided me with an advance of HK$1,000 (about $200. U.S.), and I went through a good slice of it that evening buying clothes. We went back to the hotel, and Shum departed. I changed into my new clothes, feeling like a new man. I still did not quite believe it, in a way. I was back in the West, in a nice hotel, good clothes—after the month in China it did not seem quite real. After awhile I left the hotel and walked about the brightly lighted and populated streets of Kowloon for awhile, and up and down Nathan Road. I recalled my earlier thoughts aboard the *Linda Niña II* of how nice it would be to be walking along Nathan Road, admiring cheong sams, and here I was, although a lot of unforeseen activities had arisen in the interim.

I finally wound up at a Japanese restaurant atop one of the buildings facing over Victoria Harbor and had a leisurely supper of sashimi and tempura, while looking out over the bay at the lights

Hong Kong

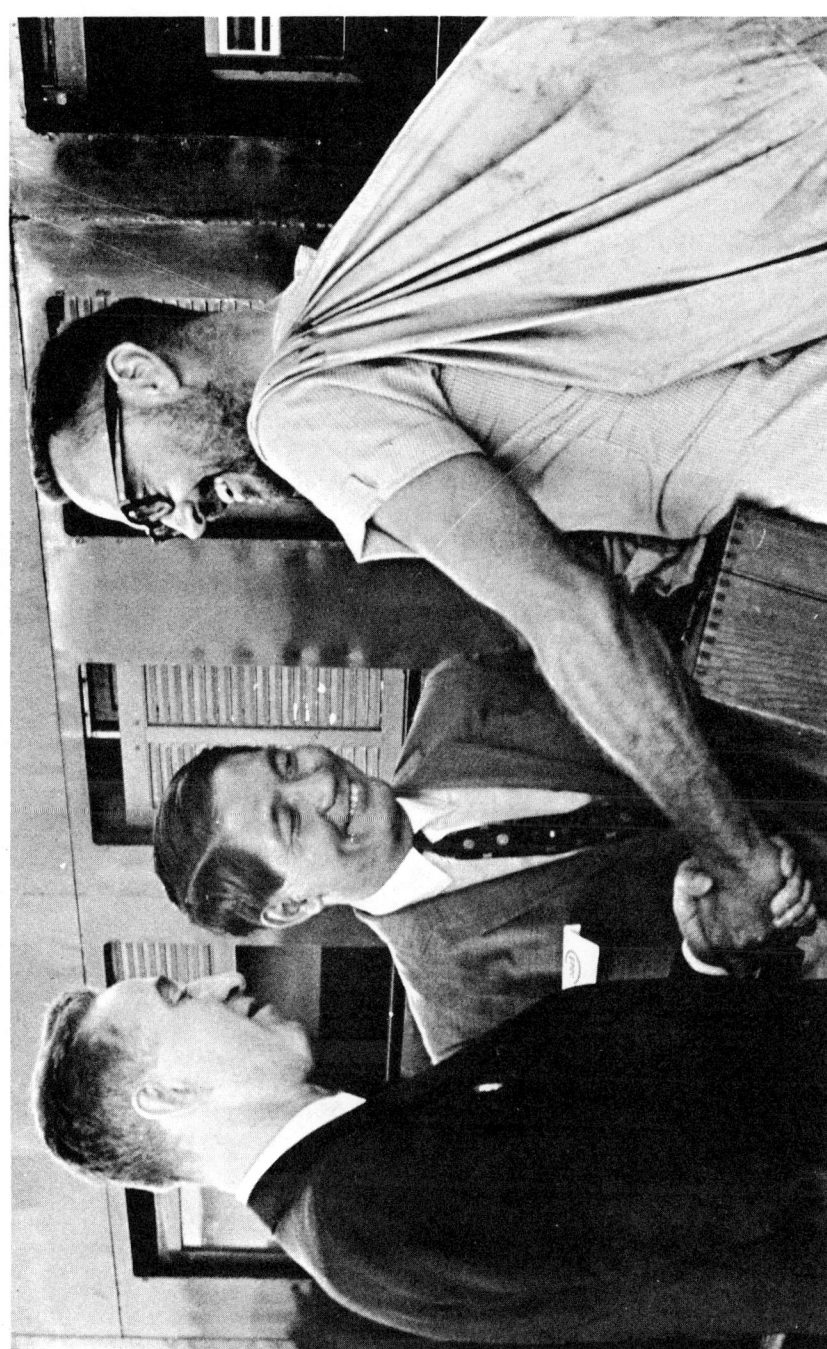

Upon his release from Red China, the author is greeted in Hong Kong by American Consul George Belcher and by Esso Public Relations Representative Karl Shum.

of Hong Kong. I was filled with a complete euphoria; one of those completely satisfying moments when you wouldn't want to be anyone else, anywhere else.

It was a real fine feeling, being back.

In the morning I was swamped with phone calls. It seemed that every reporter in Hong Kong was interested in the story, plus TV, but I told them all it would have to wait until after the discussions with the Embassy. Of course, there was nothing worth telling that I could imagine the Embassy would not want me to talk about, but it was a matter of courtesy. The reporters seemed amiable enough, and all concerned agreed to hold off until after the Embassy meeting, at which time we would have a press conference.

After breakfast, I walked over to the Star Ferry and took one across the bay to Victoria. It was a pleasant morning, and the bay was full of traffic. I thought ruefully of how I had dreamed of one day coming into the harbor with the *Linda Niña II*, and reflected that I would have had my hands full indeed trying to guide her through all that traffic. There were dozens of ferry boats and many other craft, coming and going, and crossing between Kowloon and Victoria.

The buildings on the Hong Kong side looked clean and nice, rising up the peak in the early morning sun. I recalled George Belcher and the name seemed to ring a vague bell. I mulled it over and then recalled old Captain Belcher of the H.M.S. *Sulfur*, back in the 1840's, who had played a role in the early founding of Hong Kong. As I recalled, he had surveyed the island, calculated the heights of the main peaks, and in fact was thought to have named most of them. I thought I'd rag George as to whether the Captain had been one of his ancestors.

I was swept off the ferry with the crowd of early morning commuters, and walked through Hong Kong, up past the Hilton, and up the hill to the Embassy. Belcher met me, accompanied by a comely blonde named Pat Connor, who was the press secretary. Upstairs, we met a Colonel Coon, the Military Attache, and another young man who smoked a pipe, said little, and was obviously C.I.A. We all sat in George's office and had coffee, and then I went over the whole story. They had a big chart handy on which I traced the ill-fated voyage of the *Linda Niña II*. I described the month in China in appreciable detail.

They had few questions after the story was over. They were particularly interested in the activities in the Canton area, since it was rumored that there were some uprisings being staged against Mao and his cohorts, but I could be of little help there, aside from reporting the shots that I had heard during the night.

Later in the morning Pat walked me down to the Press Club, where they had set up a reception. There was a good-sized crowd of people, perhaps fifty. They had set up a table with microphones and tape recorders, and I ran through the whole story for them, facing a phalanx of cameras grinding away from the background.

The telling of the story took about forty minutes, after which I fielded questions for awhile. Then we broke off and I went downstairs for a half-hour TV taped interview with Howard Kalb of CBS; then back upstairs for another ten minutes with NBC; then a few minutes for BBC. All this time we were followed about by a pert little Chinese newsgirl who had missed out on the main press conference and was straining to catch up.

By noon I was getting pretty tired of telling that story, and escaped to Esso, where I had lunch with the general manager and Shum. We sent out cables to all concerned, informing them of my safe arrival in Hong Kong.

Apparently the Chinese had not bothered to let anyone know what had happened to me, and my appearance in Hong Kong was the first anyone had heard of me since early August. I had been presumed lost at sea when I had not shown up in Hong Kong by late August, and air-and-sea rescue and search operations were mounted. Inquiries were made under the table via Warsaw to the Eastern Block, but no one appeared to have any news.

To this day I wonder how many people in Red China knew I was in Hainan. I must presume that so potentially sensitive an affair as holding an American captive must surely have found its way to Peking, and the Great One himself must have been informed. But I suppose I will never know.

That evening I caught myself on TV in the tranquility of my hotel room, on the David Dunkerly show. The show was preceded by a long series of advertisements for deodorants, brassieres, Schweppes, and a variety of other odds and ends. Back in the West, I grinned to myself, and remembered Mr. Shung's comments on advertising.

The next few days were spent in obtaining a new passport and health book, and a visa and tickets for Japan. I still had a week left of my vacation, and by God, I was going to relax—a few days in Nikko, a few days at Hakone, eating tempura, drinking sake, soaking in hot Japanese baths.

The big jets roared; the JAL DC-8 lifted off the runway at Kai Tak, and reached up into the sky, leaving the islands behind. I sat, nose to the window, thoughtfully watching the harbor recede and the coastline of China fade beneath the wings.

It had been quite a month. I would be thinking about it for a long time.

I thought back to the dragon, which at the time had seemed like quite an exciting undertaking, and recalled a certain degree of apprehension concerning the rate at which my adventures seemed to be escalating. What next? I had wondered.

The "what next" had turned out to be a bit more than I had bargained for! But I was back, safely, and could look back on it with reasonable equanimity. The *Linda Niña II* was gone forever, of course—a shame. I had spent a year building her, and had gotten to sail her for a week and a half. Rather a poor return on the investment.

And yet, perhaps it was not a bad investment, at that. I had traded her for a rather unique experience.

We flew at 33,000 feet towards Japan. I relaxed in my seat, musing over the past, and wondering what would come next.

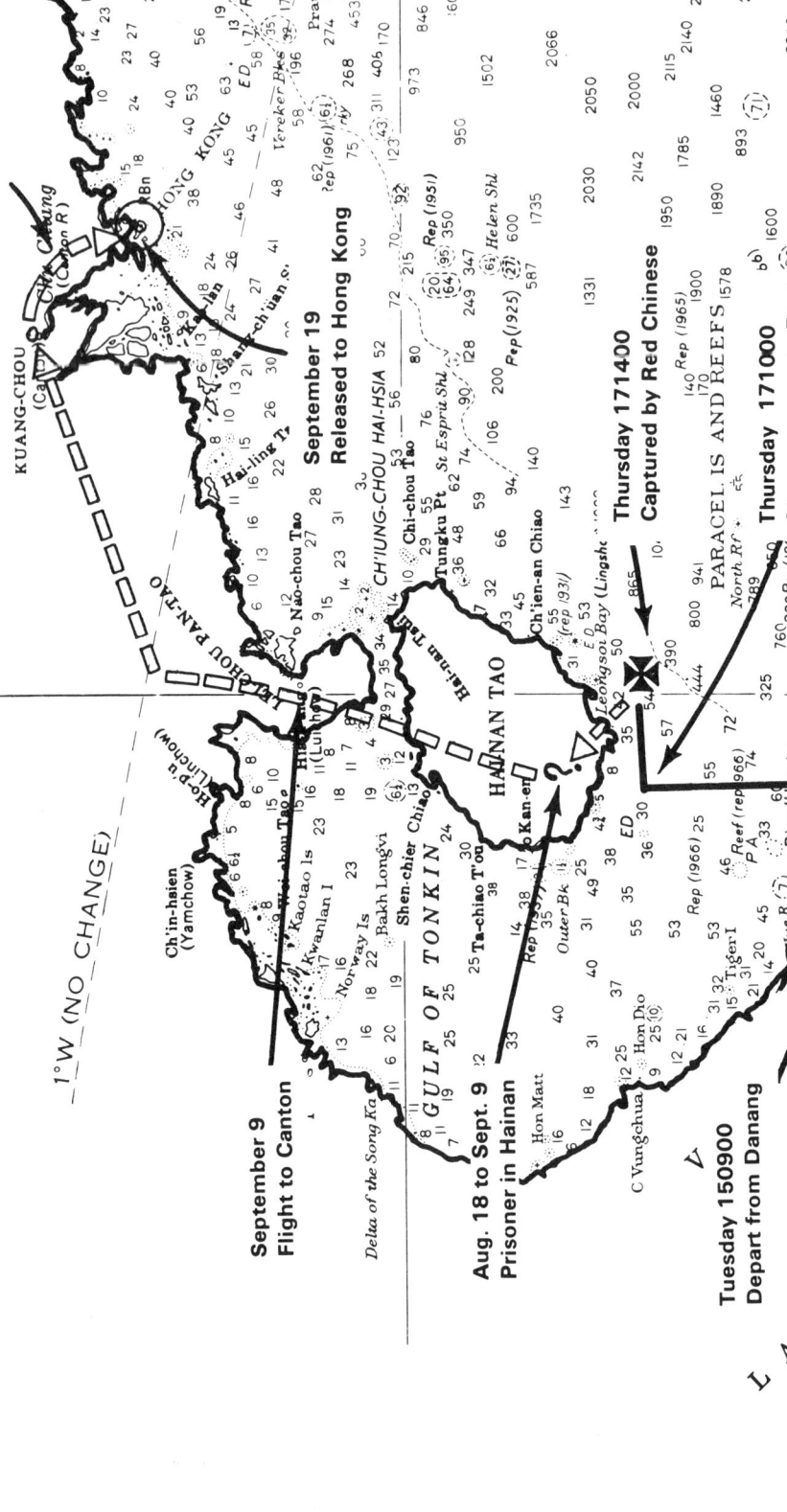

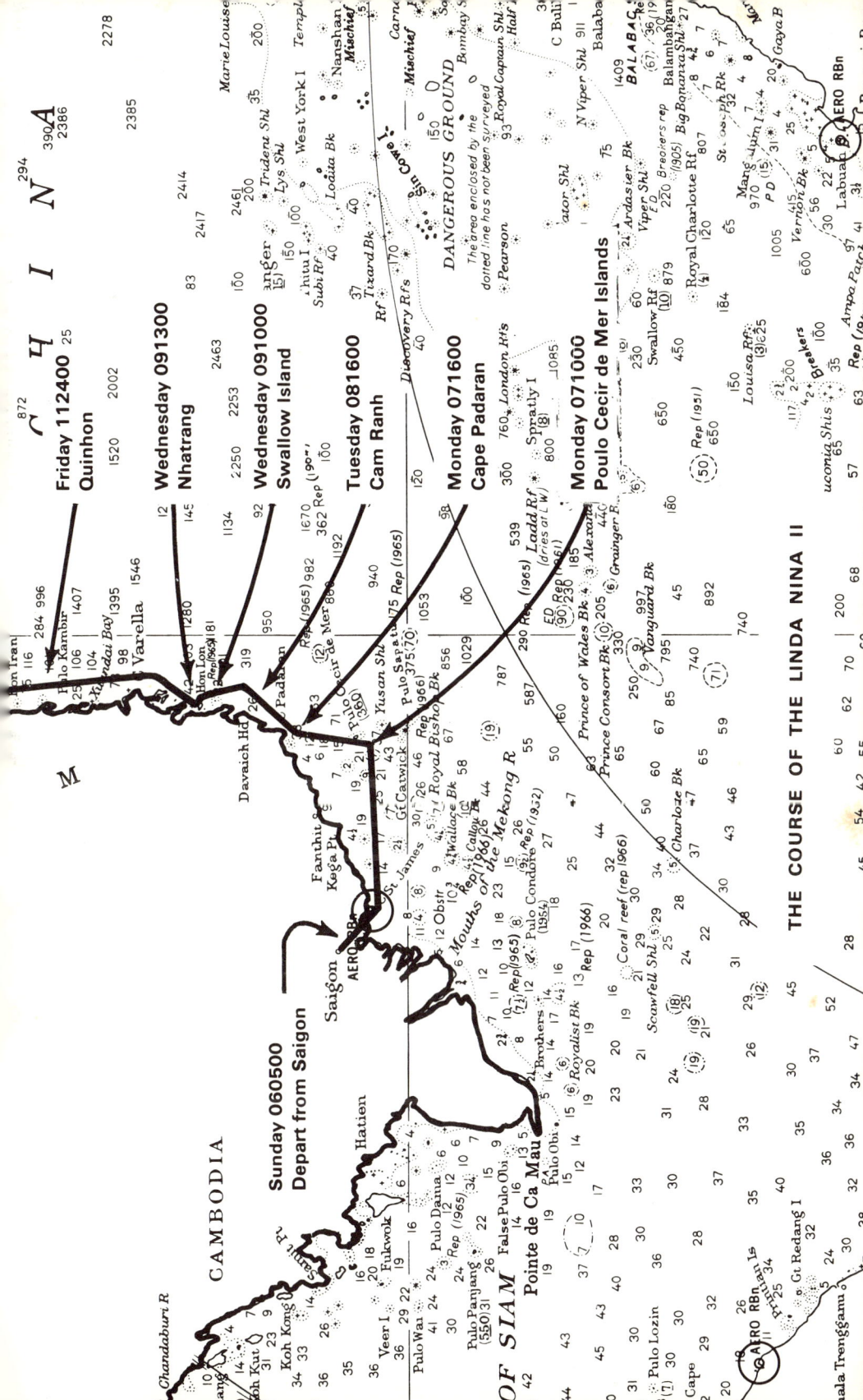